Imperialism, the State and the Third World

Talking with Kwame Nkrumah at the time
of Ghana's independence.

Imperialism, the State and the Third World

Edited by

MICHAEL TWADDLE

British Academic Press
London · New York

Published in 1992 by
British Academic Press
45 Bloomsbury Square
London WC1A 2HY

An imprint of I.B. Tauris & Co Ltd

In the United States of America
and Canada distributed by
St Martin's Press
175 Fifth Avenue
New York
NY 10010

A CIP record for this book is available from the British Library

Library of Congress Catalog card number: 91-68002
A full CIP record is available from the Library of Congress

ISBN 1-85043-488-3

Printed and bound in Great Britain by
WBC Limited, Bridgend, Mid Glamorgan.

For Kenneth Robinson, CBE,
scholar and administrator extraordinary

CONTENTS

1

IMPERIALISM AND THE STATE IN THE THIRD WORLD

Michael Twaddle

Imperialism, interpreted as the rule of foreigners by strangers, is as old as human history. But, seen as the rule of foreigners by capitalist strangers, it is a much more recent phenomenon, considered by Lenin to have commenced as late as the 1890s when, in his view, most advanced capitalist countries entered a monopolist mode and competed amongst themselves for direct control of most of the world's last unconquered land masses.[1] Almost all of these areas were situated in what has become known subsequently as the Third World.

The Third World was largely an invention of the Cold War.[2] Earlier political geographers had divided countries more simply, between an Old World on the eastern side of the Atlantic Ocean, and a New World on its western shores. But increasingly after 1945 this division was replaced by a three-fold partition between a First World, espousing, or at least partly espousing, capitalist policies; a Second World, occupied by communist-dominated states; and a Third World consisting of countries which came to independence from colonial rule by more advanced capitalist countries during and immediately after the Second World War, and whose populations' ultimate loyalties were courted continuously by statesmen from both the First and Second worlds for as long as the Cold War lasted.

To be sure, this is an oversimplified version of recent international relations. But it is not an essentially incorrect one. The first substantial number of Third World states to be created in the modern era arose out of colonies in Central and Southern America revolting against Spain and Portugal in the early nineteenth century; this was very shortly after the successful slave rebellion of the 1790s in the then-French plantation colony of Saint Domingue in the Caribbean Sea laid the foundations of the independent black republic of Haiti.[3] The next big batch of 'new states' to be created were the successor states to the Ottoman and Austro-Hungarian empires in the Middle East and Eastern Europe at the end of the First World War, though many of those in Europe were to fall under communist control twenty to thirty years later.[4] Then, as a consequence of the Second World War amongst other things, large numbers of Asian, African, Caribbean and Pacific countries came to independence.[5] Finally, there is a miscellaneous group of countries falling into no particular category, among whom should be noted Ethiopia (which managed to retain political independence for most of the time that its neighbours succumbed to white colonial rule, only very briefly being ruled by Italy), and various newly industrializing countries – (NICs) on the western Pacific rim such as Hong Kong, South Korea, Singapore and Taiwan. The European instances excepted, these together comprise the contemporary Third World, the NICs being at present by far the most economically successful amongst them.[6] Imperialism, however, had been a contentious matter both before and after the onset of the Cold War, and remains so.

Marxist theories of imperialism were originally fleshed out during the first two decades of the twentieth century, principally in order to explain why the expected final collapse of capitalism was taking so long. The outbreak of the First World War and the promptness with which European working peoples attacked one another rather than their bosses added fresh urgency to thought. Nationalism, in retrospect, seems to have had something to do with this, as well as the autonomy of political choice at the time of outbreak of the war from anything approaching economic rationality. But Marxist writers mostly looked elsewhere for explanation and for ammunition with which to pursue more sectarian concerns. Rosa Luxemburg provided in *Die Akkumulation des Kapitals* (1913) an analysis of imperialism which is still read respectfully today because of its pioneering probing of articulations between expanding capitalist and pre-capitalist social formations outside Europe. But during and after the 1914–18 War it was her advocacy of the mass revolutionary strike in order to speed up the final collapse of capitalism, otherwise given a new lease of life by imperialist expansion, that excited more immediate attention.

Marx himself had seen the expansion of capitalism outside its original heartlands as both a less important phenomenon and a more benign one than had Luxemburg; it was a marginal matter, in at least two senses. Luxemburg, however, considered that capitalism could only survive if it expanded its territory continually. One problem with this view, as Mommsen has pointed out, is that

> Rosa Luxemburg's basic adherence to Marx's complicated and controversial theory of surplus value, which by definition accrued to capitalists alone, prevented her from considering whether, if the consumer capacity of the masses were increased, internal markets might not afford suitable opportunities for the profitable investment of unconsumed i.e. reinvestable, surplus value.[7]

Another defect was that Luxemburg undoubtedly misunderstood the significance of the enormous rise in overseas investment at the start of the twentieth century. She assumed that it was closely associated with colonial annexation. Yet, as Robinson and Gallagher amongst others have reminded us more recently, it diverged widely from it.[8] Hilferding had taken a slightly different view. In *Das Finanzkapital* (1910), he was more concerned to explain why capitalist crises had recently become less frequent (there had not been one since 1896), and he argued that free trade had been replaced by finance capital, whose dominance and ability to intervene with state help anywhere in the world had temporarily delayed the final catastrophe. But it was the British journalist and free-trader J. A. Hobson, with his wide array of attacks upon overseas investment and colonial annexations in *Imperialism* (1902), whom Lenin used most extensively in his own famous study of *Imperialism, the Highest Stage of Capitalism* (1917). This was written in order not only to explain the First World War but to attack the reformism of Karl Kautsky, who had suggested that the final collapse of capitalism might be still further delayed by the emergence of an 'ultra-imperialism' stopping for the time being further intra-imperialist wars. In retrospect, Lenin's work on imperialism reads more like a tract than a treatise, but its subsequent importance was of course vastly increased by the success of his faction in seizing power in Russia in 1917; for many years afterwards it retained unquestionable status as unholy writ.

Shortly after the Bolshevik Revolution, Lenin also latched onto one of the greatest uses of imperialism as political ideology, namely, as a weapon against non-communist empires. This tendency was continued by Stalin, who told the Twelfth Congress of the Russian Communist Party in 1923: 'Either we succeed in stirring up, in revolutionizing, the remote rear of imperialism – the colonial and semi-colonial countries of the East – and thereby hasten the fall of imperialism; or we fail to do so and thereby strengthen imperialism and weaken the force of our movement'.[9] Such statements reversed Marx's original view that imperialism was good for capitalism but only of marginal importance in its development, and substituted a new conventional wisdom that (1) imperialism was bad news for all backward areas of the world, and (2) imperialism was of utterly central importance to the development of capitalism itself.

The first view has been developed further, particularly by scholars associated with André Gunder Frank, who stress the uniquely distorting effect, the 'development of underdevelopment', no less, capitalism has had in the Third World.[10] The second stress, on the other hand, has led to an oddly focused debate among historians over the colonial partition of Africa at the close of the nineteenth century; the 'theory of economic imperialism' being something of a straw man in this debate, as imperialism, on most Marxist views, did not arise until after the scramble for Africa had taken place; and even after this date Lenin was clearly wrong about the direction of most overseas investment, let alone its political significance.[11] Only as regards the US invasion of Cuba in 1898[12] and the outbreak of war in South Africa in 1899 are there really plausible cases for economic imperialism being identical with colonial annexation, the South African war in particular being popularly termed, in continental Europe at the time, 'les Boers contre la Bourse'. This is the subject to which Shula Marks and Stanley Trapido return with vigour in Chapter 4.

Other difficulties with many Marxist views of imperialism derive from Lenin's use of Hobson's *Imperialism* (1902). Hobson was a bitter critic of British overseas investment, but for very un-Marxist reasons. He was a free-trade liberal who saw colonial annexations and wars as a hugely expensive way of propping up the power and profits of a very small class of rentier capitalists, who pursued profit abroad to the detriment of investment at home. Only by manipulating the masses through an appeal to their patriotism did this tiny class of capitalists get away with this, in Hobson's view, huge confidence trick; ideally, social reform should increase the purchasing powers of the masses and thereby render imperialism powerless. Lenin ignored Hobson's theories and only used his facts. In retrospect, Hobson's theories seem less unbalanced than Lenin's facts regarding the supposed coincidence of overseas investment with colonial annexation. Hobson's views on 'under-consumption' were later taken up and given some seminal twists by John Maynard Keynes,[13] while his intuitions about connections between overseas annexation and metropolitan social structures were subsequently developed further by Joseph Schumpeter and Hannah Arendt (for her analysis of the origins of fascism).

Schumpeter wrote his essay *Zur Soziologie der Imperialismen* (1919) as an explicit attack upon contemporary Marxist theories of imperialism. Capitalism he considered to be essentially anti-imperialist in character, and such monopolistic and expansionist tendencies as characterized pre-1914 capitalism he put down to the malevolent influence of an anachronistic militarism surviving from the European feudal past. Schumpeter defined imperialism as 'the objectless disposition on the part of a state to unlimited forcible expansion'.[14] The basic trouble with this particular formulation is that while the European colonial annexations of the late nineteenth and early twentieth centuries were certainly sometimes this, they were not always so. Similarly, while much European overseas investment in the late nineteenth century certainly did not go to areas of European colonial annexation, some of it did. Furthermore, while the 'theory of economic imperialism' may well be a straw man as far as debate about the causes of the scramble for Africa is concerned, it would be absurd to suggest that the partitioners did not believe that there was something economically useful about Black Africa. Imperialism needs to be demythologized, not simply wished away.

One influential attempt to demythologize imperialism was made in the 1950s, and subsequently, by Ronald Robinson and John Gallagher, in their elaboration of an earlier historian's throwaway phrase about 'informal empire' into an 'imperialism of free trade'.[15] In their view, European imperialism throughout the nineteenth and twentieth centuries in the Third World was essentially empire on the cheap: 'informal control if possible, formal rule if necessary'.[16] In Robinson's view especially:

The excentric idea ... contains two basic theorems: one is that European imperialism generated its main force through linking and exploiting relative inequalities in local and regional balances of wealth and power, which determined input-output ratios, cost-benefits and this role in economic and strategic expansion. The other is that the imperial sum of all these structural relativities is encapsulated in the changing terms for local collaboration. These indigenous linkages, it is suggested, comprise the only field of study in which the so-called metropolitan and peripheral elements come together. Consequently, the nature and extent of imperialism, with or without empire, can only be defined in terms of local collaborative systems at the point of impact.[17]

The approach has much to commend it and has proved popular with historians and political scientists alike.[18] However, there are several problems with it as overarching theory. One concerns the internal coherence of the notion of informal empire as a consequence of the sheer diversity and complexity of European and North America informal expansive pressures overseas during both the nineteenth and twentieth centuries. This is a subject which Colin Newbury discusses in detail in Chapter 2. Other problems arise from the era in which Robinson and Gallagher first wrote. For, as Andrew Porter remarks, while they were conscious of the 'expansiveness of the United States under the banner of free trade', and probably remain sounder in their understanding of certain aspects of the metropolitan economy than more recent advocates of a more 'gentlemanly capitalism' shaping European expansion overseas, they were very much 'influenced by an anti-Marxism characteristic of the 1950s'.[19] Their excessive anti-Marxism distorted some of their attacks upon theories of economic imperialism then current[20] as well as perhaps encouraging them to take Western capitalism itself too much for granted. For, as another scholar points out in criticism of their views, 'The extent and character of the European lead [in economic and military power] surely varied over time, which may help to explain the relative costs of different options, while the opportunities of gain from (formal or informal) control also varied over time as a result of economic and political changes in capitalist centres'.[21]

This is an important point. Nowadays the ending of formal empires throughout most of the Third World during the last half-century must be seen as a much more complicated matter than principally the breakdown of local collaborative networks underpinning European imperial control systems. The global crisis of the Second World witnessed the outright defeat of some European empires and the severe weakening of others. Then what D. A. Low and John Lonsdale have called the 'second colonial occupation' immediately after the Second World War, with its stress on welfare as well as law and order in British colonies and protectorates,[22] further shaped their transition to independence as well as sharply increasing their costs to the metropolitan power in the 1940s and 1950s. There was also continuous pressure during and after the Second World War from the US Government for more rapid formal decolonization as well as for the possibility of remaining European dependencies passing under some form of international control.[23] To be sure, US pressure here was little more disinterested than it had been at the time of the US takeover of Cuba at the close of the nineteenth century, but this did not diminish its effectiveness as yet another constraint upon European imperial powers already strapped financially in the wake of the Second World War.

The South African War (1899–1902) was another time when political and economic factors were extremely closely intertwined, in both causing the war and in shaping its aftermath. To start with, the Boer leaders appear to have expected

a short war and a rapid peace settlement – as had happened in 1881 when, after their defeat at Majuba Hill, the British restored the Transvaal's independence by the Convention of Pretoria. But in 1899, the British Government was in no mood to follow Gladstone's liberal footsteps, did not believe that the problem of the Afrikaners could be 'killed with kindness', and was determined, as the prime minister, Lord Salisbury, put it 'that the real point to be made good in South Africa is that we, not the Dutch are Boss'.[24]

And a real war did indeed ensue, and by 1900 'over 200,000 British and Imperial troops were involved in a war with Boer forces fielding no more than 45,000'.[25] 'In 1979', relates the same historian,

two of Britain's leading South African historians, Shula Marks and Stanley Trapido, fired off an exasperated salvo and have followed it with a few further squibs since. They castigated historians for their 'obsession with the immediate causes of the Anglo-Boer war, rather than with the structural context in which it occurred', and for exhibiting 'an almost neurotic absorption' in the question of the individual motivations and personalities of Rhodes, Chamberlain and Milner without at any point locating them in an analysis of late nineteenth-century imperialism. 'Milner the man has been overestimated', they declared, while 'the nature of "Milnerism", as an expression of late nineteenth-century imperialism at both the ideological and practical level has been underestimated'.[26]

In a contribution to

the *Cambridge History of Africa* Shula Marks has also pointed to the 'peculiar disjuncture' which existed between 'the enclave of advanced mining capital' and the form of the state in the late nineteenth-century Transvaal, where political power remained in the hands of Afrikaner notables representing a pre-industrial agrarian society. Although some individual Afrikaners were 'modernising' and making the transition to capitalism, notably in a more commercial attitude to agriculture, it was, she comments, 'an earlier entrepreneurial and individualistic form of capitalism which was remote from the world demanded by the new concentrations of economic power on the rand, and from the demand of the mining magnates for a new form of centralized and effectively coercive state apparatus'.[27]

These views Andrew Porter attacks in a recent article,[28] again stressing the need for a more profound understanding of British policy-makers' calculations, while Iain Smith stresses rather 'the essential seamlessness of the economic, political, cultural, ideological and military drives of imperialism in the late nineteenth century'[29] In Chapter 4 of this volume Shula Marks and Stanley Trapido attack both formulations and argue again in favour of a more consciously capitalist theory of imperialism and state-formation in South Africa during and immediately after the war of 1899 to 1902.

Debate about capitalism and imperialism in South Africa shows little sign of abating as the white rulers of the Republic of South Africa themselves come under increasing pressure from the non-white majority populations.[30] However, elsewhere in the Third World two specific questions about imperialism seem to be becoming increasingly important nowadays. One concerns the economic effects of Western imperialism in the Third World. The other concerns the political legacy of Western imperialism in this whole area, especially in the creation of post-colonial states.

Current conventional wisdom on the first question is that, NICs apart, where special factors are said to have been important[31], European imperialism has been profoundly antagonistic to sustainable economic development within the Third World. This is now widely assumed to have been the case, not so much because of direct capitalist exploitation through imperialism, nor because of any supposedly widespread 'development of underdevelopment' it caused on the periphery of the global capitalist economy, but more because of its 'statish' and 'welfarist' character, particularly during the post-1945 period. Today structural adjustment packages (SAPs) are being implemented throughout the Third World, with aid and advice from international financial institutions such as the International Monetary Fund (IMF), the World Bank and the European Community, with the aim of undoing, not only the profligacy of post-colonial regimes, but the statishness emanating from their late colonial periods of government.

This is where the contribution of David Fieldhouse in Chapter 8 of this volume is so suggestive, besides being important in its own right, not only because of the evidence from both the Colonial Office and United Africa Company's records regarding the transition to, or rather further strengthening of, corporatism in British West Africa during the Second World War, but because of the rhetorical question posed by this most Schumpeterian of British economic historians: would West African farmers really have been better off without state marketing mechanisms in the last fifty years?

Current orthodoxy in international financial institutions stresses the costs rather than the benefits of state involvement in economic planning, most of the traffic in policy-making nowadays being towards ending state involvement in economic development in the Third World in the interests of 'free trade'. But already there are at least hints of a contrary view, in the need for poverty alleviation programmes to be adopted alongside structural adjustment plans;[32] and in the discovery that richer Third World countries like Thailand and Turkey have benefited more from SAPs than the poorer generality of middle African countries which have suffered excessively from having state support and expenditure cut too much during the 1980s.[33] Clearly, SAPs by themselves have proved insufficient to promote economic development in Third World states. Furthermore, as 1993 approaches, it is regional associations that appear likely to become increasingly important in shaping more developed capitalist countries' economic policies. Hence the prospect arises of free trade being required of Third World countries at the very time that protectionism is being further entrenched within the First World, with extremely little likelihood of either the European Community or the USA providing a level playing field for the sale, say, of primary products from the Third World. Only on such a playing field is it really plausible to suggest that the Third World's farmers might have been better off without any aid from state marketing mechanisms in their own countries during the last fifty years.

This brings us to the political as well as the economic impact of Western imperialism upon the Third World. From the widespread view at independence in the 1950s and 1960s that state mechanisms would be natural, inevitable and unproblematical channels for future development assistance,[34] we have now reached the curious point at which subsequent Marxist criticisms of the 'overdeveloped post-colonial state' in Asia (Alavi)[35], in Africa (Leys)[36] and, with modification for the intensity of nearby US influence, the Caribbean (Thomas)[37], have been taken over as the dominant coventional wisdom by the IMF, World Bank and European Community.[38] This is the perception that the state apparatuses left behind in the Third World by European colonialism were 'over-developed' in excessive sources of patronage and corruption by post-colonial élites. This perception has been adopted now by the very un-Marxist heads of international financial bodies like the IMF, the World Bank and the European Community. Throughout the 1980s these bodies appeared intent upon cutting state expenditure remorselessly in the Third World, seemingly in order to re-invent the eighteenth- and nineteenth-century *laissez-faire* state at least there if nowhere else.

Here it is important not to exaggerate the antagonism to state expenditure adopted by supposedly *laissez-faire* European governments during the late eighteenth and nineteenth centuries. In fact, was private as well as public monopolies that disturbed that great high priest of free trade, Adam Smith: private conspiracies against the public interest.[39] As Professors Marshall and Bayley have reminded us too,[40] and as Donald Wood demonstrates elegantly in his account of the creation of British Guiana in 1831 in Chapter 3 of this volume, British imperialism immediately before, during and after the Napoleonic era was concerned on 'scientific' and geopolitical grounds to strengthen British power and security in those parts of the world where it was already represented in more tenuous form, especially at the expense of the Dutch.

The constraints on British imperial expansion in the century after Trafalgar were essentially three: there was the desirability of not overextending British resources in overambitious policy initiatives overseas; there was the desirability of not provoking other European powers into forming an anti-British coalition as a consequence of not leaving at least some of the spoils of overseas empire to them; and it was desirable to avoid economic conflicts within the British empire too, by pursuing a policy of free trade. For, as was remarked by D. W. Brogan,

> Free trade between India and Britain may have accelerated the decline of Indian handicraftsmen (they went the way of their class in all countries of the globe). But it also ruined British landlords and farmers ... British power provided an arena in which economic forces could work over a quarter of the globe. These 'devil take the hindmost' economics were often murderous, but the victims might be Cornish tin miners or East Anglian grain-growers ... [and] the increasing scrupulousness with which British power was wielded, the increasing pangs of conscience with which the fruits of empire were harvested, these were the contributions of the little Englanders. When we consider the relative weight of the home and Indian governments, as well as the relative weight of the two statesmen concerned, there is something edifying in a bald statement that Professor Knaplund refrains from spoiling by comment. 'Gladstone sought unsuccess-fully to convince the viceroy of India, Lord Ripon, that Indian interests in connection with Egypt and the Suez Canal justified charging her with some of the cost of British military expeditions to the Red Sea'.[41]

The military costs and benefits of empire to Britain in the nineteenth century have given rise to considerable debate in recent years,[42] but common to all the debaters, as to all British imperialists at the time, is agreement regarding the necessity of retaining at least a certain mini-mum of state capability in even the smallest colony or protectorate.

At the time of the subsequent scramble for Africa, state competi-tiveness increased enormously in intensity in Europe. Here one is not thinking primarily of European states needing overseas colonies in order to accommodate excess domestic population, because in the Third World one is dealing more with colonies of strategy or exploitation than with colonies of settlement. Nor is one thinking only of intra-state rivalry in Europe being deflected into intra-European tensions. Rather one is thinking principally of the very basic point that at the end of the nineteenth century there was a qualitative jump in the technological superiority enjoyed by European powers when dealing with non-European peoples.[43] Granted this superiority in technology as a result of the invention of the telegraph, submarine cables, the development of steam-powered shipping, and the machine gun, excessive attention to other factors accounting for the European (and the United States') seizures of further colonial territory in the non-Western world at that time seems beside the point. Only in two areas did Western imperialism in the Third World come up against powerfully countervailing forces.

One was in the Far East, where European and North American imperialism confronted all the desperation of a decaying Manchu empire on the Chinese mainland and, shortly afterwards, Japanese imperialism too. This is not the place to analyse Japanese imperialism in any detail,[44] save to note that Japan was thrown into political and economic turmoil by the appearance in Japanese waters of US Commodore Perry's warships in the 1850s, as a result of which turmoil not only were Japan's ports opened to foreign traders but new leaders brought to power in 1868 'acting in the emperor's name, who ... launched Japan upon a programme of modernization in the Western manner'.[45] This programme proved astonishingly successful. As a result of it, and of the size and complexity of China and the sheer number of differing Western interests involved, Western imperialism was forced to temper its aggressiveness to the demands of the international law which had grown up to govern inter-state relations within Europe since the sixteenth and seventeenth centuries. The British colony of Hong Kong emerged out of this maelstrom of opium war, extra-territorial rights and treaty port concessions to become one of the world's leading trading centres; but only until 1997, as Norman Miners makes clear in Chapter 14. Thereafter control of Hong Kong reverts to China.

The other major area of continuing constraint was finance. This particularly affected smaller European colonies in the Caribbean like British Guiana, whose founding Donald Wood describes in Chapter 3. There, economies of scale were more difficult to achieve than in colonies with larger populations. In the Caribbean too, financial difficulties were compounded by the further emancipation of slave workers on the region's sugar plantations between the 1830s and 1860s, and by the ending of preferential duties on sugar cane imported into Britain from British colonies in the 1840s. The situation was only slightly alleviated by the importation into Caribbean sugar plantations of indentured labourers from other parts of the Third World, South Asia especially. Economically, this 'new system of slavery', as Hugh Tinker has called it,[46] helped to keep other wages in British Guiana and comparable Caribbean colonies low, but at a ferocious social price in subsequent communal conflict between the descendants of former slaves and the descendants of indentured labourers.

By the Second World War it was clear that further economic changes were required and that British colonies in the Caribbean would soon go the political way of colonies of settlement like Canada, Australia and New Zealand, and obtain dominion status, the basic debate being over whether and how they should do this, collectively or separately. In 1942 a leading British political scientist considered dominion status to be 'as much an evasion as a solution of the problem of the evolution of colonies into nations'. But he also remarked that, to date, the British Empire had been

> most successful in exporting its political institutions as Rome was most successful in exporting its laws. How simple is the party system of India compared with the religious or social system . . . Britain has left the laws, the religions, the habits of her subjects pretty much alone, interfering reluctantly to put down widow-burning in India or feudal jurisdiction in Quebec or witchcraft in Africa. But she has insisted on imposing as much as possible of her political system on vast areas that otherwise might have got along, if not well, at least comfortably without it.[47]

That is a point whose pertinence for both the Caribbean and India might still seem clear, but its application to Africa and those colonies and protectorates that became parts of the British Empire at the close of the nineteenth century requires considerable qualification in the light of Kenneth Robinson's seminal study of *The Dilemmas of Trusteeship* over these particular dependencies between the First World War and the Second.[48]

This is because the colonial states imposed upon Africa and other areas of the Third World at that time differed from those imposed upon the Caribbean and India during the earlier mercantilist era of European imperialism in a number of ways. As a scholar following in Kenneth Robinson's footsteps puts it, the colonial state imposed there 'embodied only select . . . truncated features of their historic progeni-tor' with the 'state-limiting doctrines of constitutionalism, civil liberties and liberalism . . . selectively excluded from the ideological baggage invoked to rationalise colonial hegemony'. In their place were substi-tuted the notions of trusteeship, good government and *mise en valeur*.[49] As regards Africa,

> the Berlin conference of 1884 mandated swift accomplishment of 'effective occupation' . . . [while] the political pact between metropolitan supporters and opponents of African occupation required that each colony be self-financing. European domination had [therefore] to be quickly secured by combining force, diplomacy and collaboration to neutralise local opposition and organise local commerce, production and labor in ways that would yield state revenue.[50]

By the inter-war period colonial state systems in Africa had been largely rationalized, professionalized and legitimized in the ways analysed so splendidly by Kenneth Robinson. But during the period of colonial state-formation in the late nineteenth and early twentieth centuries a much wider and more flexible repertoire of administrative actions and programmes had been deployed in order to serve the twin imperatives of accumulation and control: accumulation, to pay for colonial administration, and control, to moderate accumulation's destabilizing social effects as well as to show ultimately who was boss.[51] This process characterized by John Lonsdale as 'syncretic articulation',[52] involved the combined and uneven development of both capitalist and pre-capitalist economic strategies in colonial Africa. Inevitably there were economic and social problems resulting from 'syncretic articulation'. But arguably the most serious difficulties arose on the political front once the processes of decolonization were set in motion in the aftermath of the Second World War. For then, though departing colonial powers hurriedly introduced democratic procedures familiar in Western Europe, these were profoundly at odds with the bureaucratic structures of colonial states established in sub-Saharan Africa. Still more ominously, argues Shaseen Mozaffar, far too frequently 'the colonial state also fostered an indigenous ruling class whose structural roots were embedded not in the underlying socio-economic foundations of African societies, but in the relations of political power centered around the bureaucratic procedures of the colonial state'.[53]

However, it was not only tropical Africa which suffered excessive bureaucratization of indigenous power as a consequence of Western imperialism. India too appears to have been a casualty, if Sudipta Kaviraj is to be believed. For the British colonial period there, though it lasted for a considerably longer period,

> saw the appearance of two types of division in Indian society. The first was a division between those who made the world they inhabited intelligible in terms of modernist discourse and those who did not. This division ran decisively between the Indian élite and the lower orders. On top of it, however, nationalism put in place a second political division between colonialism and the Indian nation.

Gandhi bridged the gap between the two discourses for a time, but Nehru and his successors widened it. Fortunately for Nehru, he enjoyed the 'silent but subtle and massively significant cultural approval of the modern élite' throughout India for his politics of modernization through state auspices, while 'the backwash for mobilisation of the national movement ensured an implicit trust of the masses in the initiatives of their leaders'. But Kaviraj stresses that 'the support that the Congress leadership received was not of the kind that the bourgeoisie in classical bourgeois revolutions of the west created for themselves, by reconstituting through a process of prior cultural movement a hegemony and directive preeminence for themselves'. Indeed, as ambitious policies of modernization were pursued by the post-colonial Indian state, increasingly it 'had to find its personnel, especially at lower levels, from groups who did not inhabit the modernist discourse'. This creates an enormous dilemma for contemporary democracy in India:

> if Indian politics become genuinely democratic in the sense of coming into line with what the majority of ordinary Indians would consider reasonable, they will become less democratic in the sense of conforming to the principles of a secular, democratic

state acceptable to the early nationalist élite . . . . It appears that
the difference between the two discourses is reappearing, now
that the lower discourse is reasserting itself and making itself
heard precisely through the opportunities created by the upper
one. The way it rewrites the political world might not be liked by
the ruling modernist élite, but it is too late to disenfranchise
them.[54]

Many of the resultant tensions and contradictions are recaptured by
Dennis Austin and Anirudha Gupta in their account of India's ninth
general election (Chapter 12), while in Chapter 11 W. H. Morris-
Jones analyses further the modernist post-colonial state during its first
years of independence from Britain, as expressed in the *Letters to Chief
Ministers* within the Indian Union.

Clearly some aspects of imperial and post-imperial history are
easier to explain than others. Jawaharlal Nehru, it has been said, is
easier to place as the product of a certain kind of education at
Cambridge University than is Mahatma Gandhi to be seen as an
entirely predictable product of the London Inns of Court. Another
conundrum, in view of the turmoil into which so many African states
have plunged since independence, is how earlier colonial officials
managed to get away with so little overt turbulence, considering their
comparatively small numbers, when they themselves were in power.
Parts of the answer have been given already: the technologically
superior fire-power available to servants of western imperialism from
the late nineteenth century onwards, and the flexibility with which
officials required to establish minimal administrations on the ground
forged alliances with a wide variety of incumbent élites. But political
imperialism necessitated particular skills where minimal rather than
maximal states were being constructed, and recruitment to the various
colonial services established for this purpose clearly requires further
study.[55] Here T. H. R. Cashmore, in Chapter 6, provides fascinating
further information on the indispensable weapon in the British
colonial administrator's political armoury: bluff. In chapters 9 and 10,
John Kent and John Hargreaves take further another important aspect
of this subject, pioneered by Kenneth Robinson at Nuffield College
during the 1940s and 1950s: the comparative study of French and
British colonialism in Africa.[56] John Hargreaves takes further Robinson's suggestions regarding differing British and French 'habits of
mind' towards colonialism and its ending in Africa, while John Kent

considers in detail an important case study of colonial boundary conflict and maintenance in two geographically adjacent areas of West Africa ruled by Britain and France respectively in the immediate aftermath of the Second World War.

Imperialism, as must be clear by now, cannot be considered to be an entirely satisfactory word for scholars to use to describe all these varied but related matters. As the etymology of the word itself suggests, however, the study of imperialism is intimately associated with empires and colonies. But this is not necessarily always the case in the modern era. In the Americas, the Monroe Doctrine (1823) vetoed the creation of new colonies by European countries in the western hemisphere, but not 'dollar diplomacy' by the United States, sometimes supported by force, sometimes just with threats and unequal financial practices.[57] Capitalism, too, has not always been closely linked with Western imperialism in the Third World, but sometimes it has been so linked, as in the many Asian and African dependencies established during the second half of the nineteenth century. In these circumstances 'imperialism' is probably best separated analytically from both 'capitalism' and 'colonialism' and defined in some median manner as the pursuit of intrusive and unequal economic policy in foreign countries supported by significant degrees of coercion.

Thus defined, imperialism as formal empire (or colonialism) may be considered nowadays to be largely a thing of the past, except for a few strategic colonies (*colonies de position*) and a number of very small island dependencies.[58] On the other hand, until a few years ago it might have appeared that imperialism as informal empire (or neocolonialism, to employ Nkrumah's terminology) had an assured future ahead of it in both the non-communist and communist-dominated worlds.[59] But that was before the Cold War had virtually ended. It was also before Colin Newbury had published his vigorous assault upon the very notion of 'informal empire' in Chapter 2 in this volume!

To be sure, some scholars might prefer a still broader approach to the study of imperialism and the state in the Third World than the one adopted here. Together with historians associated with the so-called 'British world system' approach, such scholars might prefer to view the ending of European overseas empires after the Second World War as part of a much wider process associated with possession of the nuclear deterrent, European economic integration, indeed political power more generally. But this, as Jacques Marseille has remarked,[60] is to define imperialism so broadly as to render it meaningless. Here we have treated the Marxist approach to imperialism sceptically, but not totally dismissively because, as Marseille also remarks, Lenin may have got most things wrong about imperialism but at least he got its chronology roughly right.[61] Recently some scholars have started to follow the late Italian Marxist, Antonio Gramsci, in investigating ways in which Western imperialism was legitimated in Africa as well as India by 'hegemonic' projects concerned with education and medicine,[62] and we look forward to further publications in this field. In this volume Maryinez Lyons represents this tendency, in her fascinating account of colonial medicine in Zaïre (Chapter 7). Holger Bernt Hansen's discussion of church and state in Uganda during the early colonial period (Chapter 5) also necessarily covers much culturally hegemonic ground and more, as well as providing important background to one of the country's most intractable political problems today. However, wherever the colonial state entered into structural alliances with incumbent élites, this entailed abandoning at least some of the universalistic aspects of state power considered fundamental to hegemony by Gramsci himself, therefore also undermining at the same time much of the legitimating advantage of its policies regarding medicine, more advanced education and the media.[63]

Ethiopia was an African empire which expanded considerably in size at the time of the Scramble for Africa, extending its sway over many new areas and peoples at the end of the last century with the assistance of the new firearms. For much of the twentieth century, apart from a very brief period of Italian occupation, its emperor was Haile-Selassie. But in 1974 Haile-Selassie was overthrown in a revolution whose bloodiness soon came to rival that of the French Revolution, thereby strengthening considerably a number of guerilla movements seeking independence from the surviving imperial core. The ferocity of Eritrean separatist activity is perhaps unsurprising, considering that it had been an Italian colony between 1890 and 1952, after which it was very controversially incorporated within Ethiopia. But the intensity of other movements operating in the north of Ethiopia during the 1970s and 1980s is more difficult to explain. One of the burdens of Christopher Clapham's discussion (Chapter 13) is therefore to explain why areas in the south and west, which were forcibly incorporated into Ethiopia since the late nineteenth century and thereafter subjected to capitalist agriculture, have been much less rebellious than regions in the north whose peasantries have controlled their own means of production. Capitalism appears in a very Schumpeterian form in the Ethiopian imperial story as related by Clapham, the continuing struggle for hegemonic dominance there also assuming an extremely un-Gramscian character.

Notes

1. See Wolfgang J. Mommsen, *Theories of Imperialism* (London 1980) and Anthony Brewer, *Marxist Theories of Imperialism: a Critical Survey*, 2nd edn (London 1990) for good introductions.
2. P. Lyon, 'The emergence of the Third World' in *The Expansion of International Society*, Hedley Bull and Adam Watson (eds) (Oxford 1984).
3. See Franklin W. Knight, *The Caribbean: Genesis of a Fragmented Nationalism*, 2nd edn (New York 1990).
4. 'European: multinational empires and new nations', pp. 143–91 in H. Seton-Watson, *Nations and States* (London 1977).
5. R. Emerson, *From Empire to Nation: The Rise to Self-Assertion of Asian and African Peoples* (Cambridge, Mass. 1960).
6. See Nigel Harris, *The End of the Third World: Newly Industrializing Countries and the Decline of an Ideology* (London 1986).
7. Mommsen, op. cit., p. 42.
8. Ronald Robinson and John Gallagher with Alice Denny, *Africa and the Victorians: The Official Mind of Imperialism*, 2nd edn (London 1981).
9. Quoted in Mommsen, op. cit., p. 52.
10. For good introduction and updating on Latin America, see C. Abel and C. M. Lewis (eds), *Latin America, Economic Imperialism and the State: The Political Economy of the External Connection from Independence to the Present* (1985).
11. See, further, N. Etherington, 'Theories of imperialism in Southern Africa revisited', *African Affairs 81* (1982), and references to the author's other writings on imperialism.
12. For the 'pseudo-Republic' established in Cuba after the US intervention, see Louis A. Perez Jr., *Cuba after the Platt Amendment, 1902–1934* (Pittsburgh 1986) and *Cuba and the United States: Ties of Singular Intimacy* (Athens, Georgia 1990).
13. See, further, Peter Clarke, *The Keynesian Revolution in the Making 24–1936* (Oxford 1988).
14. Quoting from the translation published as *Imperialism and Social Classes* (Oxford 1988).
15. 'The imperialism of free trade', *Economic History Review 6* (1953), pp. 1–15.
16. Ibid. p. 13.
17. Ronald Robinson, 'The excentric idea of imperialism, with or without empire', pp. 267–89 in W. J. Mommsen and J. Osterhammel (eds), *Imperialism and After: Continuities and Discontinuities* (London 1986), pp. 256–8.

18. Anthony Brewer, *Marxist Theories of Imperialism: a Critical Survey*, 2nd edn (London 1990), pp. 256–8.
19. A. Porter, '"Gentlemanly capitalism" and empire: the British experience since 1750?', *Journal of Imperial and Commonwealth History 18* (1990), pp. 271–2. See also P. J. Cain and A. G. Hopkins, 'Gentlemanly capitalism and British expansion overseas', *Economic History Review 39* (1986), pp. 501–25 and 40, pp. 1–26.
20. See Etherington, 'Theories' [cited in note 11], passim.
21. See Brewer, *Marxist Theories* [cited in note 18] p. 258.
22. See their 'Introduction' to the *History of East Africa*, Vol. 3, D. A. Low and Alison Smith (eds) (Oxford 1976).
23. Wm Roger Louis, *Imperialism at Bay, 1941–1945: The United States and the Decolonization of the British Empire* (Oxford 1977) is the definitive account.
24. Iain R. Smith. 'The origins of the South African War (1899–1902): a reassessment', *South African Historical Journal 22* (1990), p. 26, quoting A. Porter, *The Origins of the South African War* (Manchester 1980), p. 228.
25. Smith, op. cit., p. 25.
26. Ibid., op. cit., p. 42, quoting S. Marks and S. Trapido, 'Lord Milner and the South African state, *History Workshop 8* (1979).
27. Ibid., p. 52, quoting S. Marks, 'Southern Africa' in *Cambridge History of Africa*, Vol. 6, R. Oliver and G. N. Sanderson (eds) (Cambridge 1985).
28. A. Porter, 'The South African War (1899–1902): context and motive reconsidered', *Journal of African History 31* (1990), pp. 43–57.
29. Smith, 'South African War' [cited in note 24], p. 54.
30. See the special number of *Radical History Review 46–7* (1990) on 'Radical history and South Africa', especially the editorial introduction by B. Bozzoli and P. Delius, pp. 13–45.
31. See N. Harris, *The End of the Third World* (London 1986).
32. See E. A. Brett, 'Rebuilding survival strategies for the poor', pp. 297–310 in Holger Bernt Hansen and Michael Twaddle (eds), *Changing Uganda: the Dilemmas of Structural Adjustment and Revolutionary Change* (London 1991).
33. See Tony Killick, *A Reaction Too Far: Economic Theory and the Role of the State in Developing Countries* (London 1989); and Paul Mosley, Jane Harrigan and John Toye, *Aid and Power: The World Bank and Policy-based Lending*, 2 vols (London 1991), passim.
34. For a good discussion, see Martin Doornbos, 'The African state in academic debate: retrospect and prospect', *Journal of Modern African Studies 28* (1990), pp. 179–98.
35. H. Alavi, 'The state in post-colonial societies', *New Left Review 37* (1972).
36. C. Leyes, 'The "overdeveloped" post-colonial state: a re-evaluation, *Review of African Political Economy 5* (1976).
37. C. Y. Thomas, *The Rise of the Authoritarian State in Peripheral Societies* (New York 1984).
38. This is one of many shrewd points made by Jean-Francois Bayart in *L'Etat en Afrique: La politique du ventre* (Paris 1989).
39. Adam Smith's classic discussion is *An Inquiry into the Nature and Causes*

of the Wealth of Nations (1776) in which he remarks that 'The government of an exclusive company of merchants is, perhaps, the worst of all governments in any country whatever' (p. 68, Vol. 2, London, Everyman edn, 1910).

40. See, further, P. J. Marshall, *'A Free Though Conquering People': Britain and Asia in the Eighteenth Century* (London 1981): and C. A. Bayley, *Imperial Meridian: The British Empire and the World 1780–1830* (London 1989).

41. D. W. Brogan, introducing *The British Empire 1815–1939* (London 1942), pp. vii–ix.

42. See L. E. David and R. A. Huttenback, *Mammon and the Pursuit of Empire: The Political Economy of British Imperialism 1860–1912* (Cambridge 1986); A. Porter, 'The balance sheet of empire 1950–1914', *Historical Journal 31 (1988)*, pp. 685–99; P. K. O'Brien, 'The costs and benefits of British imperialism 1846–1914', *Past and Present 120* (August 1988), pp. 163–200; and P. M. Kennedy, comment in *Past and Present* 125 (November 1989), pp. 186–91 and P. K. O'Brien's reply, ibid., pp. 192–9.

43. See David R. Hendrick, *The Tools of Empire: Technology and European Imperialism in the Nineteenth Century* (New York 1981).

44. See W. G. Beasley, *Japanese Imperialism 1894–1945* (Oxford 1987).

45. Ibid., p. 30.

46. Hugh Tinker, *A New System of Slavery: The Export of Indian Labour Overseas 1830–1920* (London 1974).

47. Brogan, op. cit. [in note 41], p. x.

48. Kenneth Robinson, *The Dilemmas of Trusteeship: Aspects of British Colonial Policy between the Wars* (London 1965).

49. S. Mozaffer, 'A research strategy for analysing the colonial state in Africa', *Boston University African Studies Centre*, working paper 128 (1987).

50. Ibid.

51. See, further, John Lonsdale and Bruce Berman, 'Coping with the contradictions: the development of the colonial state in Kenya, 1895–1914', *Journal of African History 20* (1979).

52. John Lonsdale, 'States and social processes in Africa', *African Studies Review 24*, 2–3 (1981).

53. Mozaffer, op. cit.

54. S. Kaviraj, 'On state, society and discourse in India', *IDS Bulletin 21*, 4 (1990), a special number on the state in the Third World edited by James Manor.

55. There is already a small but growing literature; see, for example, R. Heussler, *Yesterday's Rulers* (Syracuse, New York 1963); L. H. Gann and P. Duignan, *The Rulers of British Africa 1870–1914* (London and Stanford 1978); R. Hunt and J. Harrison, *The District Officer in India 1930–1947* (London 1980), and F. M. Deng and M. W. Daly, *Bonds of Silk: the Human Factor in British Administration of the Sudan* (East Lancing 1989).

56. See especially Kenneth Robinson, 'A survey of the background material for the study of government in French tropical Africa', *American Political Science Review 50*, (1956), pp. 179–98, and the pioneering volume on *Five*

Elections in Africa, which he edited with W. J. M. Mackenzie (Oxford 1960).

57. David Healy, *US Expansionism: the Imperialist Urge in the 1890s* (Madison, Wisconsin).

58. This of course omits from discussion the four old sugar colonies of France (Réunion, Martinique, Guadeloupe and Cayenne), which were decolonized by incorporation within metropolitan France as *départements d'outre mer* in 1946.

59. See my article on 'Imperialism' in *The Social Science Encyclopedia* ed. Adam and Jessica Kuper (London 1985), p. 379, where a number of the arguments here appear in shorter form.

60. J. Marseille, *Empire colonial et imperialisme francais: Histoire d'un divorce* (1984), quoting from Seuil edition (Paris 1989), p. 20.

61. Ibid. pp. 28–9.

62. See Dagmar Engels, 'Conference report: foundations of imperial hegemony: Western education, public health and police in India and Africa, 1859 to independence . . . Berlin, 1–3 June 1989', *Bulletin of the German Historical Institute* 11, 3 (November 1989), pp. 28–35.

63. For further discussion of Gramsci's writings on hegemony see P. Anderson, 'The antinomies of Antonio Gramsci', *New Left Review 100* (1976–7); see also J. F. Bayart, *L'Etat en Afrique* (Paris 1989) for a brilliant application of hegemonic analysis more generally to African politics.

2

THE SEMANTICS OF INTERNATIONAL INFLUENCE:
Informal empires reconsidered

Colin Newbury

The purpose of this chapter is to examine the content of an historical metaphor derived by analogy from the political and constitutional relationship of tutelage and control by imperial powers over subordinate states. Indeed, the whole topic has been heavily influenced by literary invention. A cursory survey of the literature reveals, among the many forms of hegemony, 'missionary empires', the 'invisible empires' of multinationals, 'scientific empires' promoted by geologists, 'railway empires', 'hydraulic imperialism' by canal and dam builders, and 'paper empires' made by lawyers. Clearly, such an exercise of the imagination with considerable influence over the language of international relations calls for occasional reappraisal and is not yet ready to be discarded.[1]

The origins of this metaphorical profusion are not in doubt. The term 'informal empire' entered the historiography of imperialism in the 1930s as a casual by-product of British relations with Latin America. The reasons for its more extensive deployment by historians from the 1950s would seem to lie, first, in British influence and preponderance as an imperial power in world trade and investment in the early nineteenth century, compared with European rivals; second, in a growing concern among economic historians to explain the failure of Latin American countries to turn growth into sustained development; third, in the discontent of two pioneering imperial historians with the ways in which their subject was conceptualized in constitutonal terms during periods of economic and political expansion. There have been other influences at work, not least a recognition of the alternative preponderance of the United States in Central America and elsewhere; the rise of multinational corporations and international agencies engaged in investment and supervision of international debt; and, in the period of further decolonization and developmental failures, a persistent and much older theory of international trade concerned with locational advantage, capital exports and the international division of labour which has helped to underpin the literature of dependency as a form of economic (and neo-imperial) subordination. A short survey can only summarize the historiography of the term. But an attempt will be made towards the end to suggest that the metaphor still has its uses in particular contexts, and to identify some of the reasons why these contexts from a variety of periods and regions should give rise to conditions for control and political subordination. It will be further argued that debate about the limitations or suitability of the imperial metaphor, by emphasizing the Eurocentrism of forms of control, avoids more fundamental issues concerning the spread of influence through foreign technologies in underdeveloped countries. And, finally, it is concluded that underwriting the relocation of technology overseas and investing in its diffusion have been the necessary cause of both formal empire and informal control of production and services in societies lacking the technical and financial means to compete with or resist intrusive organization.

Historiography

The assertion that the denotation of imperialism was wider than its nineteenth-century constitutional mode and could be applied to decolonized states can be traced back to C. F. Fay's Beit lectures, given at Oxford in Michaelmas Term 1933, which alluded briefly to an 'informal empire in South America', and more specifically to the case of 'the Argentine . . . an outpost of England's economic empire, moving gradually into economic autonomy'.[2] By these off-the-cuff asides in what was a longer description of trade theories derived from the existence of empire, Fay raised in the broadest terms the question of regional influence through trade and investment and the dilemmas implicit in a debtor/creditor relationship. Writing at the period of the Ottawa Agreements, he asked quite simply whether the ties of people, currency and trade existing between Canada and the United Kingdom outweighed the equally long-standing relationship with Argentina, which had frozen dividends as well as frozen meat to be considered. Could the ties of informal empire be so easily cast aside by a free-trading nation? No grand theory was intended, and, apart from a further allusion to 'economic empire' in his contribution to the *Cambridge History of the British Empire*, Fay did not explore the concept further.[3]

One contemporary did. H. S. Ferns, in 1953, accepted the notion of an abiding economic relationship between Britain and Argentina, although he argued against the subordination of a Latin American state by Britain in an article whose title belied its contents.[4] After reviewing failures of naval intervention at Buenos Aires and the River Plate, 1806–45, he moved to the bold conclusion that Argentina in the nineteenth century enjoyed 'dominion status' ignoring the devolution of powers of constitutional amendment, judicial appeals and control of external relations implicit in that status. More useful, he noticed that economic exchanges with the industrial states of Europe 'depended upon the structure of the internal politics of the states of the River Plate', which was the germ of a much more important line of enquiry into the relationship between such states and local ruling élites. But the main conclusion was that finance and trade were based on ordinary diplomatic and commercial treaties according British subjects rights equal to those of other powers. Finally, Ferns described the regulation of external debts from 1863 in Argentina and British banking vulnerability in the 1890 crisis, without invoking official Foreign Office pressures to account for Anglo–Argentine relations which were characterized late in the century by a high level of trade and investment and a low level of political tension. This, Ferns suggested, could be explained by complementarity between the external trade partner and the *estancieros* who 'maintained their independence and served their own interests with a skill and sophistication which Europeans did not altogether appreciate or fathom'.[5]

Such was the state of the art when the topic was taken up in the same year as Ferns' article and recast as the 'imperialism of free trade', by John Gallagher and Ronald Robinson, as a method of accounting for the dynamics of British expansion in the nineteenth century and as a counter to the rigid periodization of the early and late Victorian period. By listing imperial acquisitions over three decades, from 1841 to 1870, they contested the idea of indifference, concentrating on the formalities of annexation and protection in the Pacific, Africa and South-east Asia. The point on continuity was well made. The nature of informal empire as the submerged section of the great trade-and-investment iceberg was less well explained without detailed cases of the agencies at work to establish a 'political lien control'; and there were important assumptions about the value of British interests in the regions of British hegemony, where export-led growth was notably slow, in the Levant, China, Latin America or West Africa until the last three decades of the century. Gallagher and Robinson, in short, combined two sets of cases, one of which was a series of informal steps towards incorporation in the formal empire mostly in Africa (including the important example of Egypt), the Pacific and South-east Asia, and, second, a quite different set of cases which remained unconsummated examples of British influence exercised in a variety of ways in Latin America, Turkey, Persia and China, with or without official government underwriting. Terms such as 'paramountcy', 'suzerainty' and 'influence', in any case, begged questions about the instruments of control; and it did the argument no good to draw on Fay's 'ties' of people, commerce and capital outside the empire to illustrate imperial integration by other means without stating what those means were.[6] A greater paradox arises, indeed, from the sweeping inclusion of colonies of European settlement into the general matrix of the free-trade empire of informal control, by grants of responsible government. The centrality of control implied by the term empire, whether informal or not, left thereby unstated and unexplored the degrees of autonomy or subordination existing for economic institutions in the dominions and Latin states. Qualitative differences between clients of the great source of trade and investment were ignored, which gave rise to further difficulties concerning the sub-imperial or regional factors behind the transition from informal to formal empire after 1870. If these qualitative differences expressed in terms of technology and expatriate cultures are kept in mind, then the 'radical paradoxes' and 'contradictions' discerned in a continually expansive British metropolitan imperialism in the 1953 article can be resolved in quite a different way, by looking at the ways in which imported institutions were, in fact, manned by locals and expatriates in the 'managerial hierarchy'.[7]

Latin America

The initial association of the term with British relations with Latin America led to a further difficulty which the 1953 article left vague. Informal empire has been used in both a narrow, political sense of government backing *for* economic influence, and in a much broader sense of influence and control derived *from* economic activity, through trade and investment, independent of government. Strictly speaking, if formal empire is government from abroad, then the informal metaphor also requires identification of the politics of influence in nominally independent states and societies. Where such influence is hard to identify, it is either assumed or an appeal made to the power of commercial, financial or industrial agencies to fill the role of external imperial states. Despite early acceptance of a Monroe Doctrine for the external affairs of Latin American states, Great Britain supplied a suitably ambiguous imperial factor, either through naval and diplomatic interventions, or through the predominance of British private and public investment in a region of trade and capital dependency.

The literature of dependency is too voluminous and polemical to be done justice here. But it is worth noting that its historiography coincides with the promotion of informal empire in the 1950s, when economists questioned the suitability of export-led growth models, under the influence of Ragnar Nurske, and advocated import-substitution, in the manner of Raul Prebisch. The two main arguments offered for the failure of developing economies to follow the nineteenth-century pattern of growth emphasized deterioration in the terms of trade for primary products after 1921 and, second, the harmful effects of foreign domination of an export sector. Further failures in performance, particularly in Latin American countries which ran into balance of payments difficulties, and increased dependence on foreign capital and technology hardened the resolve of the *dependentistas* in rival camps to blame structural features aggravating economic and social disparities between the export and domestic sectors, to blame the multinationals for control of capital and technology, and to argue that dependency followed historically from inherently unequal relationships between the capitalist and underdeveloped worlds. A cursory survey of the economic historiography of Latin America, starting with the Economic History Project floated in 1969, shows how pervasive these explanations have been in the acceptance of the view that eighteenth-century colonial economic patterns were perpetuated to the 1880s, and longer, and in generating acceptance of 'the imperialism of free trade' as a forerunner of other 'hegemonic powers'.[8]

The Gallagher and Robinson model of informal empire, then, was taken over by an academic *caudillo*, although it was fundamentally a political metaphor and not an economic theory. It was fairly easy, therefore, to take issue with the concept in its narrow sense, by demonstrating that political underwriting in Latin America, China and Turkey did not establish, in practice, a British paramountcy before the 1870s in any way commensurate with the scale of British interests overseas inside and outside the formal empire. Christopher Platt took the view that the British Government in general and the Foreign Office in particular rarely intervened *actively* 'to support and promote international trade and finance', unless in conjunction with national security, that is, by defending the possessions and markets already won. Much the same line was taken by M. Mathew in his denial of free-trade imperialism in Peru in the absence of 'wilful and effective subordination' or 'coercive tactics' on the part of the British Government to help merchants and bondholders involved in the guano trade and in loan replayments.[9]

It might be argued, of course, that insistence on official underwriting automatically narrows the field of informal influence and pays little attention to the ways in which immigrant communities and immigrant institutions from Britain or other European states enjoyed preponderance in particular sectors of what were immature economies in the nineteenth century. John Mayo, in his study of British relations with Chile, which tends to take informal empire for granted, concentrates on the transfer of skills by Britons in the 'technological disequilibrium between advanced Britain and underdeveloped Latin America' in conjunction with Chilean capitalists. This opens a useful alternative to the narrow view of free-trade imperialism as an officially backed strategy by shifting the focus away from official remonstrance and a free-trade treaty to private companies exploiting a technological advantage.[10] Parallel attempts to show that other nationalities, such as the Germans, constituted an element of informal empire in Latin America are less convincing, precisely because official backing was irrelevant to the necessary institutional and corporative imports into banking, transport or public utilities. Without such technological relocation, mere immigration provided no sectoral influence or control.[11]

How did foreign business firms operate in practice; and did they win such control? This direction of enquiry was advanced significantly in the same year as Mayo's thesis by the appearance of Platt's edition of case studies of foreign business operating in different sectors of Latin American economies.[12] Although designed as a reply to loose assertions about informal imperialism, the value of this collection lies in empirical data rather than new formulation of older concepts. Platt stresses that the overall trend in the relationship was against 'any permanent imbalance of power' with a measure of advantage in entrepreneurship without speculative profit on the one hand or more than temporary default on loans on the other. The rather bland conclusion is that governments were sovereign and could assert themselves, as Peru did in the guano trade, through state legislation over insurance, banking, railways and utilities.

The studies themselves reveal important distinctions between sectors and types of business organization. Merchant shippers engaged in the export trade were able to take advantage of producers' vulnerability through lack of storage, credit and information to control prices in the short term for wheat, wool, cocoa and rubber. On the other hand, merchant partnerships operating as commission houses, as in the much-examined case of Peru, worked in harmony with government and local business interests, while concessionary companies such as the Peruvian Corporation of Standard Oil disputed contractual terms and fell back on the credit weapon or technical expertise, with notable success, in the 1920s.[13] From other studies of Argentine beef, Chilean nitrates, iodine and copper, it is clear, too, that sectoral advantage operated less by pressure on governments than as a diffusion of expertise in the employment of skills and venture capital in a series of very imperfect markets, giving foreign merchants entry into commodity processing, mining and agency work for shipping lines, though, significantly, not into agriculture and ranching. Constraints as well as opportunities existed; British merchant numbers remained small; and the British share of, say, Argentina's exports hardly exceeded 34 per cent at any time to 1914. A similar technical efficiency explains the predominant role of British-owned banks, profitable and conservative in use of funds and overtaken eventually by competitors, who copied their methods, and by imported trusts and mortgage companies.[14] A verdict is more difficult in the case of shipping companies which enjoyed a high level of concentration in foreign hands and discipline over shippers, though they were not immune from government action aimed at regulating berthing facilities, encouraging Latin coasting trades and subsidizing foreign competition. Such governments could well have followed the legislation imposed on shipping rings by the United States and ended the deferred rebate system (as Brazil did in 1933).[15] Similarly, historical work on Latin American railways confirms the older conclusion by Ferns for Argentina that there was less foreign 'domination' than a long series of skirmishes over tariffs and branch lines. The alternative to guarantees for profits, which in any case ended in the 1890s, was construction by the state on borrowed money in a society which lacked the public departments and engineers supplied by colonial administrations in similar conditions of underdevelopment in India, South Africa, Australia and New Zealand.[16] The question of whether it could have been otherwise depends on what kinds of options were open to governments to operate or encourage rural banking, changes in land tenure, locally organized commodity auctions at the major points of export, or to undertake public works.

Whatever the answers, the case studies make it clear that there was a widespread belief that foreign intermediation squeezed producers and kept out local entrepreneurs in what was an undeveloped marketing structure. But popular wisdom is only one reason why the notion of informal empire has proved so tenacious. There is still disagreement between historians on the significance of some of the interventions by European governments at the River Plate in the 1840s to safeguard trade and finance in Uruguay against Argentina; the joint intervention in Mexico in 1861; the joint action against Venezuela in 1902 with Germany. It is understandable, however, that nineteenth-century challenges to the integrity of new states in Latin America should be occluded with the series of strategic interventions marking the informal empire of the United States in Central America, derived in part from the Monroe Doctrine and, in part, from the need to secure American and European investments in Cuba, Haiti and the Dominican Republic, 1900–21.[17] But it is clear enough that the British Government at least would not underwrite debt; and if such guarantees are laid down as essential to informal empire, then there was none. If, on the other hand, the emphasis is on socio-economic links with a local élite, as the essential mechanism of informal empire (as in the studies offered by John Mayo and P. Winn), then decisions taken by that élite or by its representatives in power become the main focus.[18] And it is convenient for the academic descendants of that élite to argue that it was manipulated from the outside to support an economic enclave structure which had more in common with overseas market centres than the underdeveloped hinterland. The only answer to this is political history; and political history of such events as the overthrow of Balmaceda in 1891 in Chile is still controversial.[19]

The difficulty of disentangling the exogenous economic factors from internal politics is amply demonstrated by the involved argument put forward by Richard Graham to explain the retardation of Brazil's economy down to 1914.[20] According to this thesis Britain had sufficient informal influence to control much of the mercantile and agricultural export sector, together with a dominance in finance, and was able to delay Brazilian industrialization. The evidence is complex and the detailed sections on commodity futures, banks, the fate of cotton manufacturers and loan servicing by Rothschilds do not support the general argument. What Graham's book does show is the rise of debtor-dependency through servicing charges and some manipulation of exchange rates, rather than any concerted effort on the part of immigrant merchants or Rothschilds to take decisions on behalf of Brazil's politicians who, in any case, saw the future of the country in the agricultural sector and defeated local industrialists on the question of tariffs.

Apart from the intrinsic difficulty of generalizing about the state economies of a whole region, there are differences over several key topics which would have to be resolved before historians can reach firmer conclusions on the connotation of informal empire in Latin America. If development can follow from export-led growth, with or without industrialization, then it has to be clearly demonstrated that the most promising Latin economies, (Columbia, Brazil and Argentina) in the nineteenth century, as recipients of most foreign investment to 1913, were informally impeded for the benefit of external trade partners (as André Gunder Frank and other *dependentistas* would contend). Even if this were done, the assumption that such nations were candidates for development in terms of rising *per capita* percentages of GNP rests on a counterfactual argument which takes little account of political systems, internal redistribution of income and the operation of regional markets between competing developers. In short, was it possible for Latin states to develop *pari passu*, without a greater measure of intra-regional co-operation and local government institutions, as in the United States, Canada or Australia?

More specifically, informal empire through sectoral advantage implies ownership, as Richard Graham has argued, in favour of the broad definition implicit in the Robinson and Gallagher model. Control through ownership in agriculture, mining or manufactures varied too much for a regional conclusion. There *were* significant degrees of foreign ownership in Chile, Cuba, Mexico, Peru (nitrates, sugar, mining, petroleum), especially from 1900, but in the most promising countries there was little such foreign control over production.[21] Before a collaborating élite is accepted as a mechanism for control, however, it has to be asked (as does Colin Lewis) whether a 'collaborating society' was the source of local demand for foreign innovation and the benefits of high levels of foreign imports, in the absence of sufficient levels of local capital accumulation and expertise to provide alternatives. Moreover, population increase, naturally and by immigration, needs to be taken into account. The indicators of social and economic 'advance' (urbanization, education, railway mileages as percentages of population) in the absence of national income statistics are not very impressive before 1910, and even less so if considered as averages for Latin America as a whole. It might be argued that the basis for growth was not promising, given large areas of internal underdevelopment; and the failure of states to restructure during the First World War, when ties to the hegemonic metropolis were weak, would seem to bear this out (though it is a debated period).

One final point: apart from action by a Judge Conservator in Brazil under a treaty with Portugal in 1810, no sovereignty over influential foreigners seems to have been ceded by Latin American states. By contrast, jurisdiction is the starting point for informal empire in the Near and Far East, and it is a form of control which runs through much of the frontier expansion in tropical and southern Africa and the Pacific Islands.

Courts and Credit: China and the Middle East

The privilege of jurisdiction from within a consular enclave over the subjects of European states was granted first in Turkish and Muscovy treaty capitulations from the sixteenth century, for English and French merchants, as separate traders or as regulated and chartered companies.[22] These privileges were expanded to include settlement of disputes between nationals by a governor or consul; the right of official representation in commercial cases heard by the Sublime Porte; and official representation in criminal cases. They were not regarded as especially important by the Turks, nor were they regularly enforced in the Turkish regencies, or in Egypt. But they provided an important precedent for the East India Company and other merchants in Siam in 1664 and on the China coast from the last quarter of the eighteenth century, in conjunction with the search for new ways of lowering transaction costs and extending managerial hierarchies to include local compradors.[23]

Judicial privilege became linked to the administration of debt, as the sub-imperial monopoly of the East India Company in the lucrative country trade in Far Eastern waters was challenged. The company also engaged in the export of mercantile credit and financial services, utilized by other British agencies and American traders. The scale of credit operations was revealed, when agency houses and the American enterprises failed, 1829–34, on a £15 million liability. The withdrawal of the company from financial operations in Canton, moreover, marked a shift towards official supervision through agents of the Foreign Office and the superintendents of British trade who reinforced the financial monopoly of Jardine Matheson. None of this backing could save the Hong merchants whose credit was undermined by downward pressure on prices from London tea brokers and from local middlemen. What was a victory for free traders over the privileges of the company spelled bankruptcy for the Hongs and exposed a situation where some new mechanism for debt recovery had to be tried. As in the Turkish dominions at an earlier period, the problem of adjudication in commercial disputes was compounded by deep cultural differences on legal procedures, rules of evidence, use of torture, surrender of fugitives and rights of personal or group compensation.[24] With the enforcement of free trade, from 1833, the problem of trade credit increased and was not really dealt with in the Treaty of Nanking in 1842. The principles of extraterritoriality, however, were extended by the Treaty of Tientsin in 1858 for surrender of debtors and, from 1865, for mixed tribunals at Shanghai, administering Chinese law with a gradual admixture of Anglo-American judicial concepts. With remarkable vitality, the system survived until 1943.

The origins of the customs service, which was the second point of entry for foreign informal control in China, lay in supervision of the bonded warehouse system, and a legal basis was provided by treaty in 1854, recognizing the Foreign Inspectorate, separate from the consular service. To prevent smuggling and ensure a source of revenue from foreign trade for the imperial government, French, British and

American consuls and the imperial revenue collector made joint appointments and 'injected direct foreign interference into a Chinese Government department'.[25]

The significance of the Customs Service lay in its use of revenues as security for foreign loans, beginning in 1868, authorized by signature of the customs commissioners. Thereafter, until the Sino-Japanese war 1894–5, a series of 'domestic' loans was issued at the ports for sterling or silver, and government bonds were deposited with the major lender, the Hong Kong and Shanghai Bank (HKSB). Inspector-General Hart, moreover, gradually extended underwriting from local mercantile firms to the London market; and at the outbreak of hostilities in 1894 Hart undertook to fill a depleted war chest by raising £1.6m through the HKSB followed by a further £3m in 1895.

Foreign Office approval was important, but not essential to this operation of European informal empire to China. The superintendents certainly did not control the imperial court. But they ran its most vital service for funding defence and capital investment. And the British Government was drawn into the international scramble for concessions when (again Hart's idea) collieries and railways were mortgaged to British capitalists under a mixed board of control which laid the foundations for the China Railway Company in 1888. The Germans followed the British example in 1895 by securing a loan on provincial salt dues and the customs; and a gold loan the same year, arranged through the Chartered Bank of India, Australia and China, was similarly backed. Liquidation of the war indemnity of £23m entailed a new round of borrowing through Hong Kong, Russian and French banks, secured on the customs or underwritten by the Russian treasury.

For the majority of intervening powers this phase might have followed the Russian example of a quasi-protectorate over Manchuria; but, in practice, they kept to Lord Curzon's limit of 'a preponderant interest' created by financial consortia and stopping short of international partition. From 1833 the informal empire, then, consisted in enforcement of constraints through the major revenue service, a political lien, until the imperial government asserted itself by establishing a revenue council in 1906 which effectively ended Hart's position as trustee for foreign bankers.

Historians still debate the degree of co-operation between bankers and foreign governments in this episode. Clarence B. Davis finds little substance in the theory of political and financial collusion; this accords with McLean's work on the HKSB.[26] But then official underwriting was not necessary for the operation of a system of international credit which led to intense rivalry for concessions. Indeed, the 'period of concessions' was reviewed with entire satisfaction by the British Institute of Bankers in 1901 without regret for a more active role by the Foreign Office.[27] So much of the commercial and financial business of the Chinese Government managed through the banks was in the hands of a British-dominated state service that more overt official pressures were not required.

On the other hand, R. W. Huenemann's monumental work on Chinese railways, while recognizing their centrality for foreign influence, illustrates the ways in which they were conditioned by internal political considerations and a gradual shift towards improved contract terms and greater Chinese responsibility for construction. And this is borne out by one of the few studies we have of a multinational enterprise in China, the British-American Tobacco Company, which survived with difficulty in the face of populist risings and economic nationalism, using the techniques of Western capitalism in the 1920s. Other historians, notably Osterhammel, find in this intrusion and in earlier co-operative efforts on the part of European powers evidence on which to construct an ideal type of informal control, despite the slow reception and adaptation of European technology.[28]

To the limited extent that such controls were exercised, informal empire in China was based on extraterritorial jurisdiction and the competence of an efficient revenue administration which provided a bridgehead for loans and concessions. Chinese nationalism withstood this softening up process, though imperial and provincial authorities could not make good low levels of domestic technology and corporate organization or raise internal savings to provide an alternative to co-operation except through cultural isolation.

A similar progression from courts to capital loans is discernible in the Middle East with different results. Informal empire in Egypt is so well documented that it is probably the best historical case we have of the main factors in operation from the Anglo-Turkish Commercial Convention of 1838, through the period of growth in exports and infrastructure, financed by external borrowing and internal money-lending, to the debt crises of the 1870s and foreign intermediation, occupation and closer regulation by a British administration which was not part of a formal empire until the protectorate of 1914. Differences of opinion about the motives for occupation need not detain us here. The political lien required by the application of the metaphor is not really in doubt, given the privileged position of foreign officials in the administration from the 1860s, topped by the financial controllers of the late 1870s and European ministers in Ismail's cabinet. If one wanted a model for informal empire, Egypt supplies it, at least until 1882.[29]

The case for informal empire in Turkey, however, is more debatable. It was, it is true, something of a 'mediatized state', diplomatic jargon for protection by a consortium of powers, from the period of Palmerston and Metternich, and a strong case can be made for French cultural imperialism during the Tanzimat (in Stratford de Redcliffe's phrase, the 'great game of improvement').[30] But when improvement based on French codes and British guaranteed loans, 1854–62, faltered, British commissioners were sent to Constantinople to arrange for a new consolidation of the public debt, until the next default in 1874. Analysis of what lay behind these interventions has produced contrasting explanations.

For Sevket Pamuk, foreign influence is not in doubt. The loss of Turkish economic independence is traced through successive stages of growth without development: expansion of British trade to 1853 under the treaty of 1838 and a decline in local manufactures; the beginning of external borrowing 'under very unfavourable terms', accompanied by foreign ownershp of the Imperial Ottoman Bank and a market in agricultural land; stagnation and increased foreign financial control through the Ottoman Public Debt Administration 1881; an improved balance of payments and an increased growth rate from 1895 to 1914, followed by increased deficits financed by new borrowing and Jewish Palestine immigration. But Pamuk denies the term informal empire to the Turkish case, because he plays down foreign debt administration from 1881, and finds no 'merchant–landlord' groups to service the interests of external investors and commodity exporters.[31]

Roger Owen covered much the same ground earlier than Pamuk and is more critical of Turkish reliance on short-term borrowing. Both are in agreement on the high ratio of debt to export earnings. But Owen, along with Christopher Platt, makes much more of the Istanbul negotiations of 1881 leading to foreign financial control.[32] Unlike Egypt, there was no occupation but there was a loss of sovereignty to the Imperial Ottoman Bank, the Deutsche Bank and the National Bank of Turkey, and diplomatic intervention by three powers. In short, Turkey came under international audit to safeguard shares and open the country to railway investment, and was thoroughly mediatized to save it from itself as well as Russia. Intervention through debt administration succeeded in raising the value of public bonds. Turkey obtained loans on more favourable terms; but the supervisory board was also used to allocate concessions for railways and imports; and it gave considerable leverage, or political lien, to European governments, until the Turks took effective control of taxation from the Revolution of 1908.

Sub-imperialism: Africa, the Pacific Islands

Thus far, the metaphor seems to work best not so much in the aftermath of empire, as in Latin America, but in the run-up to more formal empire, with Turkey and China as examples of incomplete imperial expansion. Informal empire was part of a softening up process through technological relocation of some of Europe's institutions specializing in the organization of trade, production, communications, investment and the administration of justice. In this kind of historical sequence we should be able to find good examples in tropical Africa and on the frontiers of British colonies in southern Africa and in the Pacific, as isolated enclaves or as the sub-imperial action of client states such as Egypt, Zanzibar, Cape Colony and Natal, or the Australian colonies and New Zealand.

When we come down to cases, doubts begin to accumulate about the effectiveness of political intervention arising from commercial intermediation, juridicial extension of the powers of colonial courts over British subjects or, indeed, the whole notion of a paramountcy over foreign territory arising from the proximity of a formal administration in a client state. The concept of informal empire in West Africa has been challenged by Martin Lynn on several grounds. Actions taken against the slave trade and to promote legitimate trade, especially at Lagos and in the Niger Delta and on the Gold Coast from the period of Palmerston to the late 1850s, did not add up to informal empire because of the ineffectiveness of consuls and officials in relations with African states. British predominance in the import–export trade at the coast was marginal to regional trade in which peasant exporters were not yet dependent on exported staples, and did not amount to the kind of command over a regional economy, as suggested by Gallagher and Robinson, in what was merely a series of market exchanges. So, later expansion is a result of a 'big bang' after 1870, not a 'steady state' or 'continuous creation' as implied by the informal empire of free trade.[33] In addition, one might stress the limitations of jurisdiction over anyone but British subjects in the areas adjacent to British settlements, before the Berlin Conference. The grand debate in the 1880s between the Colonial Office and the law officers in the case of Bechuanaland on jurisdiction over foreigners was not resolved until 1891 and the law was applied in various orders in council within protectorates at the period of formal expansion in the later 1890s.

Nevertheless, the pervasiveness of the construct is evident in its acceptance by G. N. Sanderson, who believes in a British preponderance in the 1860s and 1870s, while interpreting the limited measure of extraterritorial jurisdiction over British subjects derived from treaties and consular courts as a kind of gigantic bluff, or self-delusion, until this was called by other powers.[34]

Having supplied some of the evidence to both sides for these contradictory conclusions, one is at pains to reconcile them. I cannot agree with Lynn that the 'problem is less empirical than conceptual'.[35] It is both. On the other hand, it is hard to justify expressions such as 'dominance' either politically or economically in West Africa's relations with a major power before the 1880s. Disaggregation in economic terms and political fragmentation make the construct of 'West Africa' itself little more than a geographical expression and not the scene of co-ordinated activities between British departments of state and British traders. There is more to be said for the continuous creation of an informal influence, however, if it is recognized that defence of British interests was largely a matter for sub-imperial initiative and not a grand design at the level of Whitehall. Informal influence was more than a figment of the official mind and had its roots in the mundane operations of traders, missionaries and administrators outside the formal enclaves, with the backing of the financial and organizational infrastructure constructed in those enclaves. The necessary elements for British influence were the Crown Colonies, or settlements, under the terms of the Coast of Africa and Falklands Islands Act of 1843 and the 1860 amendment which provided for skeletal administration and juridical control of British subjects by order-in-council anywhere on the globe. And what has not been noticed in the concentration on the scale of (or limits to) British trade relations is the steady and inexorable rise in British expenditure on the settlements, despite professions of uninterest, from the 1840s until the early 1880s, when, of course, expansion began in earnest. The trend of official underwriting, excluding military expeditions and foreign office expenses for consular representation, was steadily upwards between 1848 and 1890 by some 300 per cent, the major items being police, courts, roads, steamers, missions to the interior and customs posts; in short, all the elements required to extend and fund from trade the politics of local influence among the Temne and Mende, the Fante, Yoruba, Ibo and Ibibio.[36] It might be argued, of course, that it was precisely because this modestly financed bluff was so ineffectual once trading operations penetrated beyond the Delta or the Lagos lagoons, that greater territorial acquisitions were justifiable at greater cost in the 1880s. Then, the sub-imperial agencies present as administrators, consuls and merchants came into their own with a new freedom of action as travelling commissioners, proconsuls of protectorates, and agents of chartered and joint stock companies.

There is perhaps, therefore, more to be said for an argument based on the concept of a closing frontier, than the informal hegemony of a distant metropolis over a vast region. The contributions by W. D. MacIntyre and a whole school of southern African historians, consolidated in the work of John Benyon, stress the cultural dynamics of competition for land, labour, access to markets and mines, and railway routes, from bases in settler society where the proconsuls were concerned less with the imperialism of free trade than using the British to further more limited and concrete objectives in terms of nearby British settlements.[37] The only difference in West or East Africa was the smaller scale of the settlements and the political weakness of trading and missionary agencies operating in isolation.

The essential feature of sub-imperialism at the frontier, then, was agency work from the formal colonies and dependencies of empire, nominally on behalf of that empire, but more frequently in the interests of the agents and the colony concerned. The benefit in conceptual terms is that no grand assumption about informal control exercised from the centre, as political or economic hegemony, need be entertained, though the close interest of governments in some of the managerial hierarchies left to administer trade and finance cannot be overlooked. Such agencies in the form of merchant houses and banks lend themselves to detailed examination for preponderance in sectors of an aggregated economy in an independent state, where this exists, in debt administration, in plantations and industry, and in shipping railways and other services. But how effective were they in political terms?

One source of misunderstanding can be removed at the outset. They got little help from the British legal device of investing judicial powers in a Cape or Pacific high commissioner without the means or control so desired by Lord Kimberley over foreigners or the subjects of indigenous chiefs. The dilemma of aspirations for informal empire outside regions of recognized government was how far to recognize native sovereignty as territorial or personal. If the former, rights over foreigners could be ceded; if the latter, no agreement was sufficient to provide a basis for administrative controls before the 1890s.

There were other solutions, devised by the frontiersmen and confirmed by parsimonious politicians to close off spheres of interest to competitors. The chartered British South Africa Company was one, adventuring into Mashonaland and Matabeleland on the most tenuous of legal pretexts, and acting as an imperial administration between 1889 and 1894, when legal authority was regularized and shared with the Cape high commissioner. The Royal Niger Company acted in a similar dual capacity as commercial agency and political conquistador, but it did so in a formal British protectorate. Other examples are the agents sent by the Queensland government to Papua, when the weak controls allowed by the Pacific Islands Protection Act of 1875 or the Western Pacific Order-in-Council of 1877 were seen to be insufficient. Sir Arthur Gordon, hamstrung in his own effort to control anything on a vast oceanic frontier, admired the initiative of Queensland's illegal man-on-the-spot at Port Moresby, in 1878, who exercised 'a practical, though informal, assumption of control over the country . . . he holds courts; he parades an armed force; he registers land titles etc'.[38] Such actions, as Gordon recognized, were the prelude to protectorate or annexation.

The limitations of the concept used in conjunction with sub-imperial expansion can be appreciated from the case of New Zealand before 1840. By any account, the Bay of Islands was a frontier society, but the agents of sub-imperial control were ineffective in the person of James Busby, who exercised no jurisdiction, and ambivalent opponents of colonization among the missionaries. Private or joint-stock agencies were notably absent, until the New Zealand Company triggered the rapid chain of events leading to annexation. While it has been argued that the character of eventual British settlement was shaped by trans-Tasman trade from the 1820s, the lack of any control over Maori soiety would seem to set New Zealand apart from other frontier examples, where sub-imperial agents initiated policy changes.[39] If it is allowed that the New Zealand Company was such an agent, then it might be argued that the islands were informally settled so as to drive the British Government to act. But the time scale is short; and the principal difficulty with informal empire, from New South Wales, through missions or through a land company, is the weak institutional and legal basis for control in a frontier society during the brief prelude to formal annexation.

As for New Zealand's later sub-imperial influence in Pacific partition, the verdict of Angus Ross is that much of it remained at the level of local politicians' 'aspirations', successful in the case of incorporation of the Cook Islands and Niue, but much less effective in the power politics surrounding Hawaii, Tonga and Samoa.[40] For in these groups the frontier settlers (missionaries and merchants) who were directly involved in island politics were much more influential with their consuls and the German and American governments, before final partition in the 1890s, because they operated through the churches, through trading houses with extensive credit, investments in land, and control of communications, and through *ad hoc* administrations of foreign representatives and local Polynesian or Melanesian politicians.

Cultural Imperialism

What of 'cultural imperialism' as a pathfinder for the formal kind? If we accept culture in the sense of know-how, there have been attempts to extend the notion of informal empire in this way through investigations of the place of scientific patronage in nineteenth-century exploration, through the diffusion and relocation of technology, and through assessment of the role of missionary societies as precursors to formal expansion. Studies range from a macro-diffusionist view of Europe's influence on outside economies, from the late eighteenth century, when technological exchanges with older cultures became one-sided, to analysis of specific changes within African or Asian societies as a result of introducing the hardware and organization of foreign methods of production.[41] More recent work by Daniel R. Headrick has refined earlier emphasis on the technical tools of imperial control into a more sophisticated theory which carefully differentiates between simple exports to overseas locations and diffusion of technology accompanied by education.[42] The principal sources of economic power and influence through applied science have been in communications (ships, rail and telegraph), irrigation, agriculture, mining, urbanization, and to a lesser extent in the important area of military technology. Apart from one study which explores technological diffusion through business enterprise, much less attention has been paid to the taxonomy of the most usual vehicle for relocating organized commerce and investment, that is, the private and public corporation, except in its more striking chartered and transnational forms.[43]

A great deal of this valuable work relates to formal colonies, particularly India and the dominions. But so pervasive was the influence of scientific patronage at the highest levels of government, particularly when promoted by geographical societies, that it is tempting to extend the quest for exact knowledge to informal empire as well. The dimensions of such an expanded denotation have been most usefully charted in the case of British geological and geographical societies by Robert A. Stafford. Stafford's initial conclusion from his study of Sir Roderick Murchison was that: 'The natural scientists collaborated with the government in the extension of the "empire of Free Trade" using their disciplines as instruments of espionage, reform, and development in colonies, client states and unorganized regions'.[44] The central direction of such patronage is not in doubt for the formal empire and the dominions in the nineteenth century. It is less clearly demonstrated that 'collaboration' with government produced much in the way of influence or control over developmental decisions taken in Bolivia, Equador, Siam, Armenia, Kurdistan or Turkey. There is a better case made for British influence through sub-imperial agencies, especially in India, for influence on the Euphrates, collection of specimens and cartography in China, the opening up of Indo-China and expansion for coaling facilities at Labuan. The major example for Murchison's patronage, exercised to test his geological theories by mineral exploration in Africa, yielded very mixed results, however direct his influence on expeditions to the Niger, the Zambesi, the central lakes and the Nile, Abyssinia. Later work by Stafford on this region does not claim informal empire as a consequence of government and scientific collaboration.[45] Significantly, influence over appointments to geological survey in Natal led directly to sub-imperial promotion of coal, gold and copper prospecting in the 1850s (as had happened without benefit of scientific geology in 1851 in Australia). And it is difficult to extend the range of metropolitan scientific influence into later discoveries in Griqualand, Ndebeleland or the Rand, where casual prospection, German exploration and promotion of speculative syndicates from South African bases encouraged the expansive sub-imperialism of Cape Colony. The one study we have of German scientific institutions operating in Samoa, Argentina and China denies any 'pernicious imperialist quality to scientific discourse of the periphery'.[46]

The debate will not end there, of course, as long as cultural imperialism is added to the list of metaphors for political influence in the 'unorganized regions'. But there has been a recognition that more likely agencies for cultural control are to be found in missionary societies, if only because their particular managerial hierarchies, automatically co-opted by conversion local agents. Again, the record is divided. Cases can be made out for missionary theocracy from the early nineteenth century in small Pacific societies, in Eastern Polynesia, Tonga and Hawaii, on the pattern of much older missionary enclaves in Latin America and China. But they also resulted in denominational conflict along pre-existing social divisions, and they required support from strong secular leadership. They were, moreover, ambiguous in their attitude towards intervention by an imperial power; and the occasions on which imperial powers deliberately made use of their services as agents of empire are fairly limited (France in the Eastern Pacific, and in the Wallis group and New Caledonia before annexation). In practice, they were as likely to oppose imperial administration as much as they campaigned against labour recruiters.[47]

On the other hand, historians of medical missions have made out a case for their pre-imperial 'partition' of spheres of influence in East Africa; and Anthony Dachs, by re-examination of the role of John Mackenzie among the Tswana, has breathed new life into Sillery's phrase 'Humanitarian Imperialism'.[48] Among sub-imperialists like Sir Harry Johnston, there was not the slightest doubt that there had been a good deal of useful evangelical preparation in Central Africa, where 'each Mission Station is an essay in colonization'.[49] It has to be stressed, however, that Dachs' conclusion denies to missionaries a simple agency role for the British Government or Cape expansionists, by stressing the ways in which African societies incorporated them into local politics, as well as recognizing their revolutionary contribution to social and economic change through literacy, reform of land tenure and promotion of cash crops and mineral exploitation in Bechuanaland.

In Papua New Guinea, by contrast, where Christianity was very muscular in the 1870s, missionaries sometimes established a more direct link with imperial agencies. The Methodist George Brown avenged the death of his Fijian teachers on New Ireland in 1878 by supporting a punitive naval expedition against the villages concerned. W. G. Laws and James Chalmers, on the other hand, followed the policy of the London Missionary Society by opposing extension of the planters' and miners' frontier around Port Moresby, and if they favoured imperial rule, it was not necessarily the Australian version of formal administration. In effect, they set up their own administration, with sixteen stations along the Papuan coast. More murders of Papuan teachers in 1881 and naval reprisals changed their minds, to the extent that Chalmers justified formal intervention in terms of 'payback'. While reprisal was well understood by unconverted Papuans, it did not resolve the problem underlying these episodes, namely the tensions created by Pacific islander auxiliaries in positions of considerable power at isolated stations and vulnerable to other leaders who resented their influence. On this sub-imperial frontier, therefore, the local missionaries, as opposed to their society in London, actively supported the illegal Queensland annexation of 1883 and the more welcome British Protectorate of 1884 in the opening moves of partition with Germany. Reprimanded by their directors, Laws and Chalmers conducted their own press campaign to use the imperial factor, when, as their historian puts it: 'Missionary imperialism became the logical extension of missionary paternalism'.[50]

For the Germans who lacked a sub-imperial base this was not so. Klaus J. Bade, while stressing the contribution to German expansion made by the director of the Rhenish Mission, Friedrich Fabri, in 1879, based on the experience of the mission's trading company in South West Africa, quite easily demonstrates the ways in which co-operation between pastors, merchants and the New Guinea Company broke down in the late 1880s and 1890s when German missionaries refused to act as auxiliaries and pro-company intermediaries.[51]

This last point should remind us of the importance of structure and organization in putative agency control over some sector of a nominally independent society, and the need to demonstrate the authority and effectiveness of such a structure with or without distant backing by an imperial power. Part of the strength of missionary influence in the

Pacific, Africa and in China from the 1860s lay in an ability to import an administrative hierarchy and recruit local officers, as pastors, priests or lay teachers, raise funds abroad and engage in elementary public health and education. Such structures were seen often enough as a rival source of authority and evoked appropriate reactions. Consequently, one measure of informal empire, as a virus in the local body politic, is the degree of resistance to it. The case of violence against missionary auxiliaries has been mentioned. There were more sophisticated examples of indigenous co-operatives, trade boycotts, and breakaway churches in the Pacific as elsewhere on the pre-annexation frontier, as well as a desire to take over features of imported institutions.[52] Informal empire, too, had its resisters as well as its collaborators.

It is possible, therefore, that other political reactions to the intrusive influence of economic and cultural institutions in Latin America, the Middle East, China or latter-day decolonized states are simply matters of scale. So far the big ventures have attracted the historians. The many lesser partnerships, commission houses and early joint-stock enterprises have, as yet, no complete account, though an inroad into their historical anonymity has been made by Charles A. Jones. During the period of informal empire prior to annexation, the administration and investment required to take charge of a production and bulking centre, an entrepot or a mine were notably small and relatively unspecialized. In the Pacific or Africa, the private and joint stock companies engaged in wholesaling, shipping, plantations and mineral exploitation, had generalized functions, combining financial and commercial intermediation with transport, labour recruitment and elementary construction work, policing and local politics. The examples of the Royal Niger Company in West Africa or Godeffroy and Sohn in Samoa have been sufficiently well documented to illustrate the exercise of real power, in conjunction with consular allies, in commercial enclaves.[53] Such enclaves did not always result in informal control, and in many cases, such as mining in New Caledonia, the Gold Coast or New Guinea, concessions and local control of resources coincided with formal imperial underwriting. Similarly, the shipping companies provided evidence of co-operation with government for imperial mail contracts, resulting not in informal empire, in the case of the Mackinnon group in East Africa, but in a series of temporary alliances between the company, the treasury and sub-imperial agents, such as Sir Henry Bartle Frere in his role as governor of Bombay or governor of Cape Colony.[54] What is striking, therefore, about the negative examples is the weakness of their business structures. Like the Imperial British East Africa Company, they had influence but no commercial power.

The Debt Factor

From the survey of regional examples to test the weight of the metaphor, perhaps the most pervasive theme is that of 'financial intermediation', ranging from elementary credit in societies with partially monetized economies to more sophisticated lending through banks and foreign stock markets. Even quite elementary structures such as missionary enclaves had to be paid for and not infrequently resulted in barter and cash exchanges. Such an emphasis excludes, of course, those unquantifiable and non-monetized forms of cultural and institutional influence by the mission house and the scientific survey. But, as will be argued later, these examples of exportable technology are species within the cultural genus. The more common characteristic of a European presence from the eighteenth century in the Middle East, Africa, the Pacific and Latin America is the ubiquity of credit, the spread of markets and the pervasiveness of state borrowing in immature and maturing economies, including the self-governing dominions.[55] One might indeed apply a new metaphor: 'the money-lender's empire'.

The credit lien, moreover, has long been recognized as double-edged, ever since the thirteenth century when England, as 'a kind of mediaeval Zaïre', defaulted on Florentine loans financed from wool exports, and brought down bankers.[56] Debt engenders resistance as well as control; and it is central to a survey of informal empire because of the sheer scale of borrowing and intermediation, including the growth of private investment, since the nineteenth century, and because of assumptions about the controls exercised by investors. Descriptive analysis in the post-colonial period has spawned its own metaphors on this subject, replacing informal empires by invisible ones; and the language of intermediation is full of bankspeak, such as 'enhanced structural adjustment facility' (more credit to default on later), or the infamous 'conditionalities' of the International Monetary Fund (IMF) imposed not by gun boats but by international bankers.[57] The topic also has the advantage of shifting the discussion of influence and control back to the centre from the periphery and onto the well-explored ground of capital exports and the role of public and private investment.

A number of changes in the broad pattern of capital flows has still to be taken into account by imperial historians attracted to any theory of control through financial intermediation outside the formal empires. The first is a gradual swing to direct investment over the last hundred years. There had been an imperfectly estimated amount of such investment, relative to capital called up through the London market, in the last decades of the nineteenth century, perhaps as much as 40 per cent of British capital exports to 1914 amounting to 35 per cent of the assets owned by United Kingdom investors.[58] By 1911, London may, indeed, have been 'more concerned with Mexico than the Midlands', as *The Economist* observed.[59] But in Irving Stone's analysis of the increase of private investment in Latin America, much of the British share was in minority holdings, while any control through ownership lay with Americans and Latin Americans, with the exception of foreign joint stock banks.[60] Second, the trend already noticed in the case of China towards the internationalization of foreign holdings, including government obligations, continued in other fields. Such a spread is less true of the formal colonial dependencies where, in any case, there was much less private investment. Between 1938 and the 1960s, moreover, with the expansion of direct investment by the United States, the developed, rather than developing countries, accounted for two-thirds of this form of capital export, and a new set of theories had to be devised to explain the advantages of this strategy.[61] A third long-term change has been the entry of new private banks and deposit banks onto the scene, outside the City of London, joined from 1945 by international agencies. By the end of the First World War, and after the Federal Reserve Act of 1913, American private banks began to set up their branches abroad. By sale of Latin bonds they also began to reproduce the pattern of Europe's banking experience in the East, as Chase loaned to Cuba and Citibank to Peru in the 1920s, as well as to Europe, in a reversal of the trans-Atlantic flow of money. After the Great Depression and European recovery, the largest deposit banks were joined by the World Bank and its affiliate, the International Development Association. Offering soft loans they stepped in where more traditional investors feared to tread in the developing world, because of falling commodity prices in Latin America. By the late 1960s, when the first pessimism was setting in about 'development' among the less developed countries (LDCs) and the hopes outlined in the Pearson Report, the disciplines of the IMF began to be felt (for balance of payment problems rather than public investment for infrastructure) through conditions imposed on their slices of credit and a departure from gold and dollars into Special Drawing Rights (SDRs) as a way of settling accounts. But greater largesse was on the way through externally-held Eurodollars, deployed by the City and European banks mainly for corporations in the leading markets, but with a spillover into Brazil, Mexico, Iran, Korea, the Philippines, Peru, Argentina, followed by a flood of OPEC (Organization of Petroleum Exporting Countries) money concentrated in the biggest deposit banks, that is Bank of America, Citibank, Chase, Morgans, Barclays, Lloyds, Midland and NatWest. The result was massive loans on easier terms to high-risk countries with some notorious results such as Indonesian oil (Pertamina) which had to be bailed out by a new consortium in 1977 after the sacking of General Ibnu Sutowo, and the default of Zaïre in 1975, accompanied by new loans from the IMF and the installation of Erwin Blumental in Mobutu's Central Bank.

The more general result, apart from further reschedulings all round, has been harsher conditions, regular IMF inspections, and country advisers appointed as consultants by the private investment banks in Zaïre, Gabon, Sri Lanka, Panama and Turkey, while Barings moved into advising Saudi Arabia, Morgan Grenfell Sudan and Oman, Schroders Venezuela and Trinidad, and Merrill Lynch much of Latin America.

All of this 'development' and debt crisis has spawned its own literature, much of it directed against the IMF, but with some interesting case studies on the effects of controls in Africa and the Philippines, in works by Schoenholtz, Bello and others, while one plea for an IMF reading of past economic history has been made by A. G. Hopkins.[62] Much, too, has been written about the other whipping boys, that is, the multinational enterprises (MNEs). But there are some important shifts in this form of direct investment, which have to be recognized before they earn the title of 'invisible empires'.

Transnational direct investment appears increasingly in agency work and manufacturing on the pattern of North American operations in oil refining, electrical and insurance companies from the 1880s. There were many reasons for this, as old as formal imperialism, including a search for raw materials, a response to foreign tariffs and accommodation with European cartels, and sheer expertise in developing business communications and business organization through subsidiaries. Closer to the American centre, Wilkins detects, too, a peripheral weakness open to penetration ('spillover') by investment in Mexico, in ranching, mining, plantations, railroads and utilities, as 'the border became meaningless', estimated at $1 billion by 1911, of which slightly over half was direct investment.[63] The parallel with spillover from the sub-imperial enclaves into regional trade and investment cannot be pursued here. The debate on the MNEs turns, rather, on their functions in transferring technology, their contribution to income-generation, through taxation and employment, and their political clout.[64] Given the correspondence between the growth of direct investment for control through capital ownership and management, rather than security investment for capital gain, there would seem to be a good case for regarding MNEs as bridgeheads of foreign dominance, especially in the extractive industries and plantations for exportable staples, with or without metropolitan official support. Several points are worth making:

- There *are* cases of an MNE, such as Firestone in Liberia, taking advantage of public indebtedness to secure plantation concessions and interfering directly in the administration of public revenues. The reaction in the Firestone case was a moratorium in 1932 by President Barclay on the loan to the company. Under pressure from the League of Nations and the US State Department, Liberia agreed terms in 1934 (in the first of many reschedulings) for further loans and a larger number of foreign specialists.[65] Other cases have been surveyed by Harry Magdoff.[66]
- More sophisticated analysis of how such enterprises worked in practice demonstrates that: benefits from the presence of a foreign manufacturing corporation derived less from capital imports than from the import of expertise, if this could be transferred into other industries in the local economy; that there have been substantial local gains from taxation, intelligently extracted; that manufacturing outlets depend on the prior organization of an internal or regional market; that there may be little effect on employment; and that local ownership of a multinational's equity may have little influence over politics or benefit to local entrepreneurs in the absence of a developed local market for capital.[67] In other words, advantages in the bargaining

position have been a function of the know-how available in the host society to meet the incomer and extract the best terms. And where this is present, the balance of advantages is less one-sided.

● Since the 1960s, there has been a notable increase in the ability of LDCs to squeeze better terms from MNEs. The global trend summarized by Turner and others since 1945 emphasized the unwillingness of many MNEs to invest in underdeveloped areas, and casts doubt on the political and economic ability of many LDCs to make use of transferred technology. Hence the mixed record on joint ventures with local companies which has produced disagreement on the rate of expansion (where all investment comes from the foreign partner) and trouble over transfer pricing of local components. Turner's conclusion from a survey of the very mixed record of such ventures is that the balance of power had swung to the LDCs by the late 1960s, mainly on the evidence of taxation and participation by host governments and or local firms, since the late 1930s, while the world market was expanding.

This conclusion would seem to be supported by later studies. Even in the most predatory cases, that of mineral exports with high levels of profit repatriation, lack of general investment and backward linkages in return for supplies of copper, bauxite, oil, diamonds from Jamaica, Trinidad-Tobago, Venezuela, Chile and Botswana, closer analysis of the structure of the MNEs by Girvan reveals considerable differences from any imperial model:[68] contractual relations between the host country and the head office leave little autonomy for the field subsidiary; resources are allocated to the subsidiary centrally for growth within a narrow sector and not the whole of a political economy; the local manager is not a governor. The older model of local co-optation into a managerial hierarchy by early chartered companies and nineteenth-century corporations overseas may have to be modified considerably to take into account the contemporary MNE's flexibility of movement, especially personnel and financial assets. But dominance, in the sense of control of local capital assets, can be successfully challenged by forced participation. This may take several stages, as the best case study of the Nigerian experience, by Thomas Bierstecker, shows. The MNEs have developed strategies to mitigate the effects of the first and second indigenization decrees of 1972 and 1977.[69] On the other hand, although the local share of equity capital predominates at 60 per cent, crash training programmes abroad have not succeeded in replacing expatriate management. Hardest hit have been the Nigerian banks whose equity participation went to the federal government, and not the external private investors. It is clear, too, that local businessmen may not have benefited in proportion to the loss of control and ownership by expatriate firms (there are remarkably few indigenous incorporations) in an intervention resulting in state expansion through control of finance. The Nigerian case suggests to Bierstecker that the shift in the balance of bargaining power from multinationals to host countries may have been reversed.[70]

Before we accept this verdict as a general rule, even in African cases, one other trend has to be noted in the commercial and financial power balance if deployed as evidence for invisible empires, namely, the more recent and phenomenal growth of home-grown MNEs in Pacific Asian countries. Excluding Japan, Pacific Asian MNEs account for 14 of the world's 500 largest industrial companies and 35 of the world's largest banks. As Buckley and Mirza show, of the first 60 LDC financial companies in 1986 (ranked in terms of their net assets), 53 were located in the region, compared with two in Mexico, 5 in Brazil and none in tropical Africa.[71] They also make the point for historians that the typology of MNEs is now extremely varied, and includes: expatriate companies from the colonial period; companies based on circulation of international Chinese capital, particularly in property and commodity markets; and companies originating in the newly industrialized countries (NICs) of South Korea, Taiwan, Hong Kong and Singapore, as financial and commodity intermediators, that is, domestic concerns which have gone international. The expatriates which were most relevant to informal empire have long since gone beyond that early stage in establishing the international division of labour, complementary to Western industrial multinationals. Their current role is to develop and export regional resources, to encourage regional trade and investment, in addition to maintaining links with Western economies. Like the Chinese networks, they are based on the regional circulation of capital and reinforced by Japanese expatriate outsiders. Second, the home-grown MNEs of Brunei, Indonesia, Malaysia, Philippines, Singapore and Thailand upset the usual stereotypes by reminding us that some underdeveloped economies contain sufficiently concentrated resources to expand internationally, backed by the state or as state-owned MNEs, and that the People's Republic of China also has some socialist MNEs in exports and servicing, and earning hard currency through Hong Kong. The old bipolar international division of labour, on which the original informal empire analogy was based, now has to take into account these local intermediators dependent on external markets outside Europe and North America with regional and global strategies of their own, and based on a set of intermediate economies which cut across the old industrialized/developing division among international economies.

Conclusions

A term which has become so accepted is not likely to be replaced by a short survey such as this, intended as it is to give pause for historical thought. But its persistence can be better understood from the historiography which underlies its use, while considerable discrimination is required in applying it to any region to account for the influence of any European power which was also an imperial power.

At the outset, it has been argued, informal empire and the imperialism of free trade were metaphorical descriptions applied to the political and economic imbalance perceived during the nineteenth-century expansion of world trade. Because Britain stood at the centre as a predominant exporter of manufactures, services and capital, had a formal empire and went on acquiring territory, there was an implied causality between being an imperial power and being a major trading power. World influence became equated with dominion. The commercial, financial and diplomatic functions of a major trading state were occluded with other functions in imperial government. To later historians the post-war supremacy of the United States was a suggestive parallel. A recent and timely assessment of such 'terms of art' used to explain or summarize important transition periods in imperial history reminds us quite simply that political control was always a last resort in the new British empire of the early nineteenth century.[72] What is left unexplained is the operation of the substitutes for political control.

The original assertion that political power and influence was derived from industrial and commercial expansion overseas rested, however, on a macro-economic theory of trade as an engine of growth applicable to the United States, to Latin American states and the dominions, which did have some remarkable success stories before 1913. Successful development was achieved through their export sectors and internal markets in which immigration, commercial and financial intermediation and some investment in infrastructure, mainly railways, had been predominantly British in origin and management. For historians of the politics of imperialism, informal empire also satisfied a need for historical continuity between the early nineteenth century conjunction of forms of decolonization and self-government and the late expansion by imperial powers in Africa, Asia and the Pacific.

But by the 1930s explanations for arrested growth had to be found to account for the position of primary producers, long after the last boom of 1900–13 had faded and faltered. Attention among economic historians, rather than political ones, focused on exogenous factors. Less attention was given to the evidence that, relative to the growth of world trade, Latin, Asian and African exports, despite improved terms against manufactured exports to 1913, had already suffered from low per capita growth in the nineteenth century, as a result of: competition from other primary producers; the disadvantages of distance and poor internal communications; low capital accumulation from returns on exports produced at low opportunity cost with prices little above subsistence levels. A whole set of theories was formulated to explain why nominally independent states did so little, or could do so little, to improve on the distribution of gains that did accumulate from trade growth.

By the 1950s there was a theoretical convergence between the use of informal empire to argue historical continuity and to argue economic retardation. Such theories of dependency and imperialism looked back to the nineteenth century from a period of growth in world trade marked by extreme volatility, population increase and, therefore, stagnation of exports and earnings in per capita terms. From 1921 there was a rapid decline in prices relative to 1913 levels, and the net barter terms of trade were adversely affected to the 1950s. Exports per capita in value were notably better, however, during the period 1913–48 for Latin America than for Africa and Asia, which gave point to the argument that export earnings without industrialization were not enough.

At the same time, bilateral and multilateral investment began to decline compared with private investment, in the case of Latin America, as US private investment turned to Europe. By the 1970s the largest proportion of net inflow of external resources to Latin America was from transnational banks using syndicated loans from a host of small banking institutions.[73] Since 1982 the banks have taken defensive measures to manage the debt crisis through steering committees and close co-operation with financial institutions such as the IMF, as current account deficits in Latin America have grown dramatically. The Latin experience, however, deeply influenced writings on other dependencies during the period of decolonization, which included the anachronistic view that post-colonial failures can be traced directly to colonial policies.

By now we are a long way from the elementary commercial and financial intermediation of the nineteenth century, undertaken to lower transaction costs and overcome the effects of distance and absence of local skills and infrastructures in overseas commodity markets. But the misleading sense of continuity implied by the term informal empire can be seen in the polemic surrounding the growth of private investment through multinationals and in the operations of the IMF, as well as in the more sober reflections of historians who perceive underdeveloped economies as 'marginalized' by the growth and economic co-operation of former colonial powers.[74]

As regional studies have shown, however, the nineteenth-century denotation of informal empire in the sense of Britain's influence overseas is much wider than the operations of investors and debt collectors. Influential agencies must include consular courts, missionary and scientific societies, as well as the specialized private and joint stock corporations engaged in servicing sectors of an immature economy. The connotation of the term, it has been argued, is not simply the sum of these examples, but rather rests on an analogy with formal imperial controls, more especially those of the principal source of overseas agencies in the early nineteenth century. As in the case of formal empire, there were degrees of influence within the politics and economy of a host society. But there agreement ends, because of two historically unresolved problems of evidence which have given rise to both a narrow and a broad application of the metaphor of control by external agencies. The first requires some proof of government backing for operations supporting the interests of foreign intemediation; the second sees in any sectoral predominance by foreign intermediaries a loss of sovereign control, sometimes underwritten by treaties or commercial agreements. In the first school of thought, the analogy with formal empire is pressed very hard and requires an official acknowledgement and acceptance of degrees of influence short of protectorate and annexation; in the second, the work of a foreign agency is sufficient to indicate that proto-imperialism is at work, reinforced by ownership of assets.

Perhaps the initial mistake was not to recognize the limitations of metaphor, namely, that informal empire assumed structures present in formal empire which were never analysed for the kind of political lien they were supposed to exercise in the interests of a free-trading imperial power. This is because some kind of control must be present or the analogy falls to the ground. To demonstrate this assumption, historians will have to pay careful attention to the managerial hierarchies now identified as a longstanding component of great mercantile companies in the past and their successor corporations operating in more than one country. The same component has been alluded to in a more recent description of the 'cosmopolitan bourgeoisie', which turned to the gentlemanly capitalism of the City for fresh funding after 1850.[75] But we are a long way from understanding the wide variety of partnerships and incorporated companies, or the ways in which related changes in commercial law favoured this process of commercial expansion.

The second difficulty, in the absence of analytical techniques to determine the structures of intermediation, arose from using 'free-trade imperialism' as a holdall for a wide variety of imperial purposes at the level of governments and at the level of the structures themselves, as though these were common purposes. The purposes of the British Government were not really in doubt: unimpeded circulation of goods without privilege (as embodied in commercial treaties); protection of British subjects, including the abolition of slavery in British territories; and a wider belief in the benefits of improvement though commerce and technological relocation, a kind of secular salvation (or modernization) not so far removed in nineteenth-century offical minds from its spiritual counterpart, seen in the conjunction of purposes inherent in the abolition of the slave trade.

The general methods of informal empire required to achieve these purposes need to be distinguished from specific examples of intermediation through the structures created and exported overseas. A list of methods would include: mediatization by a consortium of states (associated with the Ottoman Empire, but also present in joint actions against piracy or the slave trade); sub-imperialism through client states and outposts of empire on unregulated frontiers; scientific research and proselytization on the benefits of cultural and technological change; extension and reform of international law; trade and investment in specific forms of intermediation.

The examples of intermediation through structures designed to apply these methods include foreign banking and commercial institutions, companies engaged in transport, mineral extraction, plantations and public utilities, foreign courts and consuls, international commissions, scientific and missionary societies. Terms such as 'collaborating élites' beg too many questions about identity to be considered as institutional modes of intermediation, though local recruitment and personnel are central to analysis of structures in both formal and informal empires. But the notion has not been accepted with any enthusiasm by historians of the dominions, where concepts of local nationalism still hold sway, or by more radical historians of Europe's subversion of Africa.[76]

These are no more than shopping lists without the research required to test Charles A. Jones' challenging argument that the dynamic of commercial and financial influence in the nineteenth century is to be found in the mobility of merchant entrepreneurs and in the technological changes which required them to draw closer to the centre for corporate funding. In the end, the separation of the credit function from the handling of goods, which remained in tandem in some tropical markets, and changes in joint stock liability laws may be seen as technical innovations with wider and more immediate influence at the periphery than the fact that the City was also the capital of an imperial power. Imperial networks were useful, but not the necessary or sufficient cause of all influence overseas.

The unresolved question, moreover, is how far government departments at the metropolitan end of official sub-imperial agencies are essential components to the notion of informal empire in its narrow or wide definition. There was a temptation to assume that the Foreign Office, like the US State Department, offered through nineteenth-century free-trade diplomacy a kind of export credit guarantee to protect the bondholders. The evidence is poor, outside of Egypt. The view taken here is that government intermediation for treaty ports, concessions, consular jurisdiction and debt administration provides examples of the purposeful construction of informal empire on the China coast in the 1830s and on the West African coast from 1877. The preferred mode, after all, was an absence of political control, if the conditions of free trade could be established by other means (so the argument runs). This throws a great deal of weight on the identificiation of a political lien, without which there is no empire, not even a metaphorical one. Latin America proved the most contentious region for such an identification, without recourse to the élite, which in turn has proved difficult to project onto the stage of its history as a willing collaborator. Other forms of political lien are recognizable: debt administration (in the case of Egypt, Turkey and more recent international debtors) by British, and French, commissioners and IMF officials; large-scale settlement by immigration, with control of land and other resources establishing in time complete control of government and administration; organization of cartels for shipping, commodities and concessions (paradoxically anti-free trade); minor theocracies among missionary societies. The one set of examples least well investigated by proponents of the imperialism of free trade was curiously enough the self-governing British colonies, where it is possible to demonstrate a high degree of commercial and financial complementarity between the imperial power and the so-called built-in collaborators, from the 1860s to 1918, without much evidence of a political lien, except in the area of foreign relations.

So what examples, in the end, can be offered? On a descending scale of credibility, the metaphor might be held to apply to Egypt, Turkey and China, and, for brief periods, to West and East Africa, the Pacific islands and southern Africa. In the African and Pacific cases the operation of sub-imperialism was an important source of initiative and support for control and expansion on a closing frontier,[77] and much of the informal empire identified in these areas was influence from British enclaves, which ended either in the big bang of late imperial partition or the big revolts against intermediation, such as the Anglo-Boer War, and the overthrow of the Ottoman Empire and the Manchu dynasty from within. Much less satisfactorily, foreign intermediation leading to influence rather than informal empire is in evidence in Latin America and the dominions, after local revolution and peaceful transfer of power. Convincing analogies with 'empire' appear only where control of foreign affairs was exercised by the United States, in Central America, or as a residuum of imperial practice by Great Britain.

The basic reason for this differentiation has been the relative success or failure, not of imperial pressure but of the adaptation of mediatized societies through technological diffusion and relocation. There have been a few historians, however, who have made a more discriminating analysis of the technological imbalance between an expansive Europe and regions of imperial influence in the nineteenth century, when the gap was growing larger. As a basis for understanding informal empire, the concepts of technological transfer, by relocation through agencies, or diffusion through settlers have not been explored so well. Nor have important related topics such as changes in business organization and the financial revolution of the nineteenth century been adequately analysed in the proto-imperial context, while the advantages conferred by literacy seem to have been forgotten, as much as they were apparent to contemporary trading partners drawn from frontier societies.[78] Much of the informality of the British version of overseas influence derived from technological changes in producton and marketing and, therefore, in the capacity of a leading imperial power to export goods, people and ideas. Collaboration, shorn of its political overtones, was little more than a learning process to adapt such exports to a local political economy. If such polities lacked the organizational technology, or were overcome by conquest before they had time to evolve a state structure, informal empire can hardly be said to have operated for very long at all. For, paradoxically, the concept works least well as an imperial mode for achieving political and commercial ends in those areas of Africa or the Pacific which required formal imperial intervention to underwrite agency work in conditions of international competition, precisely because so little European technology had been relocated at the coastal markets or in transportation to the interior. Diffusion by settlement, moreover, was limited to the Cape and Natal, where settler societies undertook the expansive conquest that the metropole was reluctant to finance. On the other hand the concept works well for Egypt, Turkey, China and Persia, regions where mercantile and financial technology was relocated, in conjunction with older juridical privileges, in societies with higher levels of literacy. For Japan, there was no such informal control at all before rapid adaptation by a society which had levels of formal education comparable to mid-nineteenth century European countries. The Japanese took care to end foreign jurisdiction just at the period when they paid careful attention to the military and economic lessons of Europe's formal expansion.[79] Such a consideration gives less emphasis to the externalities of control over economic sectors, which have been the main focus in Latin America, and more emphasis in organization and legislative defence against foreign intrusion and foreign privilege based on knowledge.

For the dominions, like the more advanced economies of some

Latin American states, enjoyed a high degree of technological adaptation through diffusion and relocation, including localized forms of intermediate structures. Where these existed, informal empire was either not necessary, in the sense of establishing a political lien, or was simply not present, as foreign banks (the Anglos) and companies supplied services in conjunction with local commercial and financial structures. China was edging towards this stage of domestic control over revenue and railways in the Manchu reforms of the late 1890s, before xenophobia overtook the reformers. Relative absence of technological adaptation in other regions brought a greater degree of intermediation through foreign structures and provoked a certain amount of resistance. Where no political lien could be established, as in much of Africa, sub-imperial outposts, that is, the settlements, client states and colonies, served as bridgeheads to control the frontier, in competition with other powers, as informal empire proved inadequate.

Influence through technological transfer in all its forms, rather than through the politics of informal empire also suggests that the disjunction between early and late nineteenth-century forms of expansion is greater than the continuity implied by the metaphor. By the 1870s collaborating societies, rather than auxiliary élites, were well established with considerable purchasing power in North America and the dominions, and had every incentive, expressed through functioning democracies, to integrate into the world market for goods and capital. Popular control of the political élite is less discernible in Latin America and is hardly evident at all in the Middle and Far East. But in the Latin American cases protest against the consequences of free trade and dependency on processed exports came late in the 1930s, not in the 1890s; and, while some international conventions were able to cope with the consequences of technological innovation in the last half of the nineteenth century (for navigable waterways, postage, cable and telecommunications, and international banking), those based on consortia of powers did not work. One solution was to extend domestic sovereignty to keep others out, in the informal partition of the Pacific coast and through the Monroe Doctrine. The more usual practice, however, was to recognize the failure of political mediatization in West Africa or in Egypt, for example, to safeguard the conditions for technological innovation by assigning spheres to European administration, in much the same way as the United States arrogated this responsibility in Central America, and Imperial Russia and Japan in

Manchuria and Korea. Where the politics of informal influence through technological mediatization broke down, military technology and formal empire supervened.

Notes

1. Much of the material for this revision derives from a seminar series on informal empire by the Imperial and Commonwealth History group at Oxford in Michaelmas Term 1988. I am indebted to A. G. Hopkins, Andrew Porter and Martin Lynn for comments and to John Darwin for an impartial summary of the proceedings. For some of the earlier background to the academic debate, see William Roger Louis (ed.), *Imperialism: the Robinson and Gallagher Controversy* (New York/London 1976); and for other 'imperial' metaphors: Louis Turner, *Invisible Empires: Multinational Companies and the Modern World* (London 1970); Daniel R. Headrick, *The Tentacles of Progress: Technology Transfer in the Age of Imperialism, 1850–1940* (Oxford University Press 1988); Alfred W. Crosby, *Ecological Imperialism, the Biological Expansion of Europe, 900–1900* (Cambridge University Press 1986); W. Ross Johnston, *Sovereignty and Protection: a Study of British Jurisdictional Imperialism in the Late Nineteenth Century* (Duke University Press 1963); and other references to works by Robert A. Stafford, Monica E. Turvey, Anthony J. Dachs, below. For a new lease of life, see the collection of papers in Wolfgang J. Mommsen and Jürgen Osterhammel (eds), *Imperialism and After: Continuities and Discontinuities* (London 1986), though the term is explicitly rejected for the process of influence through loans and aid (p. 357).
2. C. F. Fay, *Imperial Economy and its Place in the Formation of Economic Doctrine 1600–1932* (Oxford 1934), p. 140.
3. C. F. Fay, 'The movement towards free trade' in J. Holland Rose, A. P. Newton, E. A. Benians (eds), *The Cambridge History of the British Empire*, Vol. II: *The Growth of the New Empire 1783–1870* (Cambridge 1940), pp. 388–414, esp. p. 408.
4. H. S. Ferns, 'Britain's informal empire in Argentina, 1806–1914', *Past and Present* (1953), pp. 60–75; see, too, his *Britain and Argentina in the Nineteenth Century* (Oxford 1960).
5. Ferns, 'Britain's informal empire in Argentina, 1806–1914', p. 74; and, for other works on Latin America, from this period, exploring British influence: J. F. Rippy, *Historical Evolution of Hispanic America* (Oxford 1946); A. K. Manchester, *British Pre-eminence in Brazil* (Chapel Hill 1933); J. H. Williams, *Argentine Internatonal Trade under Inconvertible Paper Money, 1880–1900* (Cambridge, Mass. 1920).
6. John Gallagher and Ronald Robinson, 'The imperialism of free trade', *Economic History Review* vi, 1, (1953), pp. 1–15.
7. Gallagher and Robinson, 'The imperialism of free trade', esp. p. 5; and for a recent exploration of modes of commercial expansion in response to technological change, with or without benefit of empire, see Charles A.

Jones, *International Business in the Nineteenth Century: the Rise and Fall of a Cosmopolitan Bourgeoisie* (New York University Press 1987), esp. ch. 4 'Adaptation on the periphery'. For a useful summary of earlier criticisms, Bruce Knox, 'Re-considering mid-Victorian imperialism', *The Journal of Imperial and Commonwealth History* 1, 2 (1973), pp. 155–72.

8. See Roberto Cortes Conde and Stanley J. Stein (eds), *Latin America: a Guide to Economic History 1830–1930* (University of California Press, Berkeley 1977); Theotonia Dos Santos, 'The structure of dependence', *American Economic Review* 60, 2, (1970), pp. 231–6; and for an overview, Bill Albert, *South America and the World Economy from Independence to 1930*, Studies in Economic History (London 1983), esp. pp. 17–23.

9. D. C. M. Platt, *Finance, Trade, and Politics in British Foreign Policy 1815–1914* (Oxford 1968), p. 353; W. M. Mathew, 'The imperialism of free trade: Peru, 1820–70', *Economic History Review* 3, 31 (1968),pp. 562–79.

10. John Mayo, 'British interests in Chile and their influence, 1851–1886', D. Phil thesis (Oxford University 1977); 'Britain and Chile, 1851–1886', *Journal of Interamerican Studies and World Affairs* 1, 23 (1981), p. 99.

11. Ian L. D. Forbes, 'German informal imperialism in South America before 1914', *Economic History Review* 31 (1978), pp. 384–98.

12. D. C. M. Platt, *Business Imperialism 1840–1930. An Inquiry Based on British Experience in Latin America* (Oxford 1970).

13. Robert Greenhill, 'Merchants and the Latin American trade: an introduction' in Platt (ed.) *Business Imperialism*, pp. 156–97; Rory Miller, 'British firms and the Peruvian government, 1885–1930' in Platt (ed.), *Business Imperialism*, pp. 371–94.

14. Charles Jones, 'Commercial banks and mortgage companies' in Platt (ed.), *Business Imperialism*, pp. 17–52.

15. Robert Greenhill, 'Shipping, 1850–1914' in Platt (ed.), *Business Imperialism*, pp. 119–55.

16. Colin Lewis, 'British railway companies and the Argentine government' in Platt (ed.), *Business Imperialism*, pp. 395–427.

17. See especially, Dana G. Munro, *Intervention and Dollar Diplomacy in the Caribbean 1900–1921* (Princeton 1964).

18. P. Winn, 'British informal empire in Uruguay in the nineteenth century', *Past and Present* 73 (1976), pp. 100–126.

19. H. Ramirez Necochea, *Balmaceda y la contrarevolucion de 1891* (3rd edn, Santiago 1972).

20. Richard Graham, *Britain and the Onset of Modernization in Brazil 1850–1914* (Cambridge 1968); and 'Robinson and Gallagher in Latin America: the meaning of informal imperialism' in Louis (ed.), *Imperialism*, pp. 217–21.

21. Albert, *South America and the World Economy from Independence to 1930*, p. 33.

22. Sir Reader Bullard, *Large and Loving Privileges. The Capitulations in the Middle East and North Africa* (Glasgow 1960), p. 7; G. W. Keeton, *The Development of Extraterritoriality in China* (2 vols, New York 1969); and for a suggestive reconsideration of the earlier chartered companies which

ignores jurisdiction, Ann M. Carlos and Stephen Nicholas, '"Giants of an earlier capitalism": the chartered trading companies and modern multinationals', *Business History Review* 62, 3 (1988), pp. 398–419.

23. Michael Greenberg, *British Trade and the Opening of China 1800–42*, (Cambridge 1951).

24. Keeton, Vol. 1, pp. 75–7.

25. Stanley F. Wright, *Hart and the Chinese Customs* (Belfast 1950), pp. 104–5.

26. Clarence B. Davis, 'Financing imperialism: British and American bankers as vectors of imperial expansion in China, 1908–1920', *Business History Review* 19 (1976), pp. 291–305; Frank. H. H. King (ed.), *Eastern Banking. Essays in the History of the Hongkong and Shanghai Banking Corporation* (London 1983), p. 3.

27. Henry Tipper, 'China and the West: with special reference to British interests', *Journal of the Institute of Bankers* 3, 22 (1901), pp. 83–104.

28. Ralph William Huenemann, *The Dragon and the Iron Horse. The Economics of Railroads in China 1876–1937* (Cambridge, Mass. 1984); Sherman Cochran, *Big Business in China. Sino-Foreign Rivalry in the Cigarette Industry, 1890–1930* (Cambridge, Mass. 1980); Jürgen Osterhammel, 'Semi-colonialism and informal empire in twentieth-century China: towards a framework of analysis' in Mommsen and Osterhammel (eds), *Imperialism and After*, pp. 290–314.

29. See especially works reviewed by A. G. Hopkins, 'The Victorians and Africa: a reconsideration of the occupation of Egypt, 1882', *The Journal of African History* 27 (1986), pp. 363–91; and for the ways in which debt was managed, Joseph Rabino, 'Some statistics of Egypt', *Journal of the Statistical Society* 47 (1884), pp. 415–67.

30. Cited in Bernard Lewis, *The Emergence of Modern Turkey* (Oxford), p. 113.

31. Sevket Pamuk, *The Ottoman Empire and European Capitalism, 1820–1913. Trade, Investment and Production* (Cambridge 1987).

32. Roger Owen, *The Middle East in the World Economy 1800–1914* (London 1981), pp. 193, 199–200. The Public Debt Administration consisted of a council of foreign representatives to collect revenues from the salt monopoly, stamp and spirits duties, tithes and some provincial tribute. See, also, Platt, *Finance, Trade and Politics in British Foreign Policy 1815–1914*, p. 200.

33. Martin Lynn, 'The "imperialism of free trade" and the case of West Africa, c.1830–c.1870', *Journal of Imperial and Commonwealth History* 1, 15 (1986), pp. 22–39.

34. G. N. Sanderson, 'British informal empire, imperial ambitions, defensive strategies, and the Anglo-Portuguese Treaty of February 1884' in Stig Förster, Wolfgang J. Mommsen and Ronald Robinson (eds), *Bismarck, Europe and Africa. The Berlin Africa Conference 1884–1885 and the Onset of Partition* (Oxford 1988), pp. 189–214.

35. Lynn, 'The "imperialism of free trade"', p. 36.

36. This conclusion is based on an analysis of expenditure in British West African settlements from C. W. Newbury, *British Policy Towards West*

Africa, Vol. 2, Select Documents *1875–1914 with Statistical Appendices 1800–1914* (Oxford 1971) pp. 621–5.

37. William D. McIntyre, *The Imperial Frontier in the Tropics, 1865–75: a Study of British Colonial Policy in West Africa, Malaya and the South Pacific in the Age of Gladstone and Disraeli* (London 1967); John Benyon, *Proconsul and Paramountcy in South Africa, The High Commission, British Supremacy and the Sub-continent 1806–1910* (University of Natal Press 1980); see too, Howard Lamar and Leonard Thompson (eds), *The Frontier in History: North America and Southern Africa Compared* (Yale University Press 1981) for the notion of a closed frontier through the action of magistrates and taxation.

38. Cited in W. P. Morrell, *Britain in the Pacific Islands* (Oxford 1960), p. 246.

39. Peter Adams, *Fatal Necessity. British Intervention in New Zealand 1830–1847* (Auckland 1977).

40. Angus Rose, *New Zealand Aspirations in the Pacific in the Nineteenth Century* (Oxford 1964).

41. William Woodruff, *Impact of Western Man. A Study of Europe's Role in the World Economy 1750–1960* (New York 1966), pp. 164–217 (for a diffusionist interpretation); Thomas R. de Gregori, *Technology and the Economic Development of the Tropical African Frontier* (Cleveland and London 1969) (for attention to the problem of technical and administrative organization, esp. pp. 159–60).

42. Daniel Headrick, *The Tools of Imperialism: Technology and European Imperialism in the Nineteenth Century* (Oxford 1981), for the techniques or hardware employed; *The Tentacles of Progress. Technology Transfer in the Age of Imperialism, 1850–1940* (Oxford 1988); Roy MacLeod and Milton Lewis (eds), *Disease, Medicine, Empire: Perspectives on Western Medicine and the Experience of European Expansion* (London 1988), p. 2.

43. Mira Wilkins, 'The role of private business in the international diffusion of technology', *Journal of Economic History* 1, 34 (1974), pp. 166–88. For an overview of the growth of the corporate enterprise, A. B. Levy, *Private Corporations and their Control* (London 1950). Dr Stanley Chapman of Nottingham University has undertaken a much-needed study of joint stock companies in the imperial context.

44. Robert A. Stafford, 'The role of Sir Roderick Murchison in promoting the geographical and geological exploration of the British Empire and its sphere of influence, 1855–1871' (D. Phil., Oxford University 1985), p. 363; *Scientist of Empire: Sir Roderick Murchison, Scientific Exploration and Victorian Imperialism* (Cambridge 1989).

45. Robert A. Stafford, 'Roderick Murchison and the structure of Africa: a geological prediction and its consequences for British expansion', *Annals of Science* 45 (1988), pp. 1–40.

46. Lewis Pyenson, 'Cultural imperialism and exact sciences: German expansion overseas 1900–1930', *History of Science* 22, (1982), pp. 1–43; and for contemporary French influence from a sub-imperial base, see the articles grouped under 'Géopolitique et stratégique dans le Pacifique' in *Journal de la Société des Océanistes* 87, 2 (1988).

47. A. A. Koskinen, *Missionary Influence as a Political Factor in the Pacific* (California 1941); R. Oliver, *The Missionary Factor in East Africa* (London 1952).

48. J. Y. Thomas, 'The role of the medical missionary in British East Africa, 1874–1904', D. Phil. thesis (Oxford University 1981); Anthony J. Dachs, 'Missionary imperialism – the case of Bechuanaland', *Journal of African History* 4, 13 (1972), pp. 647–58; A. Sillery, *John Mackenzie of Bechuanaland, 1835–1899* (Cape Town 1971).

49. Cited in Oliver, *The Missionary Factor*, p. 128.

50. Monica E. Turvey, 'Missionaries and imperialism: opponents or progenitors of empire? The New Guinea case', *Journal of the Royal Australian Historical Society* 65 (1979), pp. 89–108.

51. Klaus J. Bade, 'Culture, cash and Christianity: the German colonial experience and the case of the Rhenish mission in New Guinea', *Pacific Studies* 3, 10 (1987), pp. 53–71.

52. Peter Hempenstall and Noel Rutherford, *Protest and Dissent in the Colonial Pacific* (Apia 1984).

53. Frederick Pedler, *The Lion and the Unicorn in Africa. A History of the Origins of the United Africa Company 1787–1931* (London 1974); Doug Munro and Stewart Firth, 'From company rule to consular control: Gilbert Island labourers on German plantations in Samoa, 1867–96', *Journal of Imperial and Commonwealth History* 28 (1987), pp. 209–30.

54. J. Forbes Munro, 'Shipping subsidies and railway guarantees: William Mackinnon, Eastern Africa and the Indian Ocean, 1860–93', *Journal of African History* 28 (1987), pp. 209–30.

55. For example, A. G. Hopkins, *An Economic History of West Africa* (London 1973), pp. 63–4, 70–1, 109–10; C. Newbury, *Tahiti Nui: Change and Survival in French Polynesia, 1767–1945* (Honolulu 1980), pp. 159–60, 247–53; 'Ho'o Tarahu: le crédit et le commerce en Polynésie orientale vers la fin du 19e siècle', *Journal de la Société des Océanistes* 38 74–5 (1982), pp. 225–40; C. G. F. Simkin, *The Traditional Trade of Asia* (London 1968), p. 279; and for earlier systems in India, C. A. Bayly, 'Indian merchants in a "traditional" setting: Benares, 1780–1830' in Clive Dewey and A. G. Hopkins (eds), *The Imperial Impact: Studies in the Economic History of Africa and India* (London 1978), pp. 171–93.

56. Anthony Sampson, *The Money Lenders: Bankers in a Dangerous World* (London 1981), pp. 29–30; and for connections between lending and bank crises, James S. Duesenberry, *Money and Credit: Impact and Control* (New Jersey 1964), pp. 10–12.

57. 'IMF in Africa', *Africa Recovery*: 4(1987), pp. 5–6; and 'African debt continues to mount', 2, (1988), pp. 23–5; Robert E. Wood, *From Marshall Plan to Debt Crisis. Foreign Aid and Development Choices in the World Economy* (Berkeley 1986); Andrew I. Schoenholtz, 'The IMF in Africa: unnecessary and undesirable Western restraints on development', *Journal of Modern African Studies* 3, 25 (1987), pp. 403–33.

58. Irving Stone, 'British direct and portfolio investment in Latin America before 1914', *Journal of Economic History* 3, 37 (1977), pp. 690–722; Peter Svedberg, 'The portfolio-direct composition of private foreign investment

in 1914 revisited', *Economic Journal* 8 (1978), pp. 763–77; Wilfried Guth, *Capital Exports to Less Developed Countries* (Dordrecht 1963), ch. 2.

59. Cited in Patrick K. O'Brien, 'The costs and benefits of British imperialism 1846–1914', *Past and Present* 120 (1988), p. 185.
60. Stone, 'British direct and portfolio investment', pp. 702–3.
61. Mira Wilkins, *The Emergence of the Multinational Enterprise: American Business Abroad from the Colonial Era to 1914* (Cambridge Mass. 1970); Louis Turner, *Invisible Empires: Multinational Companies and the Modern World* (London 1970); Peter Hertner and Geoffrey Jones (eds), *Multinationals: Theory and History* (London 1986).
62. Schoenholtz; Walden Bello, David Kinley and Elaine Elinson, *Development Débacle: The World Bank in the Philippines* (San Francisco 1982); Antony G. Hopkins, 'The World Bank in Africa: historical reflections on the African present', *World Development* 14, 12 (1986) pp. 1473–87.
63. Wilkins, *The Emergence of the Multinational Enterprise*, p. 125.
64. See note 61; and Carl Widstrand (ed.), *Multinational Firms in Africa* (Uppsala 1975).
65. M. I. Uhomoibhi, 'Imperial and League intervention in Sierra Leone and Liberia: boundaries, finance and labour 1890–1936', D. Phil. thesis (Oxford University 1982), ch. 7.
66. H. Magdoff, *The Age of Imperialism: The Economics of US Foreign Policy* (New York 1986).
67. D. K. Fieldhouse, *Unilever Overseas: the Anatomy of a Multinational 1895–1965* (Hoover Institution Press, Stanford 1978), esp. p. 581ff; Grant L. Reuber, *Private Foreign Investment in Development* (Oxford 1973).
68. Norman Girvan, *Multinational Corporations and Dependent Underdevelopment in Mineral Export Economies* (Yale Economic Growth Center, New Haven 1972).
69. Thomas Bierstecker, *Multinationals, the State and Control of the Nigerian Economy* (Princeton NJ 1987), esp. p. 263.
70. Bierstecker, p. 292.
71. Peter Buckley and Hafiz Mirza, 'The strategy of Pacific Asian multinationals', *Pacific Review* 1, 1 (1988), pp. 50–62.
72. For a comment on such terms in imperial historiography, see Frederick Madden (ed.), with David Fieldhouse, *Imperial Reconstruction, 1763–1840. The Evolution of Alternative Systems of Colonial Government. Select Documents on the Constitutional History of the British Empire*, Vol. 3 (Westport Conn. 1987), p. xxv; and for the perceptive views of a political scientist on the ambiguities of imperialism and informal empire, Katherine West, 'Theorising about "imperialism": a methodological note', *Journal of Imperial and Commonwealth History* 1, 2 (1973), pp. 147–54.
73. Stephany Griffith-Jones and Osvaldo Sunkel, *Debt and Development Crises in Latin America: the End of an Illusion* (Clarendon Press, Oxford 1986), Table 5, 41.
74. Mommsen, 'The end of empire and the continuity of imperialism' in Mommsen and Osterhammel, *Imperialism and After*, p. 351.
75. Jones; A. G. Hopkins, 'Gentlemanly capitalism and British expansion

overseas. II: The new imperialism, 1850–1945', *Economic History Review* (series 2) XL, 2 (1987), pp. 1–26.
76. John Eddy and Deryck Schreuder (eds), *The Rise of Colonial Nationalism: Australia, New Zealand, Canada and South Africa first Assert their Nationalities 1880–1914* (Sydney 1988); Walter Rodney, *How Europe Underdeveloped Africa* (Bogle L'Ouverture 1972).
77. Lammar and Thompson (eds), *The Frontier in History*, pp. 131, 167.
78. Woodruff, *Impact of Western Man*; David S. Landes, 'Technological change and development in Western Europe, 1750–1914' in H. J. Habakkuk and M. Postan (eds), *The Cambridge Economic History of Europe*, Vol. 4: *The Industrial Revolutions and After: Incomes, Population and Technological Change* (Cambridge 1965), esp. pp. 431–6.
79. R. P. Dore, 'The legacy of Tokugawa education' in Marcus B. Jansen, *Changing Japanese Attitudes towards Modernization* (Princeton 1965), pp. 100–103; S. O. Agbi, 'Japanese contact with, and knowledge of Africa 1868–1912', *Journal of the Historical Society of Nigeria* 11, 1/2 (1981–2), pp. 153–65.

3

BERBICE AND THE UNIFICATION OF BRITISH GUIANA, 1831

Donald Wood

From 1962 to 1964 a seminar was held at the Institute of Commonwealth Studies, London, on the problems of smaller territories. A book followed, and I was left with an abiding interest in the subject.[1] As a token of gratitude to Kenneth Robinson for much kindness, and to recall those discussions, when nearly every month, so it seemed, another little colony was being fledged into independence, I have decided to discuss the formation of British Guiana, paying particular attention to Berbice, the smaller partner-to-be in the united colony; a rare instance of integration in an empire that favoured federations.[2]

When the British captured Berbice, Demerara and Essequibo in 1796, Berbice had serious weaknesses compared with its bustling neighbour and these were to haunt it throughout its undistinguished years as a single colony. Under the liberal rule of Storm van s'Gravesnede of the Dutch West India Company, the united colony of Demerara and Essequibo was opened to foreigners in the 1730s. Their coming helped to shift the centre of gravity from the Essequibo, dangerously close to Spanish settlements, to the virtually unexploited Demerara River. British sugar planters, particularly from Barbados, were attracted by fresh land and a ten-year tax remission. By the 1760s the British were in a majority among the whites and the process was underway whereby settlement expanded from the rivers and creeks, where originally the Dutch had sought Amerindian trade, to the coasts. In the same years sugar was ousting coffee and cotton as the staple crop.

In contrast, the coffee and cotton plantations which straggled along the Berbice River, and its tributary, the Canje, were governed by the Berbice Association, a joint stock company chartered in Amsterdam in 1732. The association long held to precepts of a most conservative mercantilism. All produce, whether from its own estates or those of private settlers, had to be sent in Dutch ships to the United Provinces: all supplies for the colonists had to be imported through the association.[3] For most of the eighteenth century aliens were not allowed to settle. Berbice nearly received a mortal blow in the 1763 Slave Rebellion, when the white population fell from 286 to 116 and the slaves from 4,251 to 2,464.[4] The directors, after considering whether Berbice was worth keeping, imposed extra taxes and belatedly admitted foreigners in the 1780s. Its population did recover after the rebellion and it shared in the population boom after the capitulation when British merchants, planters and their slaves flocked into the conquered colonies. Yet Berbice would always play second fiddle to Demerara. At the first capitulation – there was a second in 1803 after the fragile Peace of Amiens – there were 29,473 slaves in Demerara and 8,232 in Berbice.[5]

There was no real switch to sugar and this was occasionally serious after the second capitulation. In the days of the Berbice Association, when its store ships from the United Provinces were overdue, American traders were sometimes allowed in. The Americans happily accepted bills drawn upon Amsterdam, the financial capital of the world in the eighteenth century.[6] Yet in the wars when the United Provinces had become the Batavian Republic and a weak and blockaded puppet of France, it was different. Essential shipments could then only be obtained from American neutrals for rum or cash.[7] In 1807 there were only five sugar plantations in Berbice; three years later, four.[8] They distilled not enough rum for local consumption and the main circulating currency was Dutch paper, by then of dubious value; this, as we shall see, was to be a baneful legacy of Dutch Berbice.

Moreover, Berbice had a geographical disadvantage. Anthony Trollope summed up Guianese coastal topography in a memorable terse sentence: 'Yes; Demerara is flat, and Berbice is flat, and so is Essesquibo'.[9] Thanks to Dutch skills and British capital their swampy foreshores were being drained, dyked and poldered in the eighteenth century to create a landscape that at times reminds the visitor from northern Europe of the ordered certainties of North Holland or

Friesland. Just off shore, shallow banks of mud and silt made it impossible for any but the slightest draft boats to load or land small cargoes. The only possible wharves for ocean-going ships lay in the rivers at Georgetown or New Amsterdam but their mouths were impeded by bars. Herein lay the disadvantage of Berbice.

At the mouth of the Demerara there was 18 feet of water over a mud bar at High Water Springs and 9–11 feet at Low Water Springs. On the other hand the bar at Berbice was hard silt and only navigable for vessels drawing not more than 15 feet at High Water Springs, 7 feet at Low Water Springs, a vexing limitation for navigation and commerce.[10] If a frigate could shelter in the Demerara, no vessel larger than a sloop could easily enter the Berbice. Ships' masters dared not take risks with this hard bar when entering or leaving as they could with the soft mud bar of the Demerara.[11]

For almost half the time that these colonies were separate, Britain was fighting a maritime war in which sea trade was conducted quite differently from the leisurely procedures of peace. Nowhere was this more so than in Caribbean and Guianese waters. Not only were there threats of swarms of small privateers from French Guiana or the Orinoco and, during the war of 1812, of large ones from the United States, but the merchantmen sailed in convoy across the Atlantic. To assemble a convoy was complicated and slow in the era of sail. Ships had to gather by a set date, usually at Tortola. This was more convenient for the islands than for the Guianese colonies where crop time was later. Moreover, homeward-bound ships from the Guianas had further to sail to the rendezvous. There was a nasty snag at Berbice where a fully-laden ocean-going ship could only get over the bar twice a month, much to the chagrin of planters and their British agents who often asked for a separate Guianese convoy.[12] In 1809, for example, the Berbice ships left half empty in order to float over the bar and to reach the rendezvous in time. How much easier it was for Berbician produce to be sent in coastal schooners to Demerara and there loaded for Europe! The prevailing winds were from the north-east or south-east, depending on the season; it was usually a day's easy sail from the Berbice to the Demerara. Yet it could take four tedious days to return.

Although the old rule that all goods had to travel in Dutch bottoms was irrelevant after 1796, the humane terms of an eighteenth century surrender allowed the inhabitants to keep their constitution and with it some cumbersome and niggling taxes. All vessels, no matter how small, had to report to the Custom House where various archaic taxes, namely, Lastage Money, Hospital Money, Flag Money, Anchor Money, were exacted. While only the flintiest hearted captain would begrudge one or two guilders as Hospital Money to succour the indigent sick in New Amsterdam, there was resentment about Lastage, a tax of 1.10 guilders per ton of a ship's burden. This was unique to Berbice.[13] There were still protests about it as late as 1816 as a shackle on the commerce of the colony.[14] But it lingered on, as did Anchor and Flag Money, formerly blatant perquisites of the lieutenant governor, until unification.

Little wonder then that planters and merchants yielded to the fiscal and geographical temptations of smuggling produce to the better shipping opportunities of Georgetown. It was particularly enticing to the expanding British plantations on the West Coast whose little schooners, often under a slave captain, faced tedious beating against the wind if they sailed to New Amsterdam when they could so comfortably run before it to Georgetown. As early as 1804 the lieutenant governor of Berbice, van Batenberg, issued a proclamation against the export of produce in this manner; the public revenues were suffering; trade was getting into the hands of Demerara merchants; it would never have been allowed in Dutch times.[15] London merchants who could easily apply pressure on an administration only a coach ride away from the city protested. The proclamation was disallowed.

Symptomatic of the relative weakness of Berbice was the slave drain to Demerara. After abolition, all West Indian colonies faced the task of maintaining slave numbers. All, indeed, had failed by emancipation except Barbados. After a population explosion – there is no other term for it – in Demerara and Berbice in the first years of British rule, when the majority of African imports went to the Guianas, the slave population of Demerara had grown from 29,473 in 1795 to 80,915 in 1807, the second highest population after Jamaica; and that of Berbice from 8,232 in 1795 to 28,480 in 1807. But a slow decline began as plantation deaths went on exceeding births. By 1820 the Demerara slave population had sunk to 77,400, that of Berbice to 23,400. By 1831 there were 66,860 in Demerara and in Berbice 20,645.[16] The rate of decline was, in fact, similar in both colonies: 17 per cent in Berbice and 17.6 per cent in Demerara.

In Tudor England sheep were said to eat up men; sugar did so in slave societies. In the early nineteenth century sugar needed one slave per acre whereas cotton cultivation needed one slave for two acres.[17] Understandably enough, the Demerara planters sought slaves from Berbice where shortages of capital and credit were leading to the foreclosure of mortgages, the abandonment of estates and the selling of slave gangs. Both Demerara and Berbice were hit by the fatal competition from United States cotton and from Jamaican and, later, Ceylonese coffee.

After abolition there was no free trade in British-owned slaves around the Caribbean. Some restrictions were set by the Abolition Act itself, mainly on imports into the conquered colonies; more controls to forbid illegal movements were imposed by the 1817 Slave Registration Act, the first great enactment for the amelioration of slavery. In 1825, the Consolidated Abolition Act stopped this traffic except for personal servants. Statistical information is unreliable and conflicting, and, to compound uncertainty we shall never know how many were hustled illegally across the invisible border or smuggled out by sea.

In 1818 a precocious attempt at asset stripping was reported. A Glasgow firm, Robert Bogle and Company, had bought a worn-out coffee plantation in Berbice with about 150 slaves. It planned to send them to its sugar estates in Demarara which greatly needed labour. For the first time and surprisingly, complained their aggrieved London agent to the Colonial Office, the lieutenant governor of Berbice refused his sanction, even though the firm had offered to keep the slaves in their families.[18] Perhaps the thought of so many leaving at once was too much for Henry Bentinck, the lieutenant governor, well aware of local touchiness over this exodus. Numbers were usually less, to judge from the trickle of compulsory announcements of departures in the *Berbice Gazette*. Wolfert Katz, for example, transported the gang of Plantation 27, East Coast Berbice, some 72 slaves in all, to Demerara in July 1816; in the same month Henry Burton transported 30 slaves to Demerara, and he sent 22 more in February 1818.[19] With the shortage of labour in Demerara and the lack of credit in Berbice it was an easy way for a Berbician planter to raise money when pressed by his creditors.

With the Consolidation Abolition Act of 1825 the slave drain ended. From 1808 about 1,100 slaves had been imported into Berbice with 400 arriving in that first year from Barbados, a dying echo of the unlimited trade of earlier times. An unknown but certainly large proportion of the remainder would have been servants. In the same period over 4,000 slaves were taken legally to Demerara.[20] There planters still cast longing eyes at the labour over the border. Indeed the Protector of Slaves in Berbice claimed that 50 per cent of the slaves would be on Demerara sugar estates if unification took place. Just as slaves in the Old South in the same years dreaded being sold down the river, so the slaves in Berbice feared the sugar plantations of Demerara where they believed conditions were harsher.

Courts in Demerara were sometimes thought to act arrogantly towards Berbicians. After a joint burgher militia expedition in the forests against the bush negroes in 1810, captives who had originally decamped in Berbice were sentenced in Georgetown to transportation to the islands. Their owners, in a petition requesting their return, for which they would pay, denied that Demerara courts could dispose of their property.[21] But they found themselves, so the governor of Berbice reported, the subjects of a criminal prosecution, although they were not under the jurisdiction of the Demerara courts, on the grounds that their petition had been disrespectful. Four years later a rifleman of the 60th, a company of which was stationed in New Amsterdam, murdered his sergeant. A court martial was convened at headquarters in Georgetown – another sign of the relative inferiority of Berbice – and it ordered civilian witnesses from Berbice to attend. The lieutenant governor of Berbice in an indignant despatch asked the Colonial Office why the trial could not be heard in his own criminal court, or, if it had to be legally a court martial, why this could not take place in Berbice?[22]

Although there had been occasional talk of unification during wartime, it amounted to little until the peace settlement of 1815 ensured that these colonies would stay British. The idea began to be broached seriously in the early 1820s. It came into the open in Berbice when Lieutenant Governor Bentinck died in November 1820. Following usual procedures, Major General Sir John Murray, the lieutenant governor of Demerara and the owner of two coffee plantations in Berbice, hastened to New Amsterdam to take charge until London appointed a new man. Although the Court of Policy had already sworn in the major commanding the troops in Berbice, Murray nevertheless took the opportunity to address its members. They may have expected the sombre, platitudinous reflections on the vanity of human ambition then fashionable; instead they heard an argument for what he tactlessly called, 'the long-contemplated annexation'.[23] It would cut expenses, ease communications, foster security and help prosperity. He also wrote to Lord Bathurst offering himself as governor of a united colony.[24] The Court of Policy reported mildly in its minutes that it saw no virtue in his ideas. It hoped, however, that Berbicians would be consulted if unification were considered.

Six months earlier, merchants and planters connected with Berbice had met in London. Their argument, a framework for later discussions, was probably known to Murray who seemed close to such groups in Britain. After leaving office he was elected to the influential Demerara and Berbice sub-committee of the West India Committee. These men, representing absentees rather than residents, declared that Demerara and Berbice were united by their interests; they were really one settlement. Unrestricted coastal traffic would benefit Berbice because its limited consumption did not warrant a regular direct shipping service. This could be easily provided from Demerara, and Berbician produce could be taken freely to Georgetown if only customs were abolished on coastal trade.[25] They were not yet openly asking for unification but the economic decline of Berbice in the next few years would frequently cause them to do so and finally force the British Government to act.

A mention has already been made of the Dutch paper money. Originally as secure in the eighteenth century before the French wars as bills drawn on the City of London were to be afterwards, it acquired, although more slowly and less dramatically, the dubious reputation of the *assignats* of the earliest years of the French Revolution. The Berbice Association had paid its salaries and other expenses in bills drawn on itself in Amsterdam. With the dearth of coins, these had become the circulating currency of Berbice. At Amiens Berbice was restored, not to the association but to the Batavian Republic which, in its revolutionary zeal, abolished the Dutch East and West India Companies and the governmental functions of the Berbice Association. Its rump remained as a modest private company with four estates in Berbice. The Batavian Republic also paid its garrision and other local expenses in paper. After the second capitulation, a close copy of the first, the British kept in circulation this paper money, and, indeed, at times issued their own. In 1809, for instance, Lieutenant Governor Woodley authorized the issue of 80,000 guilders in notes because of a crop failure.[26]

The first sign of trouble came after the peace convention between the Netherlands and Britain on 12 August 1815. According to article 11, the estates of the Berbice Association, which had been in British

Government hands, were to be returned to their original owners.[27] When this became known in Berbice the Court of Policy protested. There was no recognition in the convention that these estates were the only security in the colony for some 101,000 guilders of paper money issued before the first capitulation. Lord Bathurst at first was against handing them over until this problem had been settled by the British and Dutch governments. Later he weakened. The only fair claim on the association would be for bills covering the expenses of their four plantations; those issued for administering the colony should be left for a 'subsequent amicable adjustment' between the British and Dutch governments.[28] And there the problem stagnated for the next decade, a time bomb ticking away in the flimsy economic foundations of Berbice. Not even the sale of the estates to British buyers in 1818, when the association severed its links with the colony, brought any response from the British Government. Also there were, according to the Court of Policy's protest, unredeemed bills to the value of 72,000 guilders from the days of the defunct Batavian Republic.

By the end of the wars British paper issued on the security of the revenues totalled 252,160 guilders.[29] It appeared that 107,650 guilders' worth had been cancelled by the end of 1818, leaving a balance of 144,510 guilders. Another issue of 94,907 guilders followed in 1826. The Colonial Audit Office estimated that in 1828 there were 365,416 guilders in circulation.[30] This paper either had no security, if it were Dutch, or was backed merely by the dubious and waning security of the general revenue.

This still came from Dutch modes of taxation, especially from Head Money, a poll tax; Plantation Money, a tax on estates in proportion to the number of slaves; and Weigh Money, a 2.5 per cent *ad valorem* tax on exports. Thus the revenue depended upon estate prosperity. Post-war prices for produce were sinking and a few statistics will show the trend. At Liverpool in 1815 the price of cotton per pound (lb) had ranged from 18d to 25d, in 1827 it was between 4d and 7d; at London in September 1815 the average price of British West Indian muscavado was 64s 2d; in December 1828 (there are no records for 1827) it was 31s ½d.[31] According to some rare surviving figures from the receiver general in Berbice, the production of coffee had declined from 5,617,727 lbs in 1818 to 2,404,467 lbs in 1824; cotton was down from 2,375,425 lbs in 1818 to 1,020,253 lbs in 1824.[32]

The only hopeful portent was that sugar production was rising;

from 15,416 hundredweights (cwts) in 1818 to 76,924 cwts in 1824.[33] In 1815 8,318 cwts of Muscavado were imported into Britain from Berbice compared with 322,099 cwts from Demerara; this rose by 1828 to 85,154 cwts from Berbice and 717,165 cwts from Demerara.[34] By the end of 1828 there were 25 sugar estates with 9,000 slaves. Yet this was not enough to bolster finances. From the beginning of 1819 to the end of 1826 there was an excess of expenditure over revenue of £7,728 (100,464 guilders). The revenue, at its peak in 1820 at £21,644, had dwindled to £12,103 in 1826. For five of these eight years there were losses.[35] An unwelcome burden came when yet another general from Demerara administered Berbice for some months in 1825 and 1826 while Beard was on leave. Sir Benjamin D'Urban, soon to be the first governor of British Guiana and later to have his name bestowed on a town in Natal, authorized the expenditure of 74,927 guilders (£5,763) on fortifications without informing London.[36] By the end of 1828 the total debt was estimated by the Colonial Audit Office to be about 565,626 guilders (£43,509) which included 365,416 guilders (£28,109) in paper money.[37]

Anxiety in Britain and Berbice was not calmed by charges of slackness, if not corruption, in the local administration. They emerged when the Colonial Office was groping towards a more efficient control of colonies by urging on them the regular and punctual compilation of reports and statistics – the Blue Books, for example, first came out in 1821 – and in trying to stop abuses, picaresquely illuminated in the Berbice correspondence, ranging from the abolition of deputies in colonial posts, evolving procedures to deal with insubordinate or venal officials to the curbing of frequent pleas for extensions of sick leave in Bath or Tunbridge Wells.[38]

One is tempted to believe that Lieutenant Governor Beard's was a remarkably limp hand on the tiller at a time when strictness was essential. The colonial accounts for 1824 had not been received in London by July 1827 although those for 1825, compiled by D'Urban when he was administering the government, had arrived punctually. The colonial agent's salary was a year in arrears in 1827; it was still in arrears in 1829.[39] The books of the Orphan Chamber had not been audited for twenty years; money from the Poor Fund, so it was alleged, had been appropriated for the private use of some of its trustees; the receiver general had paid urgent warrants out of the funds of the savings bank, thereby depriving slave depositors in 1828 of their annual interest.[40] Beard had authorized extensive repairs to Government House without an estimate or approval; he was tartly told not to spend more than one hundred pounds on anything without the secretary of state's approval.[41] Worse still, he proposed still further paper money to tide over the 1828 deficit of 163,605 guilders.

Already in the summer of 1827 the under-secretary of state, Wilmot Horton, was sounding out Charles Wray, the president of the Court of Justice in Demerara, who was on home leave, about the constitutional and financial implications of a merger.[42] In May 1828 Henry Taylor, in a minute, summed up the advantages and disadvantages of union: the expenses of the Berbice Government would be saved; coastal trade facilitated; the raising of credit, then impossible in Berbice, eased; the transfer of slaves to Demerara sugar estates would become legal, although he wondered whether that would be beneficial to the slaves themselves; probably coffee would be abandoned; and the shopkeepers of New Amsterdam would suffer.[43]

When Wellington took office in January 1828 he induced General Sir George Murray, his quartermaster general in the Peninsula, to be his secretary of state. Murray, by 1815, was considered the best staff officer in Europe, to be compared only with Marshal Berthier a few years earlier.[44] It is tempting to imagine that he would provide meticulous and firm leadership after the long years of Bathurst, who tended only to react to problems as they arose, 'greatly averse to change but unwillingly acquiescing in many'.[45] But his contemporaries thought that he was amiable, lazy and out of his depth in a political office.[46] Although the decision to merge the colonies was taken in his time, the impetus came from the officials, Henry Taylor and James Stephen. They and the colonial auditors had to find solutions to Berbice's problems.

The dispatch telling Beard and D'Urban that a merger was contemplated was sent in October 1828. D'Urban, who had been Murray's assistant quartermaster general and then quartermaster general to the allied Portuguese army (1809–17), also received a private letter from Murray telling him that he would be the first governor of British Guiana. He accepted with a flurry of statistics and suggestions for the merger and a discussion of paper money. He pointed out rather smugly that Demerara and Essequibo had no debt at all; its annual expenditure was met by taxes raised within the year. Its paper was adequately covered by investment in the British funds. But Demerara could not be expected to shoulder the Berbician debts.[47]

After much haggling between departments, it was agreed that the British Government would be responsible for the Dutch paper because it had returned the association's plantations without any stipulation for its redemption. The fortification costs were to come from the military estimates. To the indignation of the free inhabitants, who believed themselves immune from extraordinary taxation by the charter of 1732, the remaining debt was discharged by special taxes in Berbice on income, cattle and plantains.[48]

Protests were heard in Berbice about what one memorial called 'a hated and degrading union with the neighbouring colony'.[49] Their gist was that: property values would slump in New Amsterdam; the slave drain would restart; slaves were worried at the prospect of not having a governor close by to redress grievances (a cynical suggestion by protesting planters when one quarter of the working slave population had been physically punished in the first half of 1828). With more sugar cultivation, so it was asserted, Berbice could make ends meet. Union was what wealthy absentees wanted; the inhabitants themselves were not consulted. One hundred and seven years later it would be called an *Anschluss*.

British Guiana came into being on 31 July 1831. Two years later D'Urban went on to Barbados, the Cape, Natal and Canada; Beard was retired into obscurity. Berbice was considered separate for the purpose of slave transfers until emancipation, and for taxation until its debt was paid off in 1843; the constitutional arrangements of the united colony were eventually those of Demerara.[50]

Viscount Goderich, Murray's successor, standing back from daily affairs, reflected upon West Indian smallness and upon the federal dream that has enthralled some West Indian minds until the present time. His words stand well as a prologue to those seminars on smallness in the institute a quarter of a century ago:

But the still more decisive motive with His Majesty's Government has been drawn from the conviction that the British colonies in the West Indies have been broken up into numerous separate communities in a state of mutual independence of each other to a much greater extent than sound policy can justify. The evils resulting from the contracted dimensions of these colonial socie-ties have long been, and are to this day, painfully experienced. In so narrow a sphere there is no room for the growth of that salutary public opinion which results from free discussion and even from the most ardent controversy in larger societies. Every difference of private judgement on public affairs is thus exasperated by personal animosities, and becomes the source of bitter feuds, in the pursuit of which all higher interests are neglected. These remarks involve no particular reproach on the inhabitants of any particular colony, but rather on the system which has compressed within such narrow limits the range of their public duties and interest. The legal and constitutional difficulties which impede any consolidation of colonial governments in the islands possessing representative assemblies do not arise in the case of Demerara and Berbice, and the ministers of the Crown are persuaded that they could not advise a more useful exercise of the royal prerogative ... than in combining the whole body of inhabitants into one society connected by common laws and institutions as they are already connected by a community of origin, language and rural economy.[51]

Notes

1. B. Benedict (ed.), *Problems of Smaller Territories* (London: Athlone Press, 1967).
2. The following have considered aspects of the unification: R. Farley, 'The unification of British Guiana', *Social and Economic Studies* 4, 2, 1956; D. J. Murray, *The West Indies and the Development of Colonial Government 1801–1834* (Oxford: Clarendon, 1965); M. Shahadudden, *Constitutional Developments in Guyana 1621–1978* (Georgetown 1978).
3. CO 111 73, van Batenberg to Portland, 30 Nov. 1799.
4. C. Goslinga, *The Dutch in the Caribbean and the Guianas 1680–1791* (Assen 1985), p. 492.
5. J. Rickford, *Dimensions of a Creole Continuum* (Stanford 1987), pp. 52, 58.
6. CO 111 73, van Batenberg to Portland, 30 Nov. 1799.
7. CO 111 76, Montgomerie to Castlereagh, 1 July 1807; CO 111 85, Gordon to Liverpool, 16 Dec. 1810.
8. CO 111 76, Montgomerie to Castlereagh, 1 July 1807; WIC Minute Book, 1804–27, 26 Nov. 1805.
9. A. Trollope, *The West Indies and the Spanish Main*, 2nd edn (London 1860), p. 172.
10. *A Map of Part of Dutch Guyana ... surveyed in 1798 and 1802* (London 1804); *The West India Pilot*, Vol. 1, 1872.
11. CO 111 75, J. Turnbull to E. Cooke, 12 Jan. 1805.
12. WIC Minute Book 1804–27, Minutes of 26 Nov. 1805.
13. CO 111 74, Blue Book for 1828.
14. T64 51, Minutes of the Court of Policy, 5 April 1816.
15. CO 111 74, van Batenberg to Camden, 27 Oct. 1804.

16. B. W. Higman, *Slave Populations of the British Caribbean 1807–1834* (Baltimore: John Hopkins, 1984), p. 417, Table S1, 2.
17. Goslinga, op. cit., p. 444.
18. CO 111 90, J. Cook to H. Goulbourn, 6 June 1818.
19. *Berbice Gazette.*, 17 Aug. 1816; 14 Feb. 1818.
20. CO 111 94, Beard to Bathurst, enc, 2 April 1822; CO 111 101, D'Urban to Bathurst, enc, 25 Jan. 1826; P P 1824 XXIV.
21. CO 111 85, Dalrymple to Liverpool, 18 Nov. 1810.
22. CO 111 81, Bentinck to Bathurst, 16 Aug. 1814.
23. CO 111 115, Council Minutes, 7 Nov. 1820.
24. CO 111 93 143, Murray to Bathurst, 18 Nov. 1820.
25. CO 111 93, Meeting of Planters and Merchants, 17 May 1820.
26. CO 111 77, Woodley to Castlereagh, 17 Aug. 1809.
27. CO 111 84, Bentinck to Bathurst, 13 Jan. 1816.
28. CO 112 8, Bathurst to Bentinck, 22 July 1816, 24 Feb. 1817.
29. CO 111 108, Brande to Twiss, 4 Aug. 1829.
30. Ibid.
31. L. Ragatz, *Statistics for the Study of British Caribbean Economic History* (London 1927), p. 8.
32. CO 111 99, Beard to Bathurst, enc, 4 March 1825.
33. Ibid.
34. Ragatz, p. 20.
35. CO 111 107, Beard to Murray, enc, 3 Feb. 1829.
36. CO 111 108, 'Observations on the financial state of the colony of Berbice', Colonial Audit Office, 6 Feb. 1829.
37. Ibid.
38. Murray, op. cit., chs 7 and 8 for a thorough discussion.
39. CO 112 9, Bathurst to Beard, 18 April 1827; Twiss to Beard, 8 June 1829.
40. CO 112 9, Murray to Beard, 30 Nov. 1829; CO 111 108, Power to Twiss, 25 Nov. 1829, 9 Dec. 1829.
41. Murray to Beard, 17 July 1829.
42. CO 324 99, Horton to Wray, Private, 28 June 1827.
43. CO 320 5, Taylor, minute, 6 May 1828.
44. S. P. Ward, *Wellington's Headquarters* (London: OUP, 1957), pp. 25, 60.
45. C. Greville, *Memoirs* (2nd edn), Vol. 3 (1874), p. 115; Murray, op. cit., pp. 102, 117–19.
46. Murray, op. cit., pp. 147–8.
47. CO 111 115, D'Urban to Murray, 15 March 1829.
48. CO 111 115, Stewart to Twiss, 29 Sept 1830; *Berbice Gazette*, 4 May 1829.
49. CO 111 115, Beard to Murray, 23 March 1830.
50. Shahadudden, op. cit., pp. 81–4.
51. CO 112 15, Goderich to D'Urban, 18 March 1831; quoted in Shahadudden, p. 82.

4

LORD MILNER AND THE SOUTH AFRICAN STATE RECONSIDERED

Shula Marks and Stanley Trapido

It is over ten years since we published our article, 'Lord Milner and the South African State', where we began by looking at the origins of the South African War of 1899–1902, even though our primary concern was with the state in the post-war Transvaal. We did so because we believed that an understanding of the origins of the war would help us to comprehend the rationale of the colonial state which emerged during the period of reconstruction. We argued that the origins of the war could not be sought simply in the individual motives of the key actors – or at least that these motives would not be fully understood if we did not grasp the larger meaning which these individuals gave to their stated aims. Thus, notions such as 'British supremacy' were not necessarily self-evident propositions, and their full significance could be unravelled only by setting the stated objectives of the various actors in the appropriate socio-economic and historical context.

Crucial to this context was Britain's role as the financial capital of the world and the significance of gold to the working of the international economy. The ability of the Transvaal state to guarantee the well-being of the mining industry was, therefore, of equal importance to the imperial power and the mining houses. This is not to say that the British Government was primarily concerned with ensuring the profits of the South African gold mines for its owners, but rather that only by ensuring the mines' profitability could it secure its objective of obtaining a continuous flow of gold for the London market. This was undoubtedly the outcome of the war. We are, of course, well aware that intentions cannot be read from consequences; our argument is not of the *post hoc, propter hoc* variety but that the post-war settlement saw pre-war intentions being given effect.

Recently there has been a counter critique to our arguments about the origins of the war in two major articles, one by Andrew Porter, largely reiterating the argument of his book published in 1980, the other by Iain Smith.[1] Both start by re-examining its historiography and deny any intrinsic importance to gold as a very special kind of commodity or the role of the mine magnates in the run-up to the war, although in other ways their emphases are different. In effect Smith returns, with some modification, to the analyses of Robinson and Gallagher and David Fieldhouse in attempting to integrate economic and political arguments: while the British were not interested in gold *per se*, the discovery of gold in the Transvaal transformed the regional balance of power, threatened imperial supremacy in southern Africa, and hence endangered the sea-route to India (we deal with this below). Porter takes this part of the argument for granted and moves on to contend that British intervention was 'profoundly influenced by the structure of her political institutions, by political culture and the patterns of party division, and by calculations of political ambition'.[2] We agree that these are worthy and worthwhile matters for investigation, but in the end we believe that they tell us about means and not ends.

In refuting the centrality of gold in any explanation for the outbreak of war, both Smith and Porter draw on an article on the gold standard by Jean Jacques Van-Helten, published in the *Journal of African History* in 1982.[3] Given the importance they attribute to this article, it is perhaps worth dwelling on it at some length, if only to show the areas of agreement and disagreement that exist between us and Van-Helten. Van-Helten accepts that 'during the last third of the nineteenth century the world economy was confronted with an increased demand for gold particularly from the newly industrialized countries such as France and Germany, even though world production of gold was falling', and that the expansion of world trade in the aftermath of the Great Depression 'necessitated, in part, an enlargement of the overall monetary stock' which was directly related to expansion of world gold supplies. Curiously, Van-Helten does not mention the United States of America, although, according to de Cecco, after it went off the silver standard, the USA demanded gold on an unprecedented level: not only did the US Treasury store gold 'in fantastic amounts', but the American public also 'absorbed gold at an amazing rate'. The US Treasury was incapable of putting gold back into circulation, and this represented 'a real threat to the working of the international monetary system'.[4]

Van-Helten is, however, aware that it was 'the newly mined gold from South Africa, Australia and Canada which, during this period, eased international liquidity problems by facilitating an expansion of the gold base and money supplies without the dangers of inflation . . .'.[5] He is also aware that '[t]he possibility of assaults on the Bank's allegedly slender gold supplies remained in the forefront of contemporary concern', and that when in 1898 Germany began to import raw gold directly from the South African Republic (SAR), bypassing the City of London, *The Economist* feared that Paris and Berlin would 'soon overtake London as the world's premier bullion market'.[6]

Nevertheless, Van-Helten states that he could find no evidence in the British Treasury or Bank of England correspondence which he consulted that they considered that 'the solution to Britain's apparent shortage of gold should be sought . . . by obtaining physical control over the Transvaal's gold-mining industry'.[7] Given the strength of British financial institutions, he therefore argues that the fears over the gold reserves were probably unwarranted; there is no evidence that the British Government was concerned with the problem of the gold reserves because through the 1890s the Bank of England found alternative ways of maintaining the influx of gold into London. It managed to do this through the use of the Gold Rate – which Van-Helten admits was increasingly ineffectual by the 1890s – and through what were known as the gold devices, the most notable of which was the bank's capacity to raise its purchase price of gold on the open market. As a result, according to Van-Helten, the bank did not rely 'to any great extent on . . . supplies of new gold from . . . the Transvaal, to augment its slender reserves. Newly mined gold formed only a small percentage of the total amount of bullion and specie traded daily on the London market.'[8] During the war, his argument continues, gold imports from the Transvaal declined, yet the bank rate remained low, which suggests that Britain had little trouble in maintaining gold reserves whether new gold arrived or not. Moreover, he suggests that because gold reserves remained low in the 1900s, even after the

Transvaal was conquered, fears over the gold reserve were immaterial.[9]

Van-Helten's views have been appropriated by those who deny the particular significance of gold as commodity, a significance which he himself does not deny. Rob Turrell has noted that Van-Helten's argument depends a great deal on hindsight: despite his recognition that there were fears over the reserve, Van-Helten maintains that 'because those fears turned out *in the end* to have been unfounded . . . they [therefore] had no impact on imperial strategy' (our italics).[10] It is at least arguable that a major reason why the bank rate remained low, however, was because during the South African War the British Government was able to borrow the 'unusually large sum' of £151.5 million from the United States of America. And, although in these transactions the Rothschilds remained the dominant bullion brokers, in three issues the treasury had to make use of the services of J. P. Morgan and Company. According to Turrell, 'in each case the overriding purpose was . . . to replenish the dangerously low reserves at the Bank of England'. While Turrell cites this material to counter the views of Sydney Chapman and to show the continued significance of the Rothschilds in bullion broking, it is difficult to imagine that this shift in the balance of power, which was already evident in the 1890s, had no bearing on thinking about imperial security at a time of increased international competition and insecurity;[11] next time round, the Americans might not be so accommodating.

One of the reasons why the Bank of England was able to discount fears about the size of its gold stocks was because Britain had control over Indian reserves through their conversion after the war into British securities. The India Office was thus able to prevent India 'from transforming her annual surplus into gold reserves' and this 'contributed in no small measure towards keeping British interest rates lower than would otherwise have been the case'.[12] Again this suggests rather more concern with and intervention by imperial strategists in the working of the gold standard than Van-Helten and the political historians of empire would have us believe.

More important, for our argument at least, was the second reason why the fears over the gold reserves turned out to be unfounded, and why even after the war the Bank of England permitted its gold reserves to remain low: this is the fairly obvious point made by Turrell that by then the British had secured political control over the Transvaal.[13] One of Milner's major objectives in restructuring the South African state was, as we have suggested, to ensure at least some of the conditions under which gold was produced, and thus maintain the safety net of the weekly arrival of 'Cape' bars. In the absence of this safety net and of increased gold production, the bank's expedient of raising the purchase price of gold when it found it necessary to augment its reserves could have potentially threatened the very notion of a fixed price for gold, the basis of the international standard. As Russell Ally has pointed out:

> The serious weakness of Van-Helten's argument is that while he concedes . . . that 'the real significance of the . . . gold from the Transvaal . . . was not so much that [it] found [its] way into the coffers of the Bank [but] the *knowledge* that gold was always on the way to London (eg the weekly shipments from the Cape) and that the Bank could always "tap" this flow which buttressed confidence in sterling and in the Bank's ability to maintain specie payments', he hardly takes into account at all whether the conditions under which gold was being mined in South Africa *before* reconstruction under Milner provided the basis for confidence in such a policy. In the whole of his analysis . . . Van-Helten does not develop anywhere an analysis of the role played by the Kruger state. But it was precisely the growing antagonism between the mining industry and the Transvaal state which was to have a decisive influence on British policy towards South Africa in the period leading up to the Jameson Raid and the Anglo-Boer War.[14] [Ally's italics]

It is not our contention that Britain conquered the Transvaal to ensure her *physical possession* of the gold-mines, as Van-Helten and Porter suggest. We do, however, maintain that ensuring the long-term continuation of efficient production was of the essence both to the major mine magnates and to the British Government. Hence the centrality of the state to our argument both in relation to the SAR in the 1890s and to Milner's schemes for a reconstructed Transvaal. To a very large extent Ally endorses this view. As he says, it was not physical control of the mines that was at issue: 'in a certain sense this had already been achieved by the hegemony of the British mining groups and British capital on the Witwatersrand'; what was crucial was '*political* control over the conditions under which mining took place to ensure the profitability and viability of industry'.[15]

Curiously enough, this is a view endorsed by Van-Helten in another paper not generally noted by our critics. In an article on French investment in the Rand mines, published in 1985 and based on his doctoral thesis, Van-Helten contests Kubicek's view that the war was unwelcome to French and German capitalists on the Rand, especially as it 'asserted a British presence which Europe's financiers found distinctly unwelcome'. According to Van-Helten:

> In many respects the Boer War was indeed 'unwelcome'. Total direct losses to the mining industry were conservatively estimated at £6.9 million. Indirect losses including depreciation on revenue lost between 1899 and 1902 were much higher . . ... Moreover, it was not until 1905 that the Transvaal's output of gold surpassed pre-war levels of production. Dismay at these financial losses, however, did not translate itself into ill-will against Britain, for the industry was concerned not so much with the nationality of the Transvaal's conquerors as with the fact that the Kruger administration was removed and that the mine's long-term development could proceed uninterrupted. In South Africa, as Palmade has noted of the earlier British invasion of Egypt, 'it was surely European capitalism which triumphed under British leadership'.[16]

None of this means that we believe that the war was inevitable; both the imperial government and the mine magnates would have been far happier to have achieved political control without war, provided Kruger would give way to their essential demands. Indeed Rhodes professed to the end that there would be no war, because he felt 'so sure that Kruger will concede everything HMG demand . . .'.[17]

We also continue to believe that the growing influence of Germany and the USA in the region, especially in view of the importance of gold, was a matter of British concern and gives substance to the otherwise very elusive concept of 'British supremacy'. As Van-Helten writes, almost incidentally, in 1898 'for the first time' the SAR 'emerged as a source of German imports of gold to the tune of RM38.4 million (£1.92 million)', and that 'the Anglo-Boer war . . . aborted the nascent Transvaal-German trade in raw gold'. He goes on to discount the significance of this observation by stating that whatever the gold exports to Germany, the facilities of the London market were so superior to those of Berlin and Paris that the magnates would nonetheless have needed to send the major share of the gold via Britain. While this may be true, we find it difficult to believe that in a time of heightened international insecurity British bankers and government were not aware of the need to protect this unrivalled position, particularly in relation to their two main competitors, Germany and the USA. Moreover, despite his caveats, Van-Helten cites Ford and Sayers as saying 'the mere knowledge that the Cape bars arrived in London every week reinforced London's position as the world's leading gold market and financial centre and created in itself a further sense of confidence in the ultimate strength and viability of sterling as the world reserve currency'.[18]

In view of all of this we find Porter's exhortation to historians to drop their preoccupation with gold little short of extraordinary. Certainly the alternatives he suggests seem to us to stretch credulity. He claims that the war arose out of Chamberlain's recognition of the need to protect Britain's 'world-wide but increasingly vulnerable position with a recently created democratic political system at home', and his solution, which was to mount a press campaign in which South Africa's 'injection' was 'wholly fortuitous'.[19] We are asked to believe that what at the time the *Bankers Magazine* called 'a truly exceptional circumstance' – that Britain, 'the leading monetary power in the world', was at war with the SAR, 'a country producing the greater proportion of the world's gold supply' – was completely accidental. This is like arguing that in an analysis of the contemporary Gulf crisis and war the 'banality' of oil should be abandoned because the president of the USA and the British prime minister stressed their opposition to Saddam Husein's invasion of Kuwait in terms of its illegality and the anti-democratic and brutal nature of his regime. Presumably the presence of oil in the Gulf is 'wholly fortuitous'.

It is true, as Porter says, that single cases make for bad law. Nevertheless, the South African case does have to be situated in a wider context; what is at stake is what one considers relevant to that wider context.[20] To ignore the importance of gold to the international economy when talking about a war with a country producing by the late 1890s more than one-fifth of the world's gold supply still strikes us as myopic. It leads Porter to end up reiterating that:

> Cabinet unity before the war arose not from Chamberlain's leadership but from the dominance in the cabinet of the traditional right led by Lord Salisbury, Hicks Beach and Balfour.

These were the patrician leaders of the agrarian right, seriously worried by the escalating cost of formal empire, acting to cut back the costs of defence . . . desperate not to finance wars which they feared would only be financed in ways which could increase their sectional burden of taxation . . .. That they went to war on this occasion hardly reflected sympathy for any new economic vision of empire but a very reluctant decision in pursuit of their traditional object of security.[21]

In view of the known connections between the patrician leaders of the agrarian right and the City, however, we do not need to invoke a 'new economic vision of empire' to explain their concern with the situation in South Africa. Nor does one have to accept all the ramifications of Cain and Hopkins' arguments about 'gentlemanly capitalism', or Rubinstein's arguments about landed wealth and the City, to argue for these links;[22] it is enough for our purposes that leading bankers like the Barings, Rothschilds and Grenfells had known connections with the Tory cabinet and in particular with Milner. Goschen, as merchant banker and chancellor of the exchequer and thus Milner's superior at the Board of Trade in 1891, bridged the two worlds. The Rothschilds as the most important bullion brokers between the Transvaal and London, and with their many interests in South African mining activities, were a vital link. And here the ties with the landed gentry are hardly in dispute; as Rubinstein remarks, the Rothschilds were 'nearly as important in Buckinghamshire [that is, landed gentry] as they were in the City'.[23]

It is precisely because the patrician right was desperate not to finance new wars that its decision needs explanation. Given that reluctance, what do we make of their 'traditional object of security'? Presumably this phrase refers to India, rather than to any fear of a domino effect if the Transvaalers thumbed their noses at the British. Granted the overwhelming importance of India to the British, an importance which among other things was closely related, as we have suggested, to the City's role as the monetary centre of the world and India's contribution to its financial stability, it is nevertheless difficult to accept that these very reluctant warriors fought the Transvaal to control the sea-route to India. They may, in the long term, have feared Transvaal dominance over the rest of South Africa – essentially the Robinson and Gallagher argument; but as Richard Cope has shown in relation to Carnarvon's confederation schemes in the 1870s, the imperial authorities were aware even then that intervention in the interior and annexation of the Transvaal was likely to endanger their hold on Simonstown, and that if Simonstown (the sea-route) was the focus of their concern and needing British protection then there were far simpler and safer ways of achieving this than by annexing the entire sub-continent.[24] The facts of southern African geography had not altered by the 1890s. In view of the desperate peace-brokering of the Cape's Afrikaner Bond, it is difficult to see why the British should have been propelled into action in the Transvaal by fears for imperial security unless that security involved something more substantial than the sea-route to India.

Even more perplexing is Porter's acceptance that Salisbury's goal was 'to teach the Transvaal "that we not the Dutch are Boss"' and that this 'had to be achieved even at the cost of a war "for people whom we despise, and for territory which will bring no profit and power to England"'. The charitable explanation for this pronounce- ment is that it was no more than a momentary irritation expressed in a predictably chauvinistic fashion, the less charitable that it was singularly misinformed or stupid, or both. We cannot accept, as Porter seems to, that the statements help us to resolve the issue. While Milner and Chamberlain were likely to have shared the same preju- dices, they were nevertheless likely to be better informed. It is difficult to believe that they were unaware of the views of the many economic pundits who worried over the future of the gold reserves and that, apparently like contemporary imperial historians, none of them read any of the financial papers of the day.

If the events of 1899 cannot be divorced from the working of British politics, nor can they be divorced from the working of politics in South Africa in the 1890s. While Porter largely ignores the internal politics of South Africa, Smith attempts to look again at the politics of the 1890s in the light of the recent historiography. He concludes that our work owes much to the writing of John Hobson wherein he finds the source of our error, for he argues that Hobson explained the causes of the war by resorting to 'preconceptions formed out of what had already been revealed about the conspiracy of Cecil Rhodes and a collection of capitalists and Uitlanders in 1895–6 to overthrow the Transvaal government . . .'. Although he does not refute the validity of Hobson's view of the Jameson Raid he suggests that by 1899 it was irrelevant. Thus, according to Smith, 'whoever else was behind the resort to war in 1899, it was not Rhodes who was a burnt-out case in

1899 and who remained absolutely convinced war would not break out until it did so'. Moreover, he exonerates not only Rhodes, but also the other Rand magnates and even the South African League and the Rand reformers. We need, he tells us, to revise 'the old view . . . that the issue of Uitlander grievances was largely a contrivance of the South African League, Milner and the British government and used as a stalking horse for the overthrow of Transvaal indpendence . . . the Uitlanders and Uitlander associations were not mere puppets manipulated by the mine magnates or Milner'. The mine magnates only 'finally and reluctantly, acquiesced in a war which they felt was not of their making and which they were powerless to prevent'.[25]

These opinions, Smith tells us, come from his reading of the correspondence between Rouliot and Julius Wernher in the Wernher-Beit archives, and from a number of recent works, among them Robert Rotberg's recent biography of Rhodes and Diana Cammack's study of the Witwatersrand and the South African War. Our reading of the sources suggests somewhat different interpretations. In the first place, it still seems to us implausible to argue that the defeat of the Jameson Raid meant that the raiders' objectives simply disappeared. On the contrary, once the raid turned into such a fiasco, the British Government itself seems to have determined to take control of the programme to create a more friendly environment for the Witwatersrand gold mines, in order to prevent matters of such significance remaining in the hands of bunglers. Nor should we forget that the raid owed much to the prompting, in 1893, of the British high commissioner, Lord Loch, and had the practical support of officials in the Colonial Office and the colonial secretary, Joseph Chamberlain. When, after the raid, the Colonial Office took the leading role in seeking changes in the SAR it did so with the continued support of the erstwhile raiders. Incidentally, here one hardly needs to invent a conspiracy theory; a conspiracy was manifest.

While particular individuals, especially the ill-fated members of the Reform Committee and Rhodes himself, had of necessity to take a back seat, this does not mean that they were no longer involved in the process. Thus, while Rotberg tries to establish that 'the Anglo-Boer war was not Rhodes' war' he does not attempt to portray Rhodes as a disinterested party; as he puts it, 'Rhodes had been responsible for defining the underlying issue'; 'since Milner was a war-provoker without peer and Kruger was playing his own obstinate part well, Rhodes hardly needed to help.' Rhodes may not have played an overt role in 1898–9; his financing of the press campaign against the SAR and his support of the Progressives and the South African League were, in view of Milner's determination on war, quite sufficient. And like the other mine magnates, Rhodes did not want war, provided Kruger ultimately conceded 'everything HMG demand'.[26] From the point of view of the mine magnates with a long-term future in South Africa nothing could have been better than that Milner take up the cudgels on their behalf. For capitalists, the role of the state is to ensure their continued accumulation under optimum legal and political conditions. It was certainly not their function to wage either diplomacy or war. The problem in the Transvaal was that until the advent of Milner the magnates were forced to take on a political role. Far better the new division of labour in which the imperial government now confronted the Transvaal. What they wanted was an appropriate form of state to ensure their continued profitability. If they could get it without a war so much the better; and to the last they believed that this might be possible. Like Rhodes they were prepared to take a political backseat as businessmen usually do if their interests can be protected in other ways.

This said, it is also undoubtedly true that there were differences between the different mining companies and different mine magnates over the necessity for war. Even within the largest of the companies, Wernher-Beit and Eckstein, three of the senior partners, Wernher, Rouliot and Eckstein had less of an appetite for war than others within the company. It was not, however, only the maverick Fitzpatrick who looked to war as the solution of the problems confronting the industry. Alfred Beit, however ill he may have been in 1899, and Lionel Phillips were deeply involved in the Jameson Raid and joined those who were convinced thereafter that no compromise with the Kruger state was possible.

Whatever the reluctance of individual mine magnates to contemplate war, these men were energetically engaged, like Rhodes, in preparing the ground through the South African League and the Uitlander Council, as Cammack's most recent and most closely researched account of the Rand on the eve of the war shows. According to her, the 'main goal [of the South African League] was to mobilize support for Milner in his struggle with Kruger'; its 'centralized structure was under the firm control of such professional men as Wilfred Wybergh, a mining engineer employed by Consolidated Goldfields until 1899 . . .'. The second reform organization, the

Uitlander Council, 'represented the interests of Rand capitalists and originated with J. P. Fitzpatrick, though Milner was well-informed of its inception'. According to the British vice consul, it was 'composed of men "who know what they are about and what is wanted"'. Cammack concludes, 'While the SAL [South African League] acted to mobilize mass sentiment and to generate grist for Milner's political mill, the Uitlander Council served the high commissioner by representing the portion of the Uitlander community he wished to hear . . .'.[27]

While it is perfectly true that there were various genuine Uitlander grievances, and that in the 1890s the British Government frequently seemed reluctant to engage with the Uitlanders, it is equally clear that both organizations were run by a closely knit group of highly motivated men: according to Cammack, for all the rhetoric, 'the broad mass of Johannesburgers' had relatively little to do with formulating their policy.[28] The Uitlanders were manifestly not puppets but we are unclear what the importance of this is to the argument, particularly as Smith himself maintains that they and the franchise issue 'offered the best means to a larger end; they formed the stalking horse behind which the "deep down thing" of British supremacy was advanced'.[29] It is the meaning of British supremacy that is still at the heart of the matter.

In the end this is an argument, not about finding the smoking gun but about how you think the world works. The absence so far of Bank of England or Cabinet papers setting out the importance of gold to the British financial position in the world is frustrating but does not alter our argument. It may be that to anticipate any other possibility is to expect the nineteenth-century British Treasury to have behaved as if it were constructed to deal with post-Keynsian macro-economics. The treasury's main function was to raise revenue and set limits on spending, not to manage the economy; its opinions on such matters as the gold standard may have been expressed in less obvious ways. Our explanation, built on other assumptions and a rather wider range of evidence, still provides, we believe, a more plausible interpretation than the alternatives on offer of the processes which led to the South African War.

This is not to deny that politics, political culture and public opinion played a role in the unfolding of the crisis which led to the war. Thus, for example, the widespread contempt for the Boers, so graphically displayed by Salisbury, could well have complicated negotiations in

1899. By the same token, Boer perception of British Government intentions was undoubtedly coloured by previous experience and by contemporary reinterpretation of that experience. The British annexation of Griqualand West in 1870 provided a recent precedent for an appropriation of a mineral-rich region by questionable, not to say disreputable means which was nevertheless justified by recourse to a spurious legality and arguments of British supremacy. The Transvaal Boers were bound to be even more on their guard than immediate events warranted. It was not without justification that their propagandists called their experience *A Century of Wrong*.[30] We agree wholeheartedly that wars cannot be disassociated from the history and psychology of those who find themselves overtaken by them, but neither can they be divorced from the lineaments of political economy in the way that Porter or Smith imagine.

Notes

1. A. Porter, 'The South African War (1899–1902): context and motive reconsidered', *Journal of African History* 31 (1990), pp. 43–57; I. R. Smith, 'The origins of the South African War (1899–1902): a reappraisal', *South African Historical Journal* 22 (1990), pp. 24–60. See also A. N. Porter, *The Origins of the South African War; Joseph Chamberlain and the Diplomacy of Imperialism, 1895–1899* (Manchester 1980). Our article on 'Lord Milner and the South African state' was originally published in *History Workshop Journal* 8 (1979).
2. Porter, op. cit., 'The South African War', p. 53.
3. J. J. Van-Helten, 'Empire and high finance; South Africa and the international gold standard, 1890–1914', *Journal of African History* 23 (1982), pp. 529–48.
4. Ibid., pp. 119–20.
5. Ibid., pp. 532–3.
6. Ibid., p. 541.
7. Ibid., p. 534, note 24.
8. Ibid., p. 536.
9. Ibid.
10. R. Turrell, '"Finance . . . the governor of the imperial engine": Hobson and the case of Rothschild and Rhodes', *Journal of Southern African Studies* 13, 3 (1987), p. 425.
11. Ibid., p. 430. Compare Chapman: '. . . it must be recognised that the South African War, far from being an expression of the power of London financial interests, can be identified as the first tacit acknowledgment of the power of the American dollar in international finance. It disclosed not only the vulnerability of sterling to sustained pressure but also showed the inability of the old City leaders, Rothschilds and Barings, to benefit

themselves or the economy in this period of stress'. (S. Chapman 'Rhodes and the City of London: Another view of Imperialism', *Historical Journal* 28, 3 (1985), pp. 647–66; the quotation is on p. 666). As Turrell shows, contrary to Chapman's assertion, the Rothschilds remained quite capable of benefiting themselves if not the economy in 'this period of stress', but in other respects, our argument is not substantially different to Chapman's, namely that intervention in the Transvaal was fuelled by fears already present in the 1890s of economic rivalry between the USA and Germany.

12. M. de Cecco, *Money and Empire. The international Gold Standard, 1890–1914* (Oxford 1974), p. 71.

13. Turrell, op. cit., '"Finance . . ."', pp. 425–6.

14. Russell Ally, 'Great Britain, gold and South Africa – an examination of the influence gold had in shaping Britain's policy towards South Africa, c. 1886–1914', unpublished paper presented to the symposium on 'The South Africa War, 1899–1902: the debate renewed', Institute of Commonwealth Studies, London, 25 May 1989. The paper is a 'condensed summary' of the introductory chapters to Ally's Cambridge Ph. D. thesis, 1990, which is concerned mainly with the period after 1914; it contains a far lengthier and more sustained critique of what he terms Van-Helten's 'narrowly economistic' approach to the working of the gold standard argument than we have engaged in here. His reading of the 1890s is very close to our own.

15. Ibid.

16. J. J. Van-Helten, 'La France et l'Or des Boers: some aspects of French investment in South Africa between 1890 and 1914', *African Affairs* 84 335 (April 1985), p. 260.

17. R. I. Rotberg with the collaboration of Milton F. Shore, *The Founder. Cecil Rhodes and the Pursuit of Power* (New York and Oxford 1988), p. 619.

18. Van-Helten, op. cit., 'Empire and high finance', pp. 547–8.

19. Porter, op. cit., 'The South African War', p. 55.

20. Porter's target here is Norman Etherington in his 'Theories . . . Southern Africa revisited', *African Affairs* 81, 324 (1984), pp. 385–407.

21. Ibid., p. 56.

22. See P. J. Cain and A. G. Hopkins, 'Gentlemanly capitalism and British expansion overseas. II: The New Imperialism, 1850–1945', *Economic History Review* (2nd series) XL, 1 (1987), pp. 1–26, and W. D. Rubinstein, *Men of Property* (London 1981). Martin Daunton's stimulating article '"Gentlemanly capitalism" and British industry, 1820–1914', *Past and Present* 122 (February 1989), pp. 119–58, which suggests the diversity of British bankers and the continued importance of industrial capital in the late nineteenth century, does not undermine this argument; if anything it reinforces our view (in *History Workshop Journal*, op. cit.) that, while gold was crucially important, the British government was also keeping an eye on other business interests, acting on behalf of 'capital as a whole'.

23. Rubinstein, op. cit., *Men of Property*, p. 217.

24. R. Cope, 'Strategic and socio-economic explanations for Carnarvon's

South African policy: the historiography and the evidence', *History in Africa* 13 (1986), pp. 13–34, especially pp. 18–20:

> If one believed that the naval bases were Britain's only interest in South Africa, then one would naturally regard the Cape Colony as the key to Britain's position in South Africa and the Transvaal as of importance for any effect that it might have upon the Cape. But this was not the way Carnarvon saw it. For Froude the naval bases were Britain's only interest in South Africa; for Carnarvon they quite clearly were not. Carnarvon was apparently prepared to risk endangering Britain's control over the naval bases for the sake of confederation. He wished to achieve confederation in spite of, not because, the strategic importance of Simonstown and Cape Town. (op. cit., 20)

25. Smith, op. cit., 'Origins', pp. 43, 37.
26. Rotberg, op. cit., *The Founder*, pp. 619–20. Far from being 'burnt out' in 1899–1900 Rhodes was still toying with becoming prime minister again (ibid., pp. 633–4).
27. D. Cammack, *The Rand at War 1899–1902. The Witwatersrand and the Anglo-Boer War* (London, Berkeley and Los Angeles, and Pietermaritzburg 1990), pp. 17–18.
28. Ibid.
29. Ibid., p. 46.
30. Written by J. C. Smuts, the tract was issued with departmental authority on the eve of the war in 1899 by F. W. Reitz as state secretary for the Transvaal.

5

CHURCH AND STATE IN A COLONIAL CONTEXT

Holger Bernt Hansen

Our work here is, on a small scale, so like the work and history of the Church in the 4th and 5th centuries. Many questions are just the same as were then settled. The relation of Church to State is continually cropping up.

(R. H. Walker, CMS missionary in Uganda, in 1898)

No more than a series of administrative no-man's-land poised uneasily between the well-defined 'Empires' of the major Departments of State, such marginal areas could hardly be significant in promoting that more comprehensive and co-ordinated Imperial programme which Imperialists only gradually tired of demanding and which foreign critics, especially the French, were prone to believe must exist.

(Kenneth Robinson, *The Dilemmas of Trusteeship*)

It is interesting that at the end of the nineteenth century a British missionary in Africa could compare the situation of the Church with that of the fourth and fifth centuries.[1] It was in the age of Constantine that the church–state problem became a real issue, and it was then that an official connection between church and state was first established. The parallel is especially relevant because, as in those days, there was in Uganda and most parts of tropical Africa hardly any precedent to build upon. In the African context this was further aggravated by the fact that the situation, in the language of political science, was characterized by its lack of institutions. On the one hand, there was an emergent state in the special colonial context, and on the ecclesiastical side a two-tiered structure: the European missionary society as the main representative of the church, and an embryonic African church, the founding of which was the mission's major goal.

In more than one sense it is correct, in the words of Kenneth Robinson, to speak of an 'administrative no-man's land'. On the church side there was no clear relationship between the two bodies during the process of starting a church, nor was it clear whether the state should deal with a European or African institution. On the state side the executive authority and the legislative power were divided between the local colonial representatives, and the government and parliament in London, a system which favoured ad hoc decisions and decentralization at the expense of a uniform colonial policy.

A case study from Uganda shows that the colonial state's religious policy in general and its policy towards mission and church in particular justify the above description. In Britain itself the church–state relationship was not based on detailed legislation, but was guided by long-established practice. Experience from home was thus of limited value for people faced with the problems of the newly acquired dependencies, and as already indicated it was unlikely that any central policy or even general guidelines would be available to the colonial emissaries faced with the missionaries' aspirations and expectations.

The aim of this paper is to examine, by way of a case study from Uganda, how the church–state problem was approached and solved under the specifically colonial circumstances. So far little comparative research has been done in this field, and there have been few attempts at generalizations on a wider scale.[2] The colonial church–state issue is complex, and has several dimensions, but this chapter will confine itself to the institutional and constitutional aspects of the relationship and will not consider other kinds of interaction between church and state. This means that we will not be concerned with the church's or the mission's political role as a promoter and legitimizer of colonialism, nor with their respective political activities and interchanges with the colonial government, which fall within the wider issue of Christianity and politics. Our goal will be the more narrow one of examining where to place a church in a colonial state on a scale suggested by

Talcott Parsons, who has 'the ancient European institution of the Establishment' as one extreme and the total separation of church and state as the other.[3]

One important point of departure will be the Berlin Act of 1885 which appears regularly in the Uganda material. Apart from the clauses which were meant to guide the European powers in the scramble for Africa, Article 6 of the act states some general principles of religious tolerance and missionary freedom. The aim was clearly to establish some kind of internationally accepted set of guidelines to direct the states in their religious policy and in their relationship with religious organizations, primarily as regards the growing activities of the European missionary societies. To some extent the Berlin Act served its purpose in the religious field, as we will see below, but in the present context its main significance is that it was the first attempt to establish an international code to guide the relationship between church and state.

While Article 6 of the Berlin Act had no legislative consequences for the British colonial empire and set down no general policy, it is important to notice that the principles and guidelines of the Berlin Act represented nothing new. They accorded well with the nine-teenth-century policy towards the old colonies, later called self-governing areas or dominions. Although one finds no explicit indica-tions of such a connection, nor any references to earlier colonial experience in the Uganda material, it is nonetheless unlikely that solutions worked out for Canada and older colonies were not taken into account in dealing with the newly acquired colonies.

Of course, we should not overlook the fact that the new dependen-cies represented a different type of colony with few, if any, immigrants of European stock, nor the fact that various lessons learned in the past were rarely considered by the colonial administration, nor that there was no really systematic attempt to confront the more general issues. Still, it is reasonable to assume, to quote Kenneth Robinson again, that 'British policy, as well as the demands made on it by colonial spokesmen, had indeed been influenced by the existence of the Dominions' (p. 88).

The assumption applies also to ecclesiastical policy in the African colonies. Continuity is more likely than the opposite, as the similarities with the Berlin Act indicate. Even if no systematic use was made of past experience it did after all provide some general guidelines, which formed part of the accumulated knowledge of the colonial service. It was important in defining certain minimum requirements for any settlement with the church, and in establishing a maximum limit for concessions granted to any church. Another factor to be taken into account, as pointed out by Alpheus Todd in his survey, published as early as 1880, is that by that time the situation in the old colonies had reached a stage where it doubtless formed 'a model for all the churches of the reformed Anglican confession throughout the empire' (p. 311). So it is with good reason that our first point of departure is a brief survey of the solution to the church–state problem in the dominions.

The heritage of the dominions

Around 1800 it was typical of the dominions that the Church of England held a privileged position and was favoured by the Crown.[4] This was made particularly clear by various kinds of endowment, for instance the 'clergy reserves' in Canada. In general, Canada is an interesting case for our purposes, as it led the way with changes in the ecclesiastical situation in the nineteenth century.

In the Canada Constitutional Act of 1791 there were provisions for an established position for the Church of England, primarily manifested in the extensive endowment of the 'Protestant clergy' with grants of land, the so-called clergy reserves.[5] Although the Roman Catholics' right to religious liberty and free worship, granted as early as 1763, was upheld, their position in the state was clearly inferior to that of the members of the established church. The instructions issued to a new governor-in-chief in 1818 clearly defined the restrictions to which they were subject as a religious minority. It was emphasized:

> that it is a toleration of the free exercise of the religion of the Church of Rome only to which they are entitled, but not to the powers and privileges of it as an established church, that being a preference which belongs only to the Protestant Church of England.[6]

The policy of establishment was based on two main premises, which are of general interest in the whole colonial context. In the first place, many British politicians blamed the American Revolution on the lack of an essential element in the British constitution, namely the Established Church.[7] The Church of England was seen as a pillar of state, legitimizing its institutions, and as a teacher of civil obedience. This argument was strenghtened by the second premise. The existence of the Established Church in Canada was part of the prevailing philosophy on the future of the colonies. As many British institutions as possible were to be transplanted to the colonies, to allow colonial society to develop in accordance with the British model. In this respect, Anglicanism was indispensable.[8]

But both premises were soon questioned. From the turn of the century on there was growing opposition to the principle of establishment from non-conformist and non-episcopalian circles. Even if there were freedom of worship, the privileges granted to one church were in conflict with the principle of religious equality which the state ought to observe. Establishment was a reflection of the dominance of the Anglican clique in state and society. As a matter of principle a situation characterized by denominational pluralism was incompatible with the whole idea of establishment.[9]

A little later, the idea of transplanting institutions from the mother country was also disputed. One of the first to ask the basic question whether British colonies should have British institutions was W. E. Gladstone, in the late 1830s. In view of the differences between British and colonial societies, he was rather sceptical about whether British institutions were at all appropriate for the colonies, especially the idea of established religion.[10] Gladstone, who exerted great influence on the course of change in the ecclesiastical field at home and in the colonies, for much of the century, not only questioned establishment in the colonies; he also pointed out the 'gross anomaly of principle' involved in state support for all Christian churches in the colonies.[11] It was in effect Gladstone who put two issues on the agenda: the separation of church and state and the emergence of a neutral state. Both were burning issues in Canada, at least until 1880.

The grievances expressed by the various denominations created a pressure which led to fundamental changes in church–state relations. At first the state broadened the base of religious establishment by introducing 'concurrent endowment'.[12] In a reply to the House of Lords in 1840 the judges interpreted the words 'a Protestant clergy' in the 1791 Act to include clergy other than that of the Church of England. This meant in the first instance that all Christian denominations were admitted to the benefits of official patronage and were entitled to a share of the clergy reserves. But, in accordance with Gladstone's point of view, it was also argued that the process of disendowment should extend to full separation of church and state. Subsequently the grants of land to clergy were withdrawn and distributed among the municipalities in proportion to their population.[13]

This disendowment, or rather the termination of public endowment, was part of the overall process of disestablishment implemented by various statutory measures on, for instance, university education and the celebration of marriages. The result was that by about 1880 no church had a position of preference or superiority over the other religious bodies. In that respect the state practised full religious equality. There could be no 'national church' in one colony; the churches were looked upon as voluntary associations outside the institutions of the state and outside the state's legislative power.[14]

Developments in Canada had clearly shown 'that established religion was incompatible with the religious diversities of British societies overseas'. Hence the new relationship between church and state was only a logical expression of this diversity, which again formed the background for the introduction of similar measures in other colonies.[15] Nonconformists in Britain cited the precedents from the colonies in their agitation, and the disestablishment of the Church of Ireland in 1871 was not unrelated to the changes in the colonies.[16]

Developments in Canada over most of a century can be described, in Owen Chadwick's words, as a move 'out of an age of toleration . . . into an age of equality . . .'.[17] To demonstrate the significance of the Canadian experience for other areas, it is important to identify the determining factors in the process of change. First of all there was a denominational pluralism that became more and more vociferous. It had been firmly proved beyond all doubt that multidenominationalism nullified the principle of establishment and made it unworkable.

This was strengthened by a second factor, the redefinition of the concept of establishment itself. Initially, the establishment of the church was an 'establishment of truth', the implication being that the state had the capacity to determine what was truth. Later, with the growth of multidenominationalism, it became the 'establishment of majority', the argument being that the church enjoyed the support of the majority of the people. Gladstone was the one who introduced the majority principle, and the change of emphasis in the concept of establishment was to a great extent a result of his own change of mind, from belief in a confessional state to belief in a neutral state.[18]

This leads us to the third factor, the demand on the state for religious equality. Put into practice, this leads to disengagement and disendowment, or at least to what was called 'concurrent endowment', and it puts the state on the path towards religious neutrality. The principle of equality excludes any kind of established church, but it is a moot question whether it also precludes any kind of endowment.

Irrespective of the policy-making process in the colonial administration, it is unlikely that the experience of Canada and other older British colonies did not create a precedent for future policy in the new colonies. No one seriously advocated the one extreme on Talcott Parsons' scale, 'the European institution of the Establishment', and no colonial administration could ignore the exigencies of a multidenominational situation. On the contrary, the now well-established principle of religious equality set limits within which any policy had to operate.

Yet when it comes to practical policy, the question is what is meant by equality and a neutral state. Do these lie at the other extreme of Talcott Parsons' scale, that is, the total separation of church and state?

If we view equality as a demand on the state, we must ask whether it should be interpreted on a denominational basis, that is, in a Christian context, or whether it should include other religions. The history of the dominions, and of Canada in particular, does not provide us with an answer, for the state had not been faced with the challenge. So far the quest for equality, and in a wider sense for religious liberty, had taken place in a Christian context, as part of a campaign against Anglican establishment.

Correspondingly, developments in Canada do not tell us whether a neutral state means the abolition of all state bonds with Christianity, resulting in a secular state, or whether religious neutrality implies a denominationally neutral state which still allows for a connection between Christianity and the state, provided this is done on the basis of equality between the denominations. In the latter case, endowment of the various churches would still be permissible.

We will now examine whether the Berlin Conference of 1884–5 gives an answer to these questions and in general provides us with more explicit guidelines for the relationship between church and state in the newer colonies of Africa.

The Guidelines of the Berlin Conference 1884–5

Article 6 of the General Act of the Conference of Berlin of February 1885 has the characteristic heading 'Provisions relative to Protection of the Natives, of Missionaries and Travellers, as well as relative to Religious Liberty'. It guaranteed freedom of conscience and religious toleration to Africans as well as foreigners within the regions covered by the act. This meant that the signatory powers, all of them European nations except Turkey, accepted the basic principle of religious liberty and acknowledged the accompanying obligation on the state to show tolerance. But at the same time the article clearly states that special rights will be granted to Christian missionaries, as well as scientists and explorers. In more general terms there is also a guarantee of freedom of missionary enterprise irrespective of denomination.[19]

There appears to be a dualism in Article 6. On the one hand, religious liberty is extended to all religious persuasions, not just Christians, but also to people practising African traditional religion; on the other hand, Christian missionary activity is looked upon with special favour and Christianity is placed in a special position. The reasons for this are apparent from Article 6 itself. Missionary activity is supposed to contribute to 'instructing the natives and bringing home to them the blessings of civilization'. From the point of view of the state, Christian missions were important channels for introducing 'the blessings of civilization', and in view of this joint aim it was only natural for the missions and the colonial powers to establish some sort of co-operation and to 'protect and favour' Christian activity.

The interpretation of the Berlin Act outlined here is borne out by the fact that at the next international conference on Africa, the Brussels Conference of 1889–90, convened to discuss the abolition of the slave trade, the obligation of the signatory powers to protect missions without distinction of creed was even more strongly emphasized, whereas there was no reference to the general principle of religious liberty. Once again it appears, this time in connection with the suppression of the slave trade and the supposed threat from Muslim activity in the Congo Basin, that the state and the missions share vital interests from different points of view, and this can be counted as a factor contributing to the special protection afforded by the state to the missions.[20]

In these early treaties we can identify two trends. One guarantees the general principle of religious liberty, the other emphasizes Christianity and extends special protection to missionary activity. This is confirmed when we move closer to Uganda. In the Royal Charter granted to the Imperial British East Africa Company in September 1888, Clause 11 requests that the company adhere to the principle of religious liberty and in no way interfere with the religion of the inhabitants, an understated request for religious neutrality on the part of the company. But in the agreement of 1 July 1890, between Britain and Germany, on the partition of East Africa, there is most emphasis on the other trend. Besides mentioning adherence to the principle of religious toleration and freedom, Article X is quite specific in stating that 'missionaries of both countries shall have full protection'. This means that no country is allowed to grant its own missionaries special privileges different from the ones granted to foreign missionaries. It is the principle of equal treatment that is adopted. Taking this last point one step further, it seems that the concept of religious neutrality in this case is understood in a narrow sense and applied primarily within a Christian context.[21]

These treaties, which clearly echo Article 6 of the Berlin Act, confirm the dichotomy in that act's guidelines. On the one hand in general state remains neutral in religion; on the other hand, religious liberty is conceived of in a narrower sense, defined Christian terms and seen as operating only on Christian ground. Christian missionary activity is considered by the state to be desirable and to deserve special protection. Christianity is thus placed in a special and privileged position compared to Islam, not to mention African traditional religions. The state stays neutral as far as denominational adherence is concerned, but is under an obligation to guarantee missionary freedom.

These two interpretations of the concept of religious liberty in the Berlin Act can be further explained by introducing a distinction between tolerance and neutrality. The state is obliged to tolerate all religious persuasions and allow them freedom of worship. But when it comes to the operational level, as expressed in the words 'protect and favour', the concept of religious liberty is narrowed down to the Christian sphere. The state is enjoined to stay neutral and practise equality in its dealings with the Christian missions. There is an inherent dichotomy between these two principles, and the question becomes how actively a state can practise its neutrality in the Christian sphere without violating the principle of tolerance, for instance by attaching civil privileges to a religious persuasion.

The Berlin Act legitimized a Christian bias in the colonial government's religious policy and endorsed the principle of endowment by advocating special support for the work of Christian missions. In some respects religious liberty was almost equated with missionary freedom, as it was seen as the most pressing issue. In comparison with the situation in Canada earlier in the nineteenth century, the concept of religious tolerance was explicitly being widened to include non-Christian religions, while the question of the state's neutrality was still being interpreted within an exclusively Christian framework. The requirement for a neutral state was that it was denominationally neutral, and dealt with the various Christian denominations on the basis of equality; but there was no call for all ties with Christianity to be abolished.

Given the guidelines of the Berlin Act and its inherent dichotomy, a colonial state was left with two options: either to adhere to the principle of religious liberty in its widest sense, which meant applying the principles of tolerance and neutrality within the same context without giving preference to any one religion, or, what is more likely, to take the whole context into account, to act upon the legitimization of the Christian bias and to view Christianity as a privileged religion, as expressed by various endowments. Uganda affords an example of how the latter option could be implemented.

An outline of religious policy in early colonial Uganda: tolerance or neutrality?

The religious situation in Uganda is extremely complex, and it is hardly possible to distinguish between religious feuds and political conflicts. Here it will be possible only to identify some important trends in the 1890s and the first quarter of the twentieth century.[22]

The period 1890–92 was in many ways the formative period. This was when Frederick Lugard, on behalf of the Imperial British East Africa Company, was in charge of central parts of what became the Protectorate of Uganda just a few years later.[23] Immediately on his arrival he was met by two rival European missions, the Anglican Church Missionary Society (CMS) and the Roman Catholic White Fathers. In the Kingdom of Buganda, the biggest province in the eventual protectorate, he was faced with two opposed African politico-religious parties, reflecting the dual missionary presence. While the missions demanded that Lugard adhere to the principle of missionary freedom, and requested various concessions, such as land grants, the two African parties wanted public offices involving territorial rights.

Lugard had his instructions and was fully aware of the basic principle of religious liberty, but his weak position meant that he had to give in to the various demands. He made an attempt to secure certain minimum rights for the Muslims and African traditionalists, prompted both by a genuine wish to treat them justly and an interest in reducing the monopoly-like power of the two Christian groups, but with little success. Instead most of his time and effort were spent on the equal division of goods between the Christian groups and the two missions, while trying to stay neutral in the fights between the two denominations. Without going into detail, it follows that the question of neutrality and equality only became relevant in a Christian framework.

In practice, Lugard's religious policy supported the Christians, and the Christian factor was the dominating one. Lugard applied the narrow definition of religious liberty in the Berlin Act, realizing its inherent Christian bias. This may be why his policy was acceptable in the European arena in spite of its tying of offices to religious adherence. The great issue for the Europeans was his neutrality in dealing with the two missions and the two Christian parties, and whether he followed the principle of equality when allotting concessions and distributing offices. And the Christian bias in the various treaties obviously sanctioned this kind of religious policy.

It was difficult for Lugard's successors to go beyond the pattern he set. The large section of the population which retained the traditional religion – often called 'people without religion' – did not count in the government's religious policy. While individuals were defended against oppression, the fate of their religion was of no interest to the government. 'The people without religion' were protected by tolerance, but were not seen as a party to the government's neutrality.[24]

The Muslims, who constituted a minority, were in a somewhat different position. Individually they were covered by the principle of religious liberty, and in addition were guaranteed a few chiefly offices. But they were not given equal status with the Christians, and they were kept under careful observation by a government which viewed the spread of Islam with some anxiety. In 1917 the ambivalence towards the Muslims was made very clear during a lengthy discussion between the missions and the government on how wide ranging tolerance towards all religious persuasions should be. In a circular, it was stated that equal tolerance should be extended to every form of religious belief, but Islam was singled out:

With reference to Mohamedanism it is to be borne in mind that the Moslem faith, although entitled in itself to the same tolerance as other religions, is peculiarly liable to fanatic development and as such must be judiciously watched by those who are responsible for the preservation of law and order.[25]

The principle of tolerance was here clearly circumscribed by political considerations. Islam was considered a political risk, and it was repeatedly stated that Christian doctrines and ideas consituted the best way of combating Muslim influence. Thus the greater the anxiety over the political implications of Islam, the more the instrumental value of missions was emphasized, and the idea of tolerance was scaled down.

The inferior position of the Muslims was not criticized by the home authorities; nor was the concomitant compromise of the principles of tolerance and equality the object of much debate. Although the continued tying of offices to the two Christian parties begun in Lugard's day was a sore point with the government, it was seen as acceptable and justifiable on grounds of political expedience. What mattered most was whether there was any inequity in the distribution of offices between the two Christian parties.

All in all, government policy was based on a dichotomy between tolerance and neutrality which can be traced back to the Berlin Act, and it was the principle of neutrality that carried most weight. The Christian bias, and not least the instrumental value ascribed to the missions, could easily be legitimized by reference to Article 6.

It follows that the Christian factor was the most important one in religious policy, and it is not surprising that the Berlin document was often referred to when it came to the actual implementation of the policy. In view of the significance attached to the missions' instrumental value, it was in the first instance important to create proper working conditions for them by way of the equal distribution of various concessions, especially land grants, to which we will return below. Even more important was the careful upholding of the principle of missionary freedom.[26] The government refrained from any comity arrangement and from allocating spheres to each mission, although it was fully aware that the policy of free missionary enterprise meant the export of politico-religious factionalism to all parts of the protectorate. The stipulations of the Berlin Act were taken so seriously that all such arrangements were ruled out.

The strength of adherence to the principle of freedom for Christian missionary enterprise is further illustrated by the government's attitude to a Muslim missionary initiative. In 1925, when a Muslim missionary movement from India planned to start work in Uganda, pragmatic considerations counted for more than the principle of missionary freedom. It was envisaged that the presence of such an agency would cause political trouble, and the government almost vetoed the plans by refusing to grant the same concessions as the Christian missions enjoyed.[27]

While in the latter case it was easy for the government to draw a distinction between tolerance and neutrality, there were situations where it was difficult to strike a balance between the two principles. It was sometimes difficult to decide how far the religious neutrality of the state could be kept within the Christian framework without violating the principle of tolerance. In 1916 this led to a government attempt to harmonize the two principles. During a controversy over whether the building of missionary schools should be considered a religious activity or a scheme for the general welfare of the people, it was specifically stated that 'the chiefs had no power either to order or compel their people to erect Churches or Schools or to work for religious propaganda'.[28] Instead, voluntary or paid labour must be used. And in order to clarify the principles underlying the government's policy on religion, the following statement was prefaced to the ruling:

> The Government will do all possible to promote religion and education among the native inhabitants of the Protectorate, but does not concern itself with the religious beliefs or teachings of the people, in other words complete 'religious toleration' is to prevail.[29]

This ruling was clearly seen by the missions as a new departure in government policy, as it tended to erode the state's Christian foundations. First, a distinction had to be drawn between encouraging education and putting pressure on individuals. While the latter was naturally precluded, the former was certainly permissible, as it was for the general welfare of the people. Furthermore, the mission called for a distinction between tolerance and neutrality, implying that the two were not necessarily interdependent. While the mission fully acknowledged the value of tolerance, the state's neutrality bordered on passivity or outright indifference; at the very least, the attitude of religious neutrality could be misinterpreted as religious indifference.[30]

This rejection of the state's version of neutrality brought out the dilemma with which the government was confronted in its attempts to pursue a policy of religious tolerance and neutrality. By giving absolute priority to full religious tolerance and being strictly neutral in all religious matters, the state was giving an impression of religious indifference. The alternative would be for the state to ally itself so closely with the Christian cause that the building of denominational schools could be identified with promoting the general welfare of society, thus once again justifying the use of chiefly labour tributes for Christian purposes.

The following year the government backed down somewhat from its first position and settled for the following formula:

> The Government of the Uganda Protectorate, while desirous of encouraging the spread of Christian principles by all legitimate means, extends an equal toleration to every form of religious belief.[31]

If we compare this with the statement of the foregoing year, we can see that the government, while still professing religious toleration, was now clearly committing itself to a religious policy on Christian foundations or one with a Christian bias. The distinction between tolerance and neutrality had now been recognized, if only tacitly. In the case in point this meant a legitimization of the use of the chief's tributes for Christian purposes, provided such use did not violate the individual's right to tolerance. This was not a new policy but it had been spelt out in more definite terms than before. Over the next decade it remained the most authoritative expression of the government's religious policy, and officials had occasion to cite it from time to time.[32]

The next question to arise is whether the government could maintain a neutral stand in the face of denominational pluralism and practise a policy of equality when it came to active support for the Christian enterprise. And it remained to be seen whether there was a limit to its willingness to diminish the neutrality of its policy by identifying itself with Christian principles.

Support for the Christian cause: economic links with the church

Turning to the question of how the colonial state fulfilled its pledge to further the Christian cause, one of the first questions we must ask

is whether endowment of the mission and church played any significant role. Developments in Canada had not established whether
endowment and the ensuing official link between the church and the
colonial state were possible independently of any position of establishment. At least the Berlin Act legitimized the option of endowing
Christian missions.

In the case of Uganda the question of establishment, which could
only be relevant to the CMS mission and the newly founded Native
Anglican Church, was not on the agenda. It is difficult to tell whether
the CMS had looked forward initially to some kind of established
position, but it was soon recognized that this was not a realistic
possibility. At the second meeting of the newly established synod in
1906, when some delegates suggested that the church ought to be an
integral part of the Kingdom of Buganda at least, and that the
decisions of the synod should be enforced by law, the head of the
CMS mission pointed out that there was no established church in
Uganda, and therefore no state church, as both Catholics and
Protestants were present in the country.[33] If for no other reason, it
was thus fully recognized that the denominational factor precluded
any kind of establishment. It should be added that this did not rule
out a process of Christianization of essential political institutions like
the kingship and chieftainship, nor the projection of an image of
establishment in relation to the African political system. But such a
process would not amount to a constitutional or established position,
and the possibility is beyond the scope of the present survey, which
focuses on formal and official links between the colonial state and the
mission/church.[34]

In the Ugandan setting, when the missions were in fact extensively
endowed with land, Christianization was done implicitly on the pretext
of following the guidelines set out in the Berlin Act. To secure proper
working conditions, the colonial administration confirmed the land
grants first given by the chiefs, and the whole system was codified in
the Uganda Agreement of 1900 drawn up by Sir Harry Johnston. The
CMS mission and the White Fathers were each allotted 40 sqm, while
the newly arrived Roman Catholic Mill Hill Mission was granted 12
sqm.[35] Significantly enough, the Anglican mission saw in this distribution a breach of the principle of denominational equality, and the
situation was accordingly rectified by adding 12 sqm to the Protestant
land grant.[36]

A land endowment of this size can only be seen as generous

compared to those in other colonial dependencies, and this explains Lugard's comment in *The Dual Mandate in British Tropical Africa* that 'Missions in Uganda occupy a specially privileged position' (p. 342). This makes it all the more important to examine the conditions on which the land was held, and whether it gave the church any official status. In the first place, it was given to the missions, not to the African church, and the colonial government deliberately refrained from attaching any recognition of the African church to the endowment. It was given only as an acknowledgement of an obligation to create reasonable conditions for the missions by relieving them of some of their burdens.[37]

This was further emphasized by two other measures aimed at limiting the value of the endowment. As land and the accompanying labour services from tenants were the major economic assets in society, and as the missions constantly asked for increases in their acreage, the British administration, in this case at the central level of the Colonial Office, drew up a land policy in 1914. With a few adjustments, and continued adherence to the principle of denominational equality, the endowment of the 1900 agreement was confirmed as a once-and-for-all block grant, the overall aim clearly being to stop the escalation of government support.[38]

After this decision it was also important to define the conditions on which the land was held: whether it was granted as a revenue-gathering endowment which could be used for plantations, the growing of cash crops and subletting, or simply for purposes narrowly defined as religious, such as securing housing and food for church workers. The government settled for the last option, thereby refusing to introduce the European concept of landholding. The government would not accept the mission as a major economic force in society as a great landowner or even as a pioneer of agricultural development.[39]

Besides rejecting the concept of a revenue-producing endowment, the government limited the missions' rights to landholders' tributes and privileges, as this might give the Christian missions a special status in society. Clearly the government was on its guard against the missions' constituting a 'government within the government' when rights to labour services on mission land were requested.[40] Hence the land grant is no indication of any institutional links between state and church, but represents a public endowment in accordance with the policy of support for the Christian cause. Recalling the Canadian situation, we may call it a concurrent endowment, as it followed the principle of denominational equality.

Another argument in favour of an increase in the land grant was mission education, which grew substantially after the turn of the century. Education was the other major area where there were economic links between the state and the missions, but all through the period the government maintained a distinction between support in land and labour for general missionary activity, and grants for a more specialized, mainly secular activity like education. The government clearly saw education as part of its responsibility, and grants-in-aid were given directly to the missions as the agency in charge of education, and were even earmarked for specific purposes.[41]

The employment of the Christian missions as the educational agencies was deliberate government policy. It implied that such public support entailed no recognition of the African church. What mattered more was the policy of denominational equality. Over the years a rather lax practice had developed of giving the CMS mission more than twice as much money as the two Catholic missions combined, and it was pointed out from London that this constituted denominational inequality. The local administration thereupon quickly went back to giving equal grants to both denominations.[42]

But the mixture of educational and evangelizing work still represented a dilemma for the British colonial government, as it could easily be seen as financing missionary propaganda by supporting an educational system along denominational lines. In this situation the first and most logical course for the government would have been to secularize education and start its own non-sectarian system, an option favoured by some officials in the early 1920s.[43] But the inertia of two decades, financial problems and the commitment to the Christian cause made this course of action unrealistic. After all, as we have learned from the discussion of the state's religious indifference, the implicit premise for employing the missions as educational agencies was the state's commitment to the idea that Christian values were most beneficial to the development of African society. That principle justified the government's continued support for the missionary monopoly on education along Christian lines. Instead therefore the government chose to separate education and evangelizing activities as much as possible by stipulating certain qualitative requirements and by making sure that its money was primarily spent on education rather than on evangelizing.[44]

By employing the missions as virtually the only educational agencies, the government was using public funds in support of the Christian cause, but not for general Christian purposes. The resources were earmarked for easily identifiable, mainly secular activities like education. The great importance of such a distinction is revealed when we examine requests for state financial aid for specifically ecclesiastical activities like the building of churches and the employment of official chaplains. In 1904 the Anglican bishop asked for a subscription for the building of a church at government headquarters in Entebbe. The request was firmly refused by the Foreign Office in London.[45] Again in 1907, the local administration recommended that a site of two acres should be provided for the building of such a church, together with a grant of £500. The site was granted, but the money grant was refused, this time by the Colonial Office. A grant from public funds was thus considered to be in a different category from land grants.[46]

That direct financial aid was the crucial point was confirmed in 1910, when a reply to an official inquiry from the Colonial Office stated that no government money was being paid for the maintenance of religious services or buildings, nor were there any official chaplains in the protectorate.[47] The latter issue was raised by the Anglican bishop on several occasions, and in 1924 the local administration also asked for a special grant to support a Church of England chaplain's work at headquarters. In refusing this request, the Colonial Office took the opportunity to make a major declaration of policy. It aimed at the 'gradual withdrawal of State aid for purely religious purposes in the Colonies', not least in response to 'Parliamentary pressure against the endowment of a particular form of Christianity'.[48]

It is interesting to note that cases of financial support for purely religious activities were referred to the home authorities in London. As indicated by the policy statement of 1924, the reason was that this was an area where an overall official colonial policy had been drawn up. There can hardly be any doubt that this policy was based on the lessons learned from the above-mentioned process of disendowment in the older British colonies in the nineteenth century.[49] The process originally worked against the Church of England, but the Colonial Office's reference to parliamentary opinion indicated that it was still an issue as late as 1924.

Thus the government was averse to granting direct financial support because such endowments constituted an official link with Christianity and a particular church. Although land grants served Christian missionary purposes, they were considered less of a commitment to the missionary cause, and less of an official confirmation of a close alliance with Christianity than the granting of money from public funds. Land was plentiful after the establishment of the colonial state, and this type of support made fewer demands on both sides. It could be justified with reference to the missionary situation. Grants-in-aid for education were also in a special category, because they were earmarked for a special activity and entailed no formal recognition of the missions involved.

Support for the Christian cause: formal links with the church

During the discussion of the state's 'religious indifference' referred to above, the bishops of Uganda maintained that the attitude of religious neutrality was interpreted as 'implying indifference also to moral character'. And the bishops drew a parallel to Europe in the Middle Ages 'when the authority of the State went hand in hand with the influence of the Church in doing at least what was possible to produce moral conditions in the people'.[50] Hence the question was to what extent, apart from the endowment in land, the state was prepared to act upon its Christian commitment and transform society by means of Christian legislation, thus establishing formal links with the mission and church.

Traditionally vital areas of life, especially those involving the family, were regulated by Christian principles. In Uganda the question soon arose of whether the state should uphold this Christian foundation, and whether it should allow religious institutions to administer laws touching on these issues. Soon after the turn of the century attention in Uganda was turned to the marriage laws, when the government attempted to pass a Marriage Ordinance making monogamous marriage a civil institution under the jurisdiction of the state, thus excluding the church. A remarkably strong missionary campaign blocked this attempt, and the result was that ordinances were passed allowing marriages to be celebrated according to the laws of each religious community present in the protectorate (Christian, Muslim and Hindu).[51] Thus two concessions were granted to the missions: first a marriage law based on Christian principles was passed, and monogamous marriage was not considered an exclusively civil institution; second, the church was given the right to perform legal marriages. The state in effect granted the church a legitimate role, and even more importantly gave it moral support by showing a preference for monogamous, Christian marriage. On the other hand, Christianity achieved no monopoly, as the state respected the principle of religious pluralism.

It follows that the vast field of customary, polygamous marriage remained outside the official jurisdiction. Two inter-related problems became crucial here: first, should customary marriage have the same status as religious marriage and receive full recognition by the state, or should the state also actively support the extension of Christian values in this field? second, how far should the state, in cases of conversion to Christianity and transition to Christian monogamous marriage, support such conversions by legislation?

Attempts to solve the first problem ended in a stalemate, as customary marriage occasioned intense controversy between missions and state. The realities of life forced the missionaries to recognize the validity of customary marriage, but they did so only on the condition that no more than one wife was involved. In other words, recognition involved the utterly foreign concept of a customary, monogamous marriage, and the state was asked to support this step towards monogamy by introducing a system of registration. The state wished to retain customary marriage in its original form without restrictions, but the missions prevented a special ordinance from being issued, placing customary marriages on an equal footing with Christian ones. This would have amounted to official recognition of polygamy. The customary marriage institution was not incorporated into the statute book, but was left to be guided solely by customary law.

This inconclusive state of affairs left the way open for attempts from both parties to swing the pendulum to one side or the other. The state tried to preserve the traditional marriage institution, with its polygamy option, and came close to recognizing it officially when it stated that Christians had the right to marry in the traditional way, and that they were under no obligation to marry under the Christian Ordinance. This virtually amounted to granting not only equal legality, but also equal prestige to the two types of marriage. It was naturally vehemently contested by the missions, and the government retreated somewhat. Conversely the missions made an attempt to combat polygamy by having the Christian monogamous ideal endorsed by legislation. In order to erode the dominance of customary marriage, the mission recommended that legal protection should be denied to people who had contracted polygamous marriages, and that Christians should be obliged to marry in church. The government found both requests unacceptable, and was unwilling to pass legislation which Christianized the marriage institution to such an extent at the expense of the customary system.

Thus each of the two parties was able to prevent the other from arriving at an exclusive solution to the problem of customary marriage. The church did not gain exclusive control of marriage, while the state's opposition to the extension of Christian norms did not lead to the introduction of exclusively secular legislation. This is in accordance with the point made earlier that the state did in fact favour monogamous Christian marriage, in the sense that its legislation allowed for a gradual development in that direction.[52]

This brings us to the second question posed above. To what extent was the state to support the spread of Christian values, for instance in cases of conversion to Christianity? As regards the marriage laws, part of the answer has already been given: the state rejected the mission's proposal that Christians should be compelled to marry under the Christian Ordinance. The state would go no further than to provide in the law for the conversion of a customary marriage to a Christian one in order to meet the church's conditions for baptism. All this remained optional, and the government refused to attach legal consequences to conversion to Christianity. Secular law and Christian doctrine were not made to correspond to the extent that baptismal requirements were endorsed by legislation.

It thus became clear that the British protectorate government's use of the legislative method to support the Christian cause was based on a distinction between what was optional and what was compulsory. The mission clearly wanted the latter course of action in order to secure specifically Christian legislation, while the government maintained that it was not the function of the law to set the standards; the law must follow, not lead. The state was committed to the furtherance of Christian values in vital areas of social life, but it could not establish such close links with the church that the laws of the state would be in full harmony with Christian doctrine. Consequently, the state was also hesitant to prosecute and to employ penalty clauses in cases where rules had been broken. This was the case when Christians violated the Christian Marriage Ordinance by entering into a customary, polygamous marriage, as it was with failures to comply with the fixed dowry rate and to observe the ban on Sunday labour.[53]

Another area where there could be formal links between state and church was the involvement of the church in public events and state occasions. Invoking the practice in parliament in London, representatives of the Anglican church suggested in 1916 that meetings of the council (Lukiko) in Buganda should begin with prayers, as the majority of the members, indeed the majority of the population, now professed Christianity. The Anglican bishop even wrote to the archbishop of Canterbury enquiring whether Roman Catholics had ever expressed disapproval of the prayers used in parliament, acknowledging that this could be a sore point in the Buganda context. In spite of the assuring answer from the archbishop, the provincial commissioner opposed the idea for two reasons: it would give the impression that religion was closely connected with state matters, and would thereby breach a basic principle of government policy; and it would leave the government open to accusation that it favoured the Anglican Church at the expense of the Roman Catholics, and this could create discontent.[54]

These two arguments blocked the introduction of prayers in the Lukiko, and they were also crucial to decisions on other instances of potential church involvement in public matters. Taking as its point of departure that 'amongst a simple minded people the outward sign is of much importance' the CMS mission was intent on identifying the Kabaka (King of Buganda) as closely as possible with the Protestant church.[55] In 1900 they introduced the feature that the Kabaka's Accession Day was celebrated in church. Over the following years the celebration of the Kabaka's birthday and Coronation Day began with a service in the cathedral, somewhat presumptuously called 'the usual State service'.[56] Again in 1902, on the day of King Edward VII's Coronation, and in 1910 in connection with the burial of the late Kabaka, who had died in exile, services were held in the cathedral. Thus the Anglican church was seen to be officiating at important state functions.[57]

So far the virtual Protestant monopoly of the kingship had apparently not provoked objections from the government and the Catholic mission. These came however in 1910, when it was suggested that the young Kabaka should pay a visit to Britain on the occasion of the Coronation of King George V. The Catholic bishop demanded that at least one representative of the Catholic party be included in the Kabaka's entourage, claiming that failure to do so would be a gross insult to the large Catholic majority in Buganda. And the colonial administration now realized that the Protestant establishment, with its alliance between the mission and the chiefs, was practically challenging the government to a contest 'the result of which is to decide whose authority in native affairs is paramount'.[58]

The next manifestation of the Protestant involvement with the Kabakaship occurred in 1914 when the Kabaka came of age and a proper accession ceremony was to be held. Again the CMS mission was in the forefront, emphasizing that this was 'the first coronation of a Christian Kabaka', and the coronation was carried out in accordance with Anglican prescriptions. The mission certainly managed to reaffirm the indispensability of the Anglican church on such occasions, in the face of strong opposition from the Catholic mission and the government. The governor refused to attend, and ordered the provincial commissioner and his staff, who did attend, to come in their second-best uniforms. This marked unequivocal official disapproval of the Protestants' *tour de force*.[59]

The event which best demonstrated attitudes on both sides was the consecration of the new Protestant cathedral in 1919. The governor was invited to take part in the processions and the ceremony with the Kabaka and leading chiefs. According to the CMS mission this would stress the exceptional nature of the occasion and, even more essentially, would be 'a unique opportunity for those who govern and those who are governed to meet together as members of the Christian Church professing a common creed'. The active participation of the governor and other officials would inevitably have given the impression of close identity between the Anglican church and the secular authorities, so close that it would seem to be the official church of the protectorate. The governor was well aware of this, and made the following comment: 'It is very official so far as the Church is concerned, but not as to the State'. He therefore agreed to be present, but would not participate or even wear his uniform. To make the situation even more clear he issued a statement afterwards expressing his appreciation of the growing spirit of co-operation between the government and *all* missionary societies.[60] The pattern was repeated on the occasion of the CMS Uganda mission's fiftieth anniversary in 1927. In view of the important part it had played in the history of the protectorate, the CMS asked the government to participate in the pageant and to make provision for a grant in the budget. In accordance with the general policy of economic support, the latter request was turned down, and official participation in the pageant was played down.[61]

The multidenominational factor was clearly an obstacle to any close engagement with the Anglican church. For political reasons too the government was determined to reduce its engagement with the church, although it was admitted that the church was indispensable at certain state functions. But beyond the functional level it was deliberate policy to keep the church out of state matters and vice versa. In the mid 1920s, when the issue of the bishops' precedence at official ceremonies was raised, it was made quite clear, following guidance from London, that according to the Colonial Regulations 'the precedence of the Bishop is of an honourary nature and to be accorded to him by courtesy'. The Church of England bishop had no inherent precedence over the bishops of other religions, and the guiding principle was to be seniority if more than one bishop was present. The issue was aptly summed up by the governor in 1939: 'We seem to have entirely dropped any idea of the C/E as the National Religion giving its head special precedence. I always understood that view prevailed in Uganda'.[62]

This should be seen as a reflection of an old trend in colonial policy, originating from the case of Bishop Colenso of South Africa in 1865. From then on it was not the prerogative of the state to create ecclesiastical offices in parliament, nor of the Crown to fill vacant bishoprics. It devolved upon the clergy and laity to secure effective episcopal organization for their respective churches.[63] So the various missions were simply to inform the Uganda Government as a matter of courtesy when a new bishop had been appointed. This principle was reaffirmed in 1912 when a controversy between Portugal and the Vatican threatened to change the whole system of appointment of Catholic bishops in East and Central Africa. The Foreign Office immediately informed the Uganda Government among others that it must remain neutral on this question, and that it could have 'no justificable grounds for expressing any choice as to the manner in which such ecclesiastical appointments are made'.[64]

A more direct rejection of any constitutional accommodation between state and church came in 1925, when the CMS Uganda mission made a strong attempt to obtain from the government

the recognition of the Native Anglican Church as a self-governing body with responsible officers, quite distinct from the Mission ... that the time may now have come for the drafting of an ordinance defining the position of the Native Anglican Church in

Uganda, its powers over its own members, and its relations to Government.[65]

The demand indicated that the mission considered it necessary after all to establish constitutional linkages between church and state, and to obtain a formalized position for the church within the state, along English lines. The government was asked to endorse the church constitution legally, and this involved pledging the church to adhere to Anglican doctrines and to follow certain ecclesiastical rules and regulations. This in fact amounted to asking the state to pass legislation for the church and to assume responsibility for its doctrines.

Without referring to London, the government replied that any kind of legislation for the church was out of the question. Irrespective of the labels 'mission' or 'church', both bodies were non-corporate associations, and as long as they followed the laws of the protectorate there was no reason for government intervention. As regards establishment, the Church of England model could not be extended to Uganda, despite the fact that the mission and the church were in ecclesiastical communion with the Church of England; these links did not place the church in a position different from that of any other religious body.[66]

Conclusion

Minimal formal links with the church and mission were the main trend in colonial religious policy. The roots of the trend went back to the process of disestablishment in the old colony, Canada, in the nineteenth century. The main determining factor was the denominational pluralism which was to prove a permanent feature of the colonial situation, and upon which the state's religious policy was based. But this policy did not preclude a position of favour and superiority for Christianity, a Christian bias that was endorsed and legitimized by the dichotomy between tolerance and neutrality in the Berlin Act of 1885. By extending religious tolerance to all, the government as it were acquired an alibi for neglecting its neutrality as far as non-Christians were concerned, and was able to uphold the principle of equality within a restricted Christian denominational framework.

In its actual relationship with the church the state combined 'institutional separation' with 'functional interaction'.[67] To further the Christian cause, the church was granted an endowment of land and assumed an auxiliary and instrumental role where the main areas of mutual interest were the fields of legislation and state functions. Returning to Talcott Parsons' scale, the church in the colonial state was not at either extreme. Ali Mazrui, however, has suggested a third category which may be of relevance for a final characterization: the ecumenical state.[68] This requires, first that the government is not monopolistic, but is bent on upholding religious pluralism. That distinguishes such a state from one with an established church. Second, in an ecumenical state the government takes an active interest in religion, and in view of the importance of a common set of values for the state it settles in practice for Christianity and has a clear Christian bias. This means that its active policy and its formal links with religious institutions are conducted primarily within a Christian denominational framework.

Bibliography

Owen Chadwick, *The Victorian Church*, Parts I–II (London 1966, 1970).

Hans Cnattingius, *Bishops and Societies, A Study of Anglican Colonial Missionary Expansion 1698–1850* (London 1952).

Stig Förster, Wolfgang Mommsen and Ronald Robinson (eds), *Bismarck, Europe and Africa. The Berlin African Conference 1884–1885 and the Onset of Partition* (London 1988).

W. E. Gladstone, *The State in its Relations with the Church* (4th edn), Vols I–II (London 1841).

Holger Bernt Hansen, *Mission, Church and State in a Colonial Setting. Uganda 1890–1925* (London 1984).

'The Berlin Act and religious liberty in Africa', *Swedish Missionary Journal* 3 (1985).

'Church and state in early colonial Uganda', *African Affairs* 85 (1986).

'Christian missions and agricultural change. A case study from Uganda' in Mörner, Magnus and Thommy Svensson (eds), *Third World Rural Society: the Challenge of Regional History* (London, forthcoming).

Franklin H. Littell, 'The churches and body politic', *Daedalus* 96 (1967).

F. D. Lugard, *The Dual Mandate in British Tropical Africa* (London 1922).

Ali A. Mazrui, 'Piety and puritanism under a military theocracy: Uganda soldiers as apostolic successors' in Catherine Kelleher (ed.), *Political-Military Systems. Comparative Perspectives* (Beverly Hills 1974).

Suzanne Miers, *Britain and the Ending of the Slave Trade* (New York 1975).

John S. Moir, *Church and State in Canada West* (Toronto 1959).

E. R. Norman, *Church and Society in England 1770–1970* (Oxford 1976).

Talcott Parsons, *Structure and Process in Modern Societies* (Illinois 1960).

Kenneth Robinson, *The Dilemmas of Trusteeship* (London 1965).

Leon P. Spencer, 'Church and state in colonial Africa: influences governing the political activity of Christian missions in Kenya', *Journal of Church and State* (1988).

Alpheus Todd, *Parliamentary Government in the British Colonies* (London 1880).

Michael Twaddle, 'The emergence of politico-religious groupings in late nineteenth-century Buganda', *Journal of African History* 29 (1988).

John Manning Ward, *Colonial Self-Government. The British Experience 1759–1856* (London 1976).

Notes

1. Archdeacon R. H. Walker to his brother, 31 July 1898, Walker Papers, CMS Archives, London and Birmingham.
2. For a discussion of earlier research works and the whole conceptual framework, see the author's *Mission, Church and State in a Colonial Setting* (1984); see also Leon P. Spencer (1988).
3. Talcott Parsons (1960), ch. 10.
4. Cnattingius (1952), p. 108. For Canada see in particular J. S. Moir (1959).
5. See J. M. Ward (1976), passim, and A. Todd (1880), p. 305.
6. Todd (1880), p. 316ff, Ward (1976), p. 25f.
7. Ward (1976), p. 18.
8. Ibid., p. 80.
9. Ibid., p. 44.
10. Ibid., p. 80ff.
11. See E. R. Norman (1976), p. 118, who quotes from Gladstone's book *The State in its Relations with the Church* from 1841.
12. Norman (1976), p. 117f.
13. Gladstone (1841), p. 321f, Todd (1880), p. 306. For a detailed analysis of the clergy-reserves issue see Moir (1959), chs 2 and 3.
14. Todd (1880), p. 307.
15. Norman (1976), p. 202f, Todd (1880), p. 306ff.
16. Owen Chadwick (1970), p. 433.
17. Chadwick (1966), p. 4.
18. Ibid., p. 477, Norman (1976), p. 196ff.
19. For a recent work on the Berlin Conference see Förster *et al.* (1988), esp. ch. 5 by H. Gründer. See also Hansen (1984), ch. 3, and Hansen (1985), passim.
20. See S. Miers (1975), app. I, and Hansen op. cit., passim.
21. Hansen, op. cit.
22. For a general account of the religious situation and, in particular, the emergence of politico-religious parties, see Twaddle (1988).
23. On the Lugard period in Uganda see Hansen (1984), ch. 4.
24. Ibid., p. 432ff.
25. Circular no 16 of 1917, dated 1 Nov. 1917, Secretariat Minute Paper (SMP) 4844, Uganda National Archives. See also Hansen (1984), p. 434ff.

26. Hansen (1984), p. 448ff.
27. Minutes in SMP Conf(idential), 865.
28. SMP 4219, min. 45.
29. SMP 4844, mins 6–8, June 1917.
30. Minutes from 1917 in SMP 4844. See also Hansen (1984), p. 440ff.
31. Clause 1 in Circular no 16, dated 1 Nov. 1917, SMP 4844.
32. For a discussion of the government's 'benevolent neutrality' leading to religious indifference see the three bishops' joint letter to the governor, 19 April 1918, SMP 5368.
33. Minutes of Synod, June 1906, Minute Book, Makerere University Library.
34. See Hansen (1984), ch. 17.
35. Ibid., p. 99ff.
36. SMP 4701, min. 108.
37. Hansen (1984), pp. 100ff, 451ff.
38. Ibid., p. 143ff.
39. Hansen (forthcoming).
40. Hansen (1986).
41. Hansen (1984), ch. 15.
42. SMP 1912, min. 47; Colonial Office to Governor 6 Nov. 1912, CO 536/93 file 33217, Public Record Office (PRO), London.
43. See Governor Archer, A Considered Reply by the Governor to Bishop Willis's Criticisms of the Proposed Government Educational Policy in Uganda, 14 April 1924, CO 536/130, file 23442. See also Hansen (1984), pp. 232ff and 2443ff.
44. Hansen (1984), p. 454.
45. Foreign Office to Commissioner 21 April 1904, FO 2/856.
46. Minutes from July–August 1907 in CO 536/14, file 29327.
47. Minutes in SMP 811 and CO 536/34, file 23535.
48. Minutes in CO 536/130, file 14020, and in SMP 811.
49. See Cnattingius (1952), passim, Norman (1976), p. 202ff.
50. The three Ugandan bishops' joint letter to governor, 19 April 1918, SMP 5368.
51. Hansen (1984), p. 260ff.
52. Ibid., pp. 267ff, 460ff.
53. Ibid., p. 298ff.
54. Correspondence 1916–17 in SMP 4971, and in Bishop's Files: Ab-Ar, Church of Uganda Archive, Kampala.
55. Archdeacon R. H. Walker to his father, 21 Nov. 1903, Walker Papers.
56. *Mengo Notes*, Sept. 1900; *Uganda Notes*, Sept. 1905 (both journals published by the CMS mission).
57. Minutes in CO 536/28, file 3038; and CO 536/34, file 28001. See also *Uganda Notes*, Sept. and Oct. 1910.
58. Minutes 1910–13 in SMP Conf. 77/1910.
59. Correspondence between CMS Uganda mission and CMS headquarters April–May 1914, G3 A7/010, CMS Archives, Birmingham. See Hansen (1984), p. 320ff.
60. Minutes in SMP 4491.

61. Minutes in SMP 9153.
62. Minutes in SMP 375/09; Colonial Office List for 1923, p. 778.
63. See Todd (1880), p. 308ff.
64. Minutes in SMP Conf. 104.
65. Archdeacon Kitching to CMS headquarters, 2 Feb. 1926, no 23, G3. A7/1926; Bishop Willis, Memorandum on Government, Mission and Church, 2 Nov, 1925, SMP 8897.
66. Minutes in SMP 8897.
67. For these expressions, see F. H. Littell (1967), p. 34.
68. Mazrui (1974), passim.

6

A RANDOM FACTOR IN BRITISH IMPERIALISM: District Administration in Colonial Kenya

T. H. R. Cashmore

The novelist and historian John Buchan once delivered a lecture at Cambridge on the theme of the 'causal' and the 'casual' at work in history.[1] The 'causal' were the underlying long-term trends whereas the 'casual' were those seemingly inconsequential incidents or accidents that sometimes threw the pattern awry, at least temporarily, thus deflecting the trends. Such was the tile that struck and killed King Pyrrhus; such the monkey's bite that caused the death of the young King of Greece and, so Buchan argued, made possible the Greek military disaster in Turkey in 1922. So, in addition to the great underlying trends that made or changed the course of British imperialism in this century, there were also jokers in the pack, random factors which also played a part. In colonial Kenya one such random factor was the unpredictable human relationship that developed between the expatriate district administration and the peoples of various districts.

District administration during the colonial period in Kenya often bore a resemblance to a game of blind man's bluff. Certainly there was a good deal of groping in a fog of uncertainty in which the administrator had to work and there was also an element of gamesmanship between the imperial agent and his charges.[2] And the game was made more complex both by the seeming uniqueness of each district with its differing rules and customs, and by the rivalry amongst the white strangers, for example, the conflicts with missionaries, or settlers, or even other departmental officers.

The first unwritten law of the administrator was that an order, once given, must be obeyed. In his eyes, it was vital for the prestige of government that this rule must be enforced. The second golden rule, sometimes breached with disastrous results, was that an order likely to be disobeyed ought not to be given. Here again, failure to observe this law would also harm prestige. To these might be added the commonly held view that in times of crisis, firmness early on might avoid excessive and expensive force too late, or, to put it more crudely, that a shot in time might save nine.[3]

A word about prestige, for it was a term that recurred in reports and letters throughout the colonial period. For instance, in 1898 Hardinge could write to the Foreign Office concerning the tribes coming under his control: 'Our Prestige by which we alone keep them in check, depends on their believing that our orders once given cannot be disregarded with impunity'.[4] And in the 1940s a senior officer wrote for the private guidance of his young district commissioners that 'Law and Order in the desert depend largely on the prestige of Government'.[5]

Prestige, then, meant that orders must not be allowed to be challenged successfully. It also meant that District Officers (DOs) ruled by something other than brute force, simply because that force was seldom ready to hand, often inefficient, inevitably expensive, and always liable to be embarrassing in the context of parliamentary questions. Certainly pioneer administrators believed in the stick and then the carrot: 'Smash them first and let them down lightly afterwards'.[6] But thereafter, largely because of expense, the regular use of force, as opposed to the threat, was impractical and came to be regarded as an admission of defeat by administrators, who grew used to trying to achieve their ends by prestige. The Kenya Emergency of 1952–60 was to prove a great exception.

A second element in the random factor was the environment of the district in colonial times. Administrators frequently lived isolated lives as strangers in an alien land; but the mores of Cheltenham had to come to terms with those of Chuka. Resources were limited, save in an emergency, yet results were expected. The imperial agents had to secure a modicum of law and order and the tax collection, and also use their initiative to try to bring about peaceful development. Experts were often lacking, and the amateur had to organize road-making or building, the construction of canals or wells, and be ready to operate the medicine chest. It was a case of necessity; in the kingdom of the fifth-rate the third-rate ranked high.[7]

Administration in the district tended to be a very personal thing. Writing about the new up-country areas in 1904, Sir Charles Eliot complained that 'It hangs too much on the personality of officials. A tactful Collector by long residence will gain great personal influence among a tribe, and when he is moved his successor will have to begin afresh . . .'.[8] It is hardly surprising, therefore, that administration could become egocentric, a tendency reinforced by the principle of 'trusting the man on the spot',[9] at least so long as he was successful.

An additional variable in all this was the strength or weakness in the administrative chain of command; that is, the supervision and policy guidance from above. Sir Alan Pim, who visited Kenya to report on its financial position in the 1930s, commented that the role of the provincial commissioner 'depends on his own personal qualities: he may be a stimulating and controlling influence . . . he may on the other hand tend to degenerate into a mere post office'.[10] As paperwork and the complexities of development increased, the opportunities for personal influence in a district diminished; nevertheless the administrator was always aware of its importance. The exhortation continued to be to get away from the office and out amongst the people. (In at least one province in 1961 a monthly account was still required of the days and nights spent on safari and the miles covered by vehicle or camel, on foot or by canoe.)

The district environment had marked effects on the administrator, a creature of essentially middle-class, often urban, background.[11] For one thing, he seemed to develop a countryman's devotion to things rural and to the tribal 'man in the blanket'[12] and a countryman's dislike of the urban and the detribalized 'man in trousers'. Certainly few administrators came to terms fully with the new urban problem, since this was something outside the tribal context.[13] A further consequence of the district environment was that prestige became a very personal thing. This had certain side effects: an enhanced sense of self-importance ('the rage for uniforms and precedence'[14] of early years), and a prickly sense of jealousy against all rivals.

The jealousy had both a positive and negative side, namely a paternalistic desire to protect 'his' people, or sheer negative obstruction. It led to some internal feuding between neighbouring administrators ('My district right or wrong'), but more often to disputes with other departments, particularly the police. Field officers also were critical of the secretariat,[15] which 'never understood' their problems, and issued 'impossible' circulars.[16] And, in cutting legal corners, administrators constantly collided with the Supreme Court and resented its 'interference'. Sometimes the collisions were with the missionaries, frequently with the settlers: 'When Tin God meets Tin God there's bound to be trouble'.[17] No doubt some of this could be put down to the heightened individualism[18] of a pioneer society or to the ill-effects of poor health, or fever, high altitude or alcohol. But, in essence, district administrators bitterly resented the appearance of any rival 'paramount chief'. When Francis Hall in the 1890s clashed sharply with a military officer in his district, the cause, as his PC explained, was that Hall 'does not like having any blacks in his district over whom he has not absolute personal control'.[19] The difficulty administrators had in adjusting to African nationalist politicians also stemmed in part from this jealousy of rivals.

On the positive side, there was the battle for local rights, a form of parochial trusteeship, no doubt paternalistic in its defence of 'my' people. It found particular expression in the 'protest voice' that runs through the reports and official letters of administrators at district and provincial levels: Kenneth Dundas on the iniquities of his predecessor,[20] Isaac on taxation, McClure on government expenditure,[21] Ainsworth on education, labour and the lack of a general policy,[22] Cooke and Cornell in defence of Samburu rights to Leroghi, Beech and the Kikuyu point of view, Collyer and the Masai, or a succession of officers on the need for fair sharing of the waters of the Northern Uaso Nyiro. Sometimes the theme was more general; for example, the problems of detribalization, or H. E. Lambert's wry comment on the dangers of soul erosion as well as soil erosion. Equally important, this protest voice remained persistent, sometimes shrill, during the period between the First World War and the early 1950s, a time during which the settlers had won a large slice of the local political initiative, with the district administration largely on the defensive.

The outbreak of the Emergency, however, altered the balance for a time in favour of the DO. Great Britain provided money, men and political backing for the sweeping emergency powers that underpinned the position of the men on the spot. But the Emergency powers enjoyed by DOs had been delegated and did not derive, as some may have imagined, from their own special magic. When Whitehall chose an alternative set of prefects that power, and the prestige that went with it, drained away.

One aspect of the district situation and the administrator's concern for prestige was the element of sheer bluff. On the one hand, this was the inevitable gamble in the absence of overwhelming force in support of authority; on the other, it presupposed a modicum of local consent. Once the first psychological battle was won in a district (that is, obedience to a vital order had been secured – the first unwritten law), administrators tended to rely on bluff. So a DO in Nandi in the early days got the young warriors to carry porters' loads only by concealing the loads in status-giving mail bags. James Bond Ainsworth obtained porters in the hostile conditions of Kitui by organizing dancing competitions.[23] Of course, in accordance with the second unwritten rule, it was fatal if this bluff was ever called. Charles Dundas, writing of the Kitui Kamba in 1913, noted that 'nothing makes one more helpless against him than his discovery that your threat is an empty one'.[24] And, in the years leading up to independence, possibly one of the problems facing the administrator was that not only were there new and effective rivals emerging in his district but that, as a result, 'bluff-prestige' no longer adequately operated the levers of control.

In working the levers of control – chiefs, headmen, tribal police, interpreters, drivers and other local agents, or even tribal opinion generally – administrators, at any stage of the colonial experience, faced a tussle of wills in a world of half-truths, innuendo, feuds, and that all-purpose word, *fitina*.[25] They, in their turn, were subject to considerable local scrutiny, probed for their weaknesses or idiosyncrasies, and tested for their staying power. Most officers were to a varying degree aware of this, and joined in the game with gusto, made more unpredictable in that practically every district in Kenya differed, each having its own marked peculiarities.

To be fully effective in a district, an administrator had to be *en rapport* with his people ('He is their friend and is accessible to both the rich and the poor').[26] This, however, was more easily said than done. In the first place, no one could compel tribesmen to regard an officer as *simpatico*,[27] and, when they did do so, it was for their own mysterious reasons. Second, a great deal depended on individual personalities. Here there was a spectrum that ranged from the chameleon – the administrator who totally sided with 'his' tribe – to the other extreme, totally lacking in any sympathy at all (analogous to the dog, on the old HMV records, busy *not* listening to His Master's Voice). Now for the colonial government, the danger lay in either extreme. A district officer might become over-sympathetic, hence the administration's warnings against the danger of 'Masai-itis' or 'Somali-itis', the chameleon's loss of impartiality in administering his 'pet tribe'.[28] In such circumstances the danger was that an officer ceased to be an imperial agent and became wholly the local representative, expressing only the tribal views to government. The other extreme, though unlikely to fall into this error, was almost certain to be oblivious and indifferent to crucial but hidden discontents, as Kenneth Dundas remarked to John Ainsworth: 'I cannot expect to gain the confidence of my people except I am prepared to listen to their complaints'.[29] The significance of this spectrum lay in the fact that the administrator was the hinge linking policy to action. The manner in which policy was implemented was all important, and could differ sharply according to the administrator's reading (feel) of a local situation, and the degree of local tolerance for any proposed measure.

One small point in this connection needs to be noted. On those many occasions when a general policy was lacking, absence of financial resources being a common cause, there was always scope for local initiative. But the results could, again, be highly personal and uneven. McClure, in Nyeri prior to the First World War, was the first DC there to own a motor car; it was his boast that he had 150 miles of motorable road constructed in the Nyeri district.[30] H. E. Lambert, posted to the Teita hills in the late 1920s, was urged by his PC to smother the hills with carnations which might be sold to the Mombasa housewives. Lambert compromised with cabbages, which travelled better and offered more hope of financial success for the African growers.[31] Personal enthusiasms might switch from building schools to constructing water points, from football fields to women's clubs. Not infrequently, great labour brought no tangible results. At the behest of the medical department thousands of pit latrines were dug in the 1930s but went unused, leading the DC, Meru, to remark sadly upon 'present monuments to an earlier creed [which] serve merely to give new meaning to the expression "the bottomless pit"'.[32]

Despite parochialism (the administrator's first loyalty was his district), the administration was a small and fairly close-knit body. It had a sense of caste, of clannishness,[33] and the bond of common service. In such an atmosphere more was discussed and decided than was ever put on paper. There was often an unspoken consensus of commonly held beliefs that did not require to be spelt out within the privileged circle. And much of the collective experience of the service was not recorded in standing orders but passed on in an evening over a drink.

Certainly there were interminable discussions of this sort. Much of the emphasis was on instinct and pragmatic experience rather than logic, the need to 'play a situation by ear'. The advice varied: 'a noisy and excited crowd is generally harmless, a silent and sullen one is dangerous';[34] 'remember the Secretariat wants peace and quiet, if you must be "go ahead" make sure you do so without expense or trouble'; or the advocate of King Log v King Stork, 'Look, half your decisions are probably wrong, and the other half are unnecessary'; again, 'In each district the new DC has got to have a showdown. Choose your battlefield and bluff will last you to the end of your tour'; 'Remember you rarely learn the full truth about any incident till months later'. Finally, there was the comment of a desperately over-worked DC during a critical period of the early 1950s: 'When in doubt, create a crisis'.[35]

At the same time, within the brotherhood of DOs there was a greater variation in terms of personalities than outsiders appreciated. Individualism verging on eccentricity was not unknown, despite the apparent solidarity of the 'Heavenborn', which white settlers sometimes derided with the hoary joke of 'one district officer who was so stupid that even his fellows noticed it'.[36] Indeed what appeared to outsiders as an over-rigid caste of the Heavenborn, was also a bunch of individualists, bound together by a shared work ethic, and sense of duty.

On occasions, a senior officer would record his experiences in the form of instructions for his young DCs. 'Uncle' Reece provided one such example from his years of service amongst the Somali of the Northern Frontier District. Some of the advice was personal: 'Brightly coloured shirts and jumpers are not appropriate to official duties in this territory ... silent disobedience of orders indicates a thoroughly bad civil servant ... your most important work obviously is travelling on foot ... a slovenly looking person in the bush is usually a tyro ... Most Europeans ... regard criticism of their own men ... as personal criticism of themselves ... all human beings need encouragment ...'.[37] More telling were the warnings to innocent newcomers: 'Interpreters ... are seldom if ever entirely honest and headmen are often ambitious and inclined to say only what is calculated to please when they are not in the presence of their own people',[38] or this sober advice about disobeying orders in an emergency, for officers could be faced by that age-old dilemma, the tension between public duty and private conscience (or judgement):[39] 'If you succeed you get glory and promotion, but if you are unlucky and fail, you are always harshly criticised . . .'.[40] Perhaps most significant was a circular written at the height of the Second World War, which set out the pitfalls of pastoralist administration as Reece saw them:

> As a rule a man who is very pro-Somali or very anti-Somali is a man who does not understand the Somali. The majority of officers who go to Somali countries start by being very pro and then become very anti, and eventually (if they are sensible) they are neither violently one nor the other . . .. Personally I like the Somali. I like his good manners, his manliness, his cleanness, his love of children, and his ability to fight with courage and to endure hardship and to suffer pain. I like his sense of humour and his immense zest and energy which he can put into what he is doing, if it appeals to him.
>
> As always the detribalized people are the most unpleasant members of the tribes, but one tries not to hate them too much . . . .

Reece also struck an almost evangelical note: 'I am now preaching the doctrine that, with education and better feeding, it may be possible so to adapt the qualities of the Somali that he will become one of the most useful inhabitants of Africa'.[41] Colonial paternalism did have its romantic and idealistic side!

To sum up, it is not always possible to discover in the written records of the administrators, though hints appear, especially in some of their handing-over reports, exactly what were their fundamental assumptions. In many instances these were taken for granted and so left unsaid. In other cases the DOs were unaware of them, and acted instinctively. In the corpus of assumptions and beliefs, one must include the two unwritten laws. There was also a confidence that colonialism, or rather the administrators' part in the imperial scheme of things, was 'good', that change must be gradual (though on questions of native custom they could differ as to what should be changed or how swiftly). Most of them also felt that to detribalize without first creating new values to replace the old was both harmful and immoral, and that over the slow decades self-government would come to their charges, but must not be hurried. There was sufficient time left to make a thorough job of transforming African society. But DOs had a curiously ambivalent attitude towards Western values and feared corrupting influences. They were not wholly sure of what they wanted for 'their' people, but it was not a pale imitation of the West.[42]

As a consequence, there was a lack of sympathy and understanding for the urban dwellers and a distrust of the men in trousers. Equally, there was a distrust of other rivals, be they white settlers or other officials, the men in Whitehall or local politicians. A strong element of protective jealousy existed amongst the 'Guardians'. Finally, the two unwritten laws probably applied to the local rulers as much as to the ruled. Administrators at the district level could and did drag their feet if orders from above seemed in their view to be impractical or dangerous. Unrealistic policy could be defeated, or at least deferred, in the bush.

Notes

1. John Buchan, Rede Lecture, 1929 (reprinted in *Men and Deeds*, London 1935).
2. 'They [the Wakamba] provided many pitfalls for the new and inexperienced officer, for whose benefit all the worn-out old civil cases, feuds, and bickerings are served up at the earliest opportunity.' Nairobi Archives (1963 Classification), Machakas Records, MKS 56, Chapter II.
3. Hesitation could lead to disaster as happened at Kolloa in 1950 (see the *Report of the Commission of Inquiry into the Affray at Kolloa*. Government Printer, Nairobi, 1950). Equally dangerous was '*furor africanus*', the sudden red rage that could seize an officer at the end of a long hot day when anger or frustration got the better of his judgement, as, for instance, in the death of Grant, in Narok, in August 1946 and of Elliott in February 1916.
4. Hardinge to Foreign Office, 19 August 1896, FOCP 7095/185.
5. Nairobi Archives, NFD/31. Was this concern with 'prestige' wholly wrong? Note Professor Stone's comment in *The Causes of the English Revolution 1529–1642* (1972), p. 79: 'The most important cause and symptom of the decay of any government or institution is the loss of prestige and respect'.
6. A criticism made by Lobb of the Colonial Office in minuting on the Kisii troubles: CO 533/43/15165, para. 56.
7. See 'Winslow' in C. P. Snow's *The Masters* (Penguin edn, p. 28): 'He's thought to stand a chance of the colonial service if he can scrape a Third. Of course, I'm totally ignorant of these matters, but I can't see why our colonies should need third-class men with some capacity for organised sports'. In fact, their academic record was not necessarily so modest.
8. Cd. 2231: Protectorate Annual Report 1903–04, p. 8 (see also FO 2/839, des 593 of 14 September 1904). However, the development of any personal administration was made infinitely more difficult by the perpetual game of musical chairs over postings between districts.

9. See J. R. MacDonald, *Labour and the Empire* (1907), p. 39, where he comments on the unthinking British imperialist 'trusting the man on the spot – that is his method'.

10. Colonial No. 116 of 1936, p. 85.

11. Although the pioneer administrators had very varied backgrounds, a uniform pattern was established by the time of the First World War. Between 1895 and 1914, approximately 200 men joined the Kenya administration. Of these, I have information on about five-eighths. The overall pattern (taking 200 as the figure) was that a third were university men, and a half from public schools; 1 in 20 were educated outside the UK, 1 in 5 had been in the forces, 1 in 10 had lived at some time in South Africa, 1 in 5 were parsons' sons, 1 in 20 later became governors, but 1 in 9 died whilst serving. See Cashmore, 'District administration in the East Africa Protectorate' (Cambridge Ph.D. thesis (1965); also Heussler, *Yesterday's Rulers* (1963).

12. Sir R. Furse, *Aucuparius*, p. 263: 'the natural African, "the man in the blanket", whom the men we sent out . . . chiefly lived to serve'.

13. The Latins in their colonies seem to have been much more city conscious.

14. CO Minute, CO 533/33/143757 (1907). A sense of old-fasioned etiquette also prevailed, for example, the acting commissioner to the Famine Relief Committee in Mombasa in 1899: 'I would prefer the despatch in manuscript – it is not etiquette to address a personage like Lord Salisbury in a typewritten letter' (Mombasa Provincial Records, 'Demi-Official Correspondence', letter of 29 August 1899).

15. For example, some of the light-hearted administrative verse; see G. H. H. Brown, 'The Golden Road to Habbaswein' where the DC 'sun-kippered, khaki-clad' goes to 'some cool file-stacked office hall' in Nairobi. 'There dwells a Minister who can explain This circular: in hope this may be so I take the Golden Road to Habbaswein', only to be admonished by his PC: 'Seek not excess . . . It will be countermanded by and by'. Also J. S. S. Rowlands' *A Nosegay of Cacti* and his 'But Government is tardigrade'.

16. Ravine Diary, 15 August 1899 (Nairobi, Rift Valley Province Records): 'A circular . . . from headquarters something about titles . . . but I could not understand. I fancy it's all rot though so it doesn't matter'.

17. Lord Cranworth, *A Colony in the Making* (1912), p. 76.

18. Carter Land Commission, 1934. Evidence, Vol. III, p. 3455 (Francis Traill's comments on the European pioneers' individualism.)

19. Mombasa Provincial Archives (subsequently moved to Nairobi), Shelf 75, Ukamba In 1896–1900, Ainsworth to Craufurd, 5 December 1896. See also Lord Lytton's comment in *The Desert and the Green* (1957), p. 220.

20. Nairobi Archives: Central Nyanza, CN/42.

21. Nyeri Annual Report 1915–16 (Nairobi Archives) in which McClure ironically writes: 'The advantages already conferred on the native by government are, no doubt, of considerable value comprising as they do valuable education in the matter of labour . . . by persuading them that temporary discomfort breeds eventual dignity. . . . Admirable as these concessions are it is possible that some more tangible sign of the interest

which Central Government no doubt takes in the natives . . . would still be further appreciated. . . . This might even take the form of the expenditure of some of the public funds on the public.'

22. Note Ainsworth's 1914 memo on the effects of the labour policy: 'We are in danger of losing the confidence of the tribes'. (Nairobi Archives, 'Nandi Confidential File', 20 March 1914).

23. Sir Charles Dundas, *African Crossroads* (1955), pp. 17, 20, 27.

24. C. Dundas, 'History of Kitui', in *JRAI* 42 (1913).

25. Kiswahili = malice, discord, skullduggery, malicious gossip or plotting, slanderous rumours etc. Almost anything going wrong tended to be blamed on *fitina*.

26. Mombasa Provincial Archives, Shelf 20: File 'Administration of Native Reserves'. Hobley's 'Instructions to DCs', approved by the governor, 30 October 1915.

27. The unpredictable reactions of the host community are delightfully sketched in E. Waugh's *Men at Arms*, pp. 15–16: 'He was not loved, Guy knew, either by his household or the town . . . Grafin von Gluck, who spoke no word of Italian and lived in undisguised concubinage with her butler, was simpatica. Mrs Garry was simpatica, who distributed Protestant tracts, interfered with the fishermen's methods of killing octopus and filled her house with stray cats . . .

Guy's Uncle Peregrine, a bore of international repute . . . was considered molto simpatico . . .'

28. A term used by Hobley in his 1915 Instructions (see note 26).

29. K. Dundas to J. Ainsworth, 8 August 1909 (Nairobi Archives, CN/42).

30. H. R. McClure, *Land Travel and Seafaring* (nd), p. 129.

31. HEL to THRC (1964). Some day, something must also be written about that informal institution, 'the goat bag'.

32. Meru Annual Report, 1939, pp. 40–41 (Nairobi Archives).

33. Note the young DO in 1953 who was informed by his first DC that the administration was 'a Brotherhood' ('And never use the word ("Admin"!'). A similar attitude was observed in Southern Rhodesia by A. K. H. Weinrich, *Black and White Elites in rural Rhodesia* (Manchester University Press 1973), p. 51, where one DC spoke of his colleagues as 'my brothers'.

34. H. R. McClure, pp. cit., p. 81, and, more recently, see the comment in Cmnd 4964/1972 (Pearce Commission), para. 396.

35. See Cashmore, op. cit., (cited note 11), p. 55, note 3.

36. Or Gethin's description of a young DO, an Irishman, nicknamed 'Puss in Boots', 'a typical official, most of his brains were in his boots' (Matson Papers, Gethin Ms, p. 31).

37. Nairobi Archives: NFD/31, extracts from various circulars of the Officer in Charge, Northern Frontier District in the 1940s. Reece (subsequently Sir Gerald Reece) later became governor of the British Somaliland Protectorate.

38. Ibid., Circular 16/1945.

39. A dilemma well put by Sir Edmund Verney in the seventeenth century: 'I have eaten his (the King's) bread and served him near thirty years . . .

and choose rather to lose my life (which I am sure I shall do) to preserve and defend those things that are against my conscience to preserve and defend'.

40. NFD/31, Circular, 18/1945.
41. Ibid., Circular 6/1942.
42. For other recent views of the men on the spot see *The Transfer of Power* ed. A. H. M. Kirk-Greene (Oxford 1979) and *The Desert's Dusty Face* by Charles Chenevix Trench (Blackwood 1964), or John Butter's *Uncivil Servant* (Edinburgh 1989).

7

MEDICINE AND EMPIRE:
The Funding of Sleeping Sickness Research in the Belgian Congo[1]

Maryinez Lyons

Today more money is spent researching the trypanosome than any other pathogenic parasite.[2] The trypanosome is the parasite which causes trypanosomiasis, or African sleeping sickness, a disease of both animals and humans. There are two forms of the human disease: *gambiense*, a slower-developing, more chronic form found throughout western and central Africa, and, *rhodesiense*, a virulent and much faster-acting form found in the savannas of eastern and southern Africa. There are other important diseases caused by parasites such as malaria, filariasis, leishmaniasis and schistosomiasis which account for appalling morbidity and mortality in Africa, so why is there such massive investment in the trypanosome? Part of the answer lies in the history of sleeping sickness which, as we shall see, was bound up with the history of tropical medicine itself.

Today, the trypanosome is of particular interest to molecular biologists researching immunology. Its unique ability to undergo rapid antigenic changes in response to antibodies produced by infected people and animals makes it especially valuable in this rapidly developing field. A molecular biologist at Stanford University, John Boothroyd, recently said that 'If the number of investigators working in a field is any indication of its importance, the study of African trypanosomes must be ranked high', and he explained that the field is still 'expanding very rapidly'.[3] The emphasis of this research, however, is very much upon the pathogen and not the disease it causes, nor the victims who suffer from it.

Sleeping sickness, as an insect-borne parasitic disease, consolidated the dominant tropical diseases paradigm early this century, it has been remarked.[4] Almost 80 years ago metropolitan scientists moved in and out of Uganda, alienating local medical officers. They regarded sleeping sickness as 'their disease', but local medics were disgusted with the lack of regard on the part of the scientists for prevention and treatment. It is worth noting that despite great investment of funds in basic research, the treatment for African sleeping sickness remains archaic, while there is still no treatment for the American form of the disease. According to one eminent specialist, 'We are in a state of total ignorance', still relying upon drugs used in the late 1940s when the first really effective ones appeared.[5] 'There is almost no work on drug development going on [for the reason] that such drugs would not be profitable ... the people living in trypanosome-infested countries are frequently desperately poor'.[6] With so little prospect for profit, pharmaceutical firms simply have not been motivated to investment in research until very recently. These facts are common knowledge among all those working on sleeping sickness in Africa today.[7] In 1976 the World Health Organisation (WHO) launched a programme to encourage research on six tropical diseases, one of which was sleeping sickness.

There have been no significant advances in the chemotherapy for this disease for nearly half a century. WHO reported in 1985 that the drugs available were grossly inadequate.[8] For instance, suramin, currently used to treat *gambiense* sleeping sickness in the early stages, was introduced in the Belgian Congo well over half a century ago, in 1916. Clearly, we are still in the dark ages of treatment in the primary stages of sleeping sickness.

The first drug used was an organic arsenical, called atoxyl. The great German chemist, Paul Ehrlich, experimented with the drug as early as 1903, and two years later it was developed for clinical use by Wolferstan Thomas at the new Liverpool School of Tropical Medicine. In fact, the science of specific chemotherapy, or 'magic bullets', evolved in connection with the search for trypanocidal drugs. Atoxyl was so named because, within the spectrum of arsenical compounds, it was considered to be reasonably non-toxic to humans. Nevertheless, it contained 38 per cent arsenic, and soon after it was administered to Africans in the Belgian Congo and Tanganyika, an unfortunate side effect was noticed by researchers. Atoxyl caused the optic nerve to atrophy, so it blinded about 30 of those Africans who received it. In spite of this dreadful 'side effect', its use continued in the Belgian Congo, as well as in the French colonies, well into the 1920s.[9] Melarsoprol, the drug currently used for the advanced stages of sleeping sickness when the central nervous system is affected, is far less toxic than was atoxyl. Even so, this is a difficult drug to administer and it too causes serious side effects in 5 per cent of the patients who suffer nausea, diarrhoea, vomiting and abdominal pain. It can damage the liver, and for another 1–5 per cent of the patients, injections of melarsoprol are fatal.[10]

To add to this depressing scenario, in recent years sleeping sickness has been on the increase. WHO estimates there are currently some 50 million people at risk, with approximately 20,000 cases appearing each year. Serious epidemics have been underway in Sudan, Uganda and Zaïre in recent years. In 1988 in Zaïre alone there were 11,000 new cases, while 7,000 were recorded in 1986,[11] and early in 1989 Dr David Molyneux said that 5,000 new cases were reported in Zaïre in 1988 and 8,000 cases in Uganda. The disease is greatly underreported according to the WHO (perhaps only 10 per cent of victims are known), so the numbers are only indications of the true scale of affliction. I attended a trypanosomiasis meeting of the British Society of Parasitology in September 1987, an impressive gathering of several hundred tryps specialists, most of whom were researching the parasite, not the disease. Yet, many of the scientists appeared surprised when Dr David Smith of the Liverpool School of Tropical Medicine gave his eyewitness account of the terrible epidemic taking place in Uganda. His slides, vividly illustrated the terrible plight of victims, who, if left untreated, will all die. I overheard a lab scientist exclaim, 'Gee, that really brings home the human dimension'. With this disease, it seems that the parasite is more important than the patient.[12] With so much funding going into research on the parasite and so little going into the therapy, the history of sleeping sickness reveals some of the broader political and economic issues involved in scientific and medical research.

I am not going to discuss the role of the trypanosome in the new and exciting field of molecular biology and its importance to pure research or to immunology except to say that trypanosomes can be thought of at present as the 'white mice' of parasites; nor am I going to enter into debate regarding the relative merits of pure versus applied research. It is important to note, however, that in the past, as now, scientists who were keen to pursue pure research were guided by the needs and, most importantly, the funding of the agencies employing them.

The early history of sleeping sickness research has a political dimension as well, for it illustrates the close relationship which existed between tropical medicine and European imperialism in Africa. This chapter focuses upon two aspects of that history: its international quality, and events in the Belgian Congo between 1900 and 1930.

Tropical medicine and imperialism

In the late 1890s, Patrick Manson helped to lay the foundation of a new medical speciality with his definition of tropical diseases. They were, he explained, geographically confined to warm climates and most often they were insect-borne parasitical diseases, the chief example of which was trypanosomiasis, or sleeping sickness.[13] He was the first to show that insects could transmit diseases to humans with his studies on filariasis. Manson's view of tropical medicine became widely accepted after the discovery by Ronald Ross, in India, that the parasite which causes malaria is transmitted by the anopheles mosquito. Manson's ideas continued for most of this century to influence greatly the new fields of tropical medicine and parasitology. Perhaps more importantly, for many researchers, tropical medicine and parasitology were one and the same thing.

Sleeping sickness was one of the main subjects in the new professional journals for tropical medicine, the *Transactions of Tropical Medicine and Hygiene* and the *Annals of Tropical Medicine and Parasitology*. In the *Annals*, for instance, 25–50 per cent of the first seven volumes (1907–15) were about sleeping sickness while the remainder of the articles focused on protozoology and helminology. Over 60 years later, in 1987, 80 per cent of the articles still concentrated on these subjects.[14]

Tropical medicine from the beginning was intimately connected to imperial politics. In 1899 Joseph Chamberlain, the British secretary of state for the colonies, made explicit the relationship between the new field of tropical medicine and overseas expansion when he said, 'The study of tropical diseases is a means of promoting imperial policy'[15] and 'The pioneers of tropical medicine were [to be] put on a par with Empire builders like Raffles and Rhodes'.[16] Soon after the turn of the century, most colonial powers perceived one disease in particular to be a major obstacle to their plans for Africa: 'The elucidation of [sleeping sickness]', explained a researcher in 1905, 'has a large bearing upon the development and prosperity of Africa'.[17] It must be understood that the main health concern at the time was the protection of Europeans in hot climates, a concern shared by all colonizing powers in Africa as elsewhere. Many early scientific researchers agreed with Manson that the future of imperialism lay with the microscope.

It was no coincidence that 1899 also saw the establishment of the two British schools of tropical medicine, at Liverpool and London. The creation of both schools was very much a result of the pragmatic concern of both government and the business community to protect their agents in difficult climates. The Liverpool school was founded mainly through the efforts and support of that city's commercial and trading sector led by Sir Alfred Jones. Among his many business interests was the Elder Dempster Shipping Line which plied along the west African coast. Chairman of the African Section of the Chamber of Commerce, Jones was a principal figure in the establishment of the School of Tropical Medicine and he was the first Chairman of the Board. He also happened to be a personal friend of King Leopold II of Belgium. The story of Leopold's exploitation of the Congo Free State between 1885 and 1908 is one of extreme brutality to the Africans and their land. Yet, in spite of much publicity of that brutality from 1904 onwards, one critic of Jones reported that 'Posterity will forget his attitude on the Congo and only remember that he was a powerful captain of industry, a man of great energy and the creator of the Liverpool School of Tropical Medicine'.[18]

Leopold II and African sleeping sickness

King Leopold was an astute business man and a capitalist on a grand scale. Exhibiting what J. S. Galbraith has called a kind of 'Afromania'[19], Leopold suggested in 1885 that the 'great powers' of Europe meet in Berlin to divide among themselves most of sub-Saharan Africa. Europeans had been conducting business along the west coast of Africa for centuries but the Berlin Conference systematized their presence with official boundaries and agreed zones of influence. While previously the trade had been more blatantly profit oriented, around the turn of the century European business enterprises in Africa were accompanied increasingly by platitudinous expressions of philanthropic motives. A common example of this was the view that Europeans were engaged upon a 'civilizing mission'. Such moralizing of the work ethic and its role in improving and uplifting the lower orders was not limited to colonized Africans but was addressed equally to the new proletariat emerging in rapidly industrializing Europe.[20] Thus, the colonial powers regarded themselves as bringing to the dark continent the benefits of European or Western civilization. An important adjunct of the new progressive order was, naturally, the new bio-medical science. The main attractions in Africa for most Europeans were the cheap or even free raw materials in the early Belgian Congo, like ivory, rubber and gold. In addition, there was the anticipation of an equally cheap (or free) and plentiful labour supply for European enterprises.

As a shrewd businessman, Leopold was not without perception and foresight and he established a precedent for later colonial administrations by his grasp of the importance of tropical medicine and medical provision as essential features in both the success and the justification of the colonial enterprise. His decision to invite British scientists from the Liverpool School of Tropical Medicine in 1902 to investigate sleeping sickness in his African state must be understood in this wider political context.

One of the Liverpool scientists, John Lancelot Todd, researching in the Congo Free State in 1905, explained that Leopold is:

> absolute sovereign here and this is not a Belgian colony in the proper sense of the word. The King of the Belgians made the state, and it is practically his. He must be a very smart man indeed to have made use of his position as a Ruler to so successfully exploit the country. He is boss of the state both as ruler and in the same way as some of the big mine owners out West are sovereigns of certain towns . . .

Todd possessed a lively understanding of the political nature of scientific research. In August 1906, he along with two other scientists from the Liverpool school, Rupert Boyce and Ronald Ross, were invited to visit the Belgian king. The young and ambitious Todd later reported: 'After we'd finished telling the old man how to make the Congo healthy and promised to administer a lovely coat of whitewash to his character in the eyes of the English, he created Boyce, Ross and myself officers of his Order of Leopold II . . .'[21]

There are many examples of contemporary awareness of the relationship between tropical medicine and European imperialism. For instance, in the 1920s, Andrew Balfour's publication of 'Medical Science as a Factor in Imperial Development, 1870–1921' and 'Malaria as an Enemy of the British Empire' illustrates this. In 1924 Todd explained in clear terms that 'medicine is now more than the healing of the sick and the protection of the well. Through its control of disease, medicine has come to be a world factor of limitless power'.[22]

A few years later the language was somewhat more restrained and the emphasis slightly changed to reflect new considerations of colonial 'development', but the connections between tropical medicine, sleeping sickness and European imperialism in Africa were quite clear. In 1928 at the international conference on sleeping sickness organized by the League of Nations, the British under-secretary of state for the colonies explained that:

The various European powers have undertaken the great responsibility of penetrating and establishing their administration throughout the greater part of the Dark Continent. They have found nature bountiful in her resources, but guarding those resources with formidable armaments in the way of malaria, yellow fever, blackwater fever, filariasis and sleeping sickness. From the wider point of view, from which I, as a lay administrator, must look upon it, animal trypanosomiasis in the British dependencies is still a tremendous factor in stopping the development of Africa.

And in 1943 the director of the Congo medical service emphasized the necessity to:

see medical provision, not as a justification for colonisation, but as a justification after the fact of colonisation. It is a compensation offered to the natives for certain misfortunes that colonisation brought them . . . the spread of certain scourges, like the fearsome sleeping sickness . . . the native population has suffered and diminished because of us.

Sleeping sickness became inextricably linked to public health policy and medical research in much of early colonial Africa.

Until the outbreak of the Second World War, the 'great powers' of Europe who were consolidating their colonial holdings and attempting to rationalize them in both the economic and the moral senses were convinced that the new field of tropical medicine and research into sleeping sickness were vital keys to the potential riches of their newly acquired African territories.

Sleeping sickness research: tropical medicine and international prestige

Research into sleeping sickness was from the beginning very much an international affair with a great deal of competition, and collaboration, among both the individual scientists and among nations. By the turn of the century, there existed a well-established forum for collaboration and the exchange of health information among European nations in the form of the international sanitary conference which began in 1852 and continued throughout the nineteenth century. The original impetus for those conferences was the great epidemics, especially cholera, which punctuated the century and, with no drugs, the emphasis was decidedly upon sanitation meaning isolation, separation and segregation. From 1903, 'colonial hygiene' was included in the conferences, and that year the Belgian scientist, Emile Van Campenhout, reported on sleeping sickness in the Congo.

At the turn of the century the new field of tropical medicine presented the opportunity for bright young men to gain considerable prestige at the international level. While researching in the Congo Free State in 1903, Todd confessed to his family that, 'Tryps are a big thing and if we have luck, I may make a name yet!'[23] According to J. N. P. Davies, 'the discovery of the cause of sleeping sickness was one of the greatest triumphs of tropical medicine'.[24] But it was a triumph tainted by unpleasant aspects of the keen competition often prevailing among scientific researchers. So intense was the competition and so great the potential for prestige that the history of sleeping sickness research contains one of the more notorious examples of a scientific wrangle. That was the great Castellani–Bruce controversy which arose as the international scientific community early this century took sides over which of these two researchers, the Italian or the

Englishman, should receive credit for being the first to establish the aetiology of sleeping sickness.[25]

Agencies involved

A variety of agencies and institutions became involved in the research. In Great Britain the colonial, foreign and war offices, the Royal Army Medical Corps, the Royal Society and the new schools of tropical medicine were all keen to enter the field. In 1896, after David Bruce discovered the relationship between tsetse flies and the animal form of trypanosomiasis (*nagana*), the Royal Society established a special Tsetse Fly Sub-committee. In the 1920s further committees and commissions were established to investigate sleeping sickness and to co-ordinate results.

The situation was considerably different in Belgium where the African holding was very much the private enterprise of a businessman and his colleagues. King Leopold and his business associates initiated and funded scientific research in the Congo Free State until his death in 1909. For instance, the laboratory at Leopoldville was established privately with funding from the grandly named Belgian Society for Colonial Studies, which was in effect a commercial company very deeply involved in the economic exploitation of the territory. In 1908, a year before his death, Leopold had ceded his state to the Belgian parliament and for the next half century the Congo was administered from Brussels by that body which set research priorities and allocated major funding. Until 1960 and political independence, the private and voluntary sectors played quite significant roles in both scientific endeavour and medical provision in the Congo, as indeed they did in Belgium itself.

An important example of international collaboration in sleeping sickness research was the jointly administered Belgian-French Permanent International African Office for Tsetse and Trypanosomiasis which was established at Leopoldville in 1948. There were meetings nearly every year thereafter at which research findings and policy matters were discussed among the representatives of most African territories affected.

It was not unusual for national agencies to employ the services of foreign scientists and it was certainly the norm to expect collaboration within the international scientific community. Yet patterns emerged based upon old cultural and historical ties. At the outset the Belgians found it quite natural to look to the German and French scientific communities, and much of the early Belgian data was published in journals in those countries. Of particular importance to research on trypanosomiasis chemotherapy was the collaboration between the Belgian scientists, Jerome Rodhain and Anton Broden, and the great German scientist, Paul Ehrlich.

The first truly international health organization was of course the health section of the League of Nations. The First World War and influenza pandemic stimulated international co-operation on disease and public health. The league was founded in 1920 and created a European Health Committee which became its official health organization. After the Second World War and the formation of the United Nations, the WHO took over the activities of the league's Health Office which had concerned itself with sleeping sickness research. Sleeping sickness was also a concern of the Food and Agriculture Organisation (FAO), the United Nations Development Programme (UNDP) and UNESCO.

Sleeping sickness conferences

Between 1907 and 1930 there were nine major, international meetings on the subject of African sleeping sickness, held in England, Switzerland, France and Angola. The Society of Tropical Medicine was formed in January 1907 at the British Colonial Office, with Patrick Manson as the first president and Ronald Ross the first vice president. The Colonial Office, pressed by the Advisory Committee for the Tropical Diseases Research Fund, organized a Sleeping Sickness Conference the folowing June.[26] Although the League of Nations was the venue of the first official international health organization, in fact the 1907 British Colonial Office conference was the first attempt to bring together representatives of all the nations with interests in Africa to discuss the disease.

After the First World War, the league set up an International Commission on Human Trypanosomiasis with a committee of experts to look into the problem.[27] The four experts met in September 1924 at the London School of Tropical Medicine to formulate their recommendations. National chauvinism remained. In spite of attempts by some to break away from narrower national interests, many scientists remained keenly jealous of research within their own colonies. For example, in 1924 Van Campenhout warned the league not to send again independent teams of scientists to study sleeping sickness in Africa, as the Royal Society had done in 1902 and 1903 with its commissions to Uganda. Instead, suggested the Belgian, it would be more satisfactory for scientists resident in a colony to conduct investigations. Any interested governments could send their experts on temporary attachments to local laboratories. However, added the Belgian, turning to the important subject of funding, the league should allocate finance for three to five years for all of the studies of the disease.[28] Clearly, Van Campenhout was concerned to retain control over scientific results which he considered to be an important and potentially prestigious national asset. Nevertheless, he expressed the widely held view that funding for that research should derive from international sources.

The First International Sleeping Sickness Conference was organized by the league in May 1925 in London, followed by a second one in Paris in November 1928.[29] Much discussion concerned clarification of the precise role and function of scientists researching sleeping sickness. In contrast to Van Campenhout's more nationalistic view, it was generally held that research teams should be international in character and visit a selected region affected by the disease. After much debate, Entebbe, Uganda, was chosen as the headquarters for the League of Nations commission. (As an aside, it is interesting to note how today Entebbe has once again surfaced as a focus of the efforts of the international community to research a devastating disease, this time, AIDS.) The league saw its role as a facilitator helping to co-ordinate research within the international community and assisting to communicate results. To achieve this, international guidelines were issued *vis-à-vis* sleeping sickness research and control programmes. Sleeping sickness was an important aspect of the development of agencies and mechanisms for the international co-ordination and co-operation necessary to control diseases which, after all, observe no national borders.

Expeditions, documentation and information

The early years of sleeping sickness research formed an important chapter in the history of tropical medicine. Motivated by political and economic needs, national governments looked to their scientists to solve problems in the new colonial territories, and each national group was alert to the activities and findings of the others. But by the early

1920s, it can be said that genuine international co-operation was very much on the agenda.

The great epidemic in Uganda, which between 1901 and 1905 had killed some 300,000 people, was much publicized at the time and was the occasion of the first major sleeping sickness expedition. In 1902 Patrick Manson, by then medical advisor to the Colonial Office, urgently requested the Royal Society to send out a team of researchers. In the same year, the Liverpool School of Tropical Medicine had its sleeping sickness researchers in place on the west coast of Africa, in Senegambia, where another epidemic was underway.

'Expedition' expresses the wider connotations of these scientific enquiries, as research in the rapidly growing fields of tropical medicine and parasitology took scientists far from their urban laboratories to 'exotic' regions of the globe and immersed them in the adventure of safari in the bush. The satirical magazine, *Punch*, expressed it as follows in September 1903:

> Men of Science, you that dare
> Beard the microbe in his lair,
> Tracking through the jungly thickness
> Afric's germ of Sleeping Sickness,
> Hear, oh hear my parting plea,
> *Send a microbe home to me!*

By 1930 nearly 20 major scientific expeditions had investigated sleeping sickness in Africa, 8 before the First World War. They were often international in composition with funding deriving frequently from a variety of public and private sources. The League of Nations' expert committee on sleeping sickness advised and supervised the international team of researchers based at Entebbe. From 1926 on, researchers representing England, Belgium, Germany, France and Portgual made field trips into Uganda, Tanganyika, the Belgian Congo and Kenya. Each colony was already involved in some sort of campaign to combat the disease. Competition remained. In 1926, a Belgian researcher was pleased to explain how proud he had been to show the English what the Belgians were doing about sleeping sickness in Congo. He added that the Belgian effort was 'one hundred times more than they were doing'![30]

Documentation

Massive documentation was generated by the research. Some was produced under the aegis of specialist institutions and agencies while many results were published in the evolving specialist journals of tropical medicine. The Sleeping Sickness Bureau was established in 1908, in London. The bureau was supposed to be an international effort but that did not work, so Lord Elgin, the secretary for the colonies, established it as a British institution. By 1912 four volumes had appeared of the *Bulletin of the Sleeping Sickness Bureau*, which eventually became, and remains to the present time, the *Tropical Diseases Bulletin* of the Bureau of Hygiene and Tropical Diseases, based at the London School of Hygiene and Tropical Medicine. Other publications on the disease included the reports of the Royal Society Sleeping Sickness Commission (1903–19); the Liverpool School's *Memoir* series; and the League of Nations reports.

Over two decades after the first flurry of response to human sleeping sickness in Africa, a significant portion of the international scientific community, including the national governments which supported this flurry, still maintained that the disease posed the gravest threat to the economic and social development of Africa. In 1923, the French scientist Gustave Martin reported to the League of Nations that:

> It would be of course inaccurate to hold sleeping sickness exclusively responsible for the depopulation and mortality in countries where nutrition is often inadequate and always defective, and where the bad conditions, diseases of the lungs, syphilis, malaria, intestinal parasitism, physical debility and lack of stamina are the causes of a terrible morbidity, but trypanosomiasis is the first and most important of the endemic diseases to be contended with.

In 1965 a Belgian scientist repeated the warning that 'The African trypanosomiases do not represent a threat like the other diseases, they constitute the calamity of Africa'.[31]

For many decades sleeping sickness either dominated or remained a high priority on tropical medicine research agendas in both the international and individual colonial scientific communities. Institutions proliferated in direct response to the increasing emphasis given to the one disease. Research can generate its own momentum as new participants are attracted not only by the problems to be solved but by the funding made available for that research. It was certainly true that funding was made available for further research into sleeping sickness.

Tropical medicine in the Belgian Congo

By the late 1930s, the Belgians had established at home and abroad a total of 13 research laboratories and 3 major research institutes which until the Second World War concentrated primarily upon sleeping sickness. Public and private finance was involved and the larger enterprises such as the railway and mining companies established and staffed their own scientific institutions. The Red Cross, religious missions and both the Catholic and Free Universities of Belgium, as well as other charity organizations, established their own research centres as well as medical delivery systems.

The laboratory at Leopoldville became over time an important sleeping sickness hospital and research centre. It remains today an significant facility in Kinshasa, the capital of Zaïre. Two Zaïrian and two Belgian doctors in co-operation with a tropical medicine foundation (FOMETRO) maintain a research and surveillance programme for sleeping sickness in Zaïre, so continuing over 80 years this centre's focus on the disease.

Research Expeditions

The first major expedition to study sleeping sickness in the Congo arose from the concern of Leopold II that his private state might be the scene of a disastrous epidemic like the one in Uganda. There was still no specialist institution for tropical medicine in Belgium in 1902 so, while the Belgian scientific community collaborated with German and French scientists, the king used his personal business and commercial connections. He was intimately involved in the commercial activities of Liverpool and a close personal friend of Alfred Jones. Since Jones had been involved recently in the establishment of the Liverpool School of Tropical Medicine, it was unsurprising that Leopold turned to that school for assistance. We have here a good example of the complex relations pertaining among the political, commerical and scientific communities of the time. In 1902 Leopold asked the school to send a team of tropical experts to research sleeping sickness in his private state. The expedition was heavily subsidized by the king who, in addition, contributed major funding to the Liverpool school. Other major expeditions followed to research the epidemiology, pathology, and chemotherapy of the disease and possible public health and control programmes.

Institutionalization of sleeping sickness missions

By the 1930s programmes to research and combat the disease were institutionalized, with a whole industry of scientific researchers, health workers and a public health programme. The latter had become, by the 1930s, almost impossible to control because of its sheer scale and entrenched nature. In 1929 and 1930 the attention focused upon sleeping sickness caused some researchers and practitioners to complain about the 'creaking bureaucracy' and 'cumbersome' nature of the special campaign against this one disease. In 1938, it was reported that 'a vast organization works against sleeping sickness ...'. That year, the itinerant survey teams examined more than five million Congolese. Sleeping sickness had generated a scientific and medical response on such a scale that attempts to monitor that response were extremely difficult. In classic style, the focus upon a single disease had resulted in a vertical campaign to the detriment of other important public health problems as widespread and basic as malnutrition, infant mortality and the enormous morbidity caused by other endemic diseases such as measles and malaria. It was not until the late 1930s that the colonial medical programme began to respond to these wider issues.

Conclusions

This survey of some of the factors involved in the early history of African sleeping sickness research has drawn attention to its international aspect. From the beginning, there was a political dimension involved. Sleeping sickness and the scientific response to it were related to the development of the speciality of tropical medicine. In the Belgian Congo, enormous attention was devoted to this one disease for over three decades.

In 1976, WHO set up its *Special Programme for Research and Training in Tropical Diseases* (TDR), and the trypanosomiases became one of the six major endemic diseases targeted, along with: malaria, schistosomiasis, filariasis (including onchocerciasis), leishmaniases and leprosy. Important new developments include diagnostic techniques and a drug for advanced sleeping sickness. Yet, today, 50 million people are at risk with the trypanosomiases while only five to ten million have access to some protection and treatment.

Notes

1. This chapter is based upon work more fully set out in *The colonial disease: a social history of sleeping sickness in Northern Zaïre, 1900–1940* Cambridge University Press, forthcoming.
2. Kenneth Warren, personal communication, 1988 (former director of Health Sciences Division, Rockefeller Foundation).
3. John Boothroyd, 'Scrutinizing sleeping sickness', *Science* 226 (November 1984), 956.
4. M. Worboys, 'Science and British imperialism, 1895–1940', D. Phil thesis, University of Sussex (1979), p. 121.
5. David Smith, Liverpool School of Tropical Medicine, lecture at London school on 20 April 1989. With no SF, use suramin for both forms of the disease or pentamadine for *gambiense*. With CSF, use melarsoprol and suramin.
6. Boothroyd, op. cit., p. 959.
7. L. S. Goodwin, personal communication. 'Chemotherapy and tropical disease: the problem and the challenge' in (ed.) M. Hooper *Chemotherapy of Tropical Diseases*, (Chichester 1987), pp. 1–18.
8. World Health Organisation. UNDP/World Bank/WHO Special Programme for Research and Training in Tropical Diseases. *Tropical Disease Research*, Seventh Programme Report (1985).
9. MAEAA 4404.170, 10 December 1925. Dr A. Broden explained that its use had been abandoned because of its toxicity and lack of stability in the tropics.
10. Dr L. S. Goodwin, The Wellcome Trust.
11. David Molyneux, lecture at London School of Hygiene and Tropical Medicine, 27 April 1988.
12. Dr David Smith, 27 April 1988.
13. Michael Worboys, 'The emergence and early development of parasitology' in K. S. Warren and J. Z. Bowers (eds), *Parasitology: a Global Perspective* (New York 1983), pp. 1–18.
14. K. S. Warren, ibid: 25 per cent of articles in first volume were on trypanosomiasis in both *Transactions* and *Annals*, while over the next six volumes of *Annals*, the percentages ranged from 25 to 50.
15. Lesley Doyal, *The Political Economy of Health*, p. 241.
16. Michael Worboys, 'Tropical medicine and colonial imperialism, 1895–1914' in *Science and British Colonial Imperialism, 1895–1940*, Ph.D. thesis, University of Sussex (April 1979), p. 99.

17. Dr Louis Sambon, quoted in 'Tropical Medicine and the Congo State', *West Africa* 22 (August 1905), p. 195.
18. E. D. Morel in *History of the Congo Reform Movement* J. Stengers and Wm. Roger Louis (eds), (1968), p. 50.
19. J. S. Galbraith, 'Gordon, MacKinnon and Leopold: the scramble for Africa, 1876–84', *Victorian Studies* 14 (1971).
20. William J. Samarin, *The Black Man's Burden: African Colonial Labor on the Congo and Ubangi Rivers, 1880–1900* (London: Westview Press, 1989), p. 12.
21. Bridget T. Fialkowski, *John L. Todd 1876–1949: Letters* (Quebec 1977): 23 and 27 August 1906, Brussels.
22. J. L. Todd 'Tropical medicine, 1898–1924', 25th-year commemorative talk for the United Fruit Company.
23. Todd to brother, in Fialkowski, op. cit., 8 July 1903.
24. J. N. P. Davies, 'The cause of sleeping sickness? Entebbe 1902–03', *East African Medical Journal* 39 (March 1962), p. 81.
25. Ibid., pp. 81–99.
26. MAEAA AE 321. 2 May 1907. Arthur Hardinge to Chevalier de Cuvelier (Brussels).
27. The experts were: Andrew Balfour of the Wellcome Bureau of Scientific Research representing Britain; Emile Van Campenhout who was director of public health at the Ministry of Colonies representing Belgium; Gustave Martin, chief medical officer of French African territories; and A. G. Bagshaw from the Tropical Diseases Bureau.
28. MAEAA 4461.56. 1924, Emile Van Campenhout.
29. Representatives came from Great Britain, France, Portugal, Spain, Italy and Belgium.
30. MAEAA 4461.228, 28 November 1926, L. Van Hoof, Entebbe to E. Van Campenhout.
31. F. M. J. C. Nevens, 'Projet de plan general de l'organisation de la lutte contra les trypanosomiases en Afrique', *Bulletin of the Academie Royal des Sciences d'Outre-Mer 17* (1965), p. 7.

8

WAR AND THE ORIGINS OF THE GOLD COAST COCOA MARKETING BOARD, 1939–40

David Fieldhouse

Much has been written about the origins and utility of marketing boards in Africa. This chapter is intended merely to provide some revisionary detail on the genesis of the Gold Coast Cocoa Marketing Board, the parent of all marketing boards in tropical Africa, during its first year of operation, from 1939 to 1940.[1]

The official account of the creation of state marketing of cocoa was given in the White Paper of September 1944.[2] That document described the origin and rationale of state purchasing in the following brief and bland statement:

> From the outbreak of war, His Majesty's Government has guaranteed the purchase of the total cocoa production of the British West African Colonies ... The merchant firms themselves realised the necessity for this action on the part of His Majesty's Government and their co-operation assisted in the smooth working of the scheme.[3]

While strictly true, these statements are economical with the truth. It will be shown here that the cocoa control was not imposed at the start of the war on merely acquiescent merchants, that there is no reason to think the British government had any initial plan to set it up, and that it was the merchant firms, in alliance with the Colonial Office, which succeeded, in pursuit of their distinct but momentarily coincidental interests, in persuading the Ministry of Food and the Treasury to establish and pay for such a system.

The roots of the story, of course, lie earlier, in the 1930s, and more particularly in the Gold Coast cocoa hold-up of 1937–8. That story cannot be recounted here; but the logical starting point of later developments must be the report of the Nowell Commission of September 1938, which was to be the point of reference of most later thinking on the matter.[4]

After investigating several causes of the refusal of Gold Coast cocoa producers to sell their cocoa to the 'Agreement' firms, whose pool had reduced prices in response to a dramatic drop in the world market price in 1937, the three commissioners and their secretary spent a month in the Gold Coast, ten days in Nigeria and four days in London taking evidence from all interested parties. Their general aim was not to pass judgement on those concerned in the hold-up but to discover some device by which, in future, African producers could be sure of getting a fair payment for their cocoa and so have no incentive to mount further potentially dangerous protest movements. More specifically, as they put it in their report, they hoped:

- to remove various undesirable features of the marketing system;
- to strengthen the economic position and morale of producers in relation to the buyers;
- to recognize the legitimate interests of both the African community and the shippers;
- to maintain free competition in the purchase of the cocoa crop; and
- to avoid unnecessary expense in marketing.[5]

These were admirable objectives, but taken together they ruled out many considered solutions, for example: fixing marketing centres and licensing buyers and middlemen; imposing export quotas on buyers; setting up a monopolistic cartel of buyers ('Cocoa Union Ltd') with fixed seasonal prices and a fixed commission to the company as buyer; Sir Ofori Atta's proposed Gold Coast Farmers' Federation, which would have been a cartel of producers to bargain with the buyers; and finally price fixing by the government (because a colonial government could not take the risk in a speculative market, and in such a market prices could not be accurately predicted).[6]

Instead the commissioners proposed setting up a statutory association of all cocoa producers whose function and right would be 'to assemble and sell on their behalf the entire crop'.[7] All producers would be organized in local groups of about 500, each with its own committee. Buyers could buy cocoa only from the association at its local selling points. They would buy from the association, not the individual producer or his group, and the association would pay each group for its produce on the basis of an average price, calculated by pooling the proceeds of all cocoa sales during an appropriate period, deducting a levy for such things as operating expenses and reserves, and dividing the remaining sum by the number of tons sold. It would be a matter of expediency whether short or long pool periods were used.

The commissioners claimed that their scheme would provide three main benefits: to producers, by strengthening their bargaining position, while maintaining competition among buyers to ensure maximum prices; to buying firms, by ending 'indirect forms of competition', making advances unnecessary and 'In general, cocoa buying would be rendered less speculative, expensive and laborious'. Other desirable consequences might be that the Gold Coast could avoid hold-ups, Africans would be educated in commercial matters, and employment would be provided for literate Africans. The association, however, would need money: an estimated £300,000 capital for stores and about £250,000 a year for running expenses. The former should come as a grant from colonial development funds or as a low interest loan, while the latter should be covered by the association's profits plus a grant from the colony's export tax on cocoa.[8] In this scenario the co-operative societies, the darlings of colonial administrators, would, however, play no part. They should stop cocoa marketing and concentrate on acting as savings banks and providers of credit to Africans.[9]

That scheme, based explicitly on comparable producer organizations in Britain, New Zealand and Australia,[10] had no effect before 1939. The Nowell Commission proposals found few friends: a local committee worked out that both capital and running costs would be much higher than Nowell had estimated; the firms disliked the proposed producer monopoly; African chiefs found little support from their subordinates; and African middlemen and the co-operative movement both opposed it because it would have deprived them of business. Government officials were divided, some fearing financial disaster if the proposed association miscalculated market trends. As a result nothing happened. The hold-up ended, even though prices did not rise significantly. The average fob price of cocoa exported, which had dropped from £42.2 per ton in 1937 to £17.3 in 1938 was only £18.2 in 1939.[11] At the outbreak of war in September 1939 the Gold Coast and Nigerian cocoa marketing systems were exactly as they had been before the hold-up.

War caught the exporting firms on the hop. As members of the pool they had to buy their share of the total crop, and the 1938–9 Gold Coast crop was a big one. With the important German market closed, uncertainty over the position in neutral countries in Scandinavia, eastern Europe and the Mediterranean, and the problem of shipping to the USA,[12] the most important of all cocoa markets, the exporting firms were in danger of holding huge amounts of an unsaleable crop. In this situation the merchants swallowed their objections to state interference without apparent difficulty and approached the British Government for help. Their appeal is important because it proved to be the genesis of state control of this and other commodity trades and the beginning of the end of the traditional system of produce marketing in West Africa.

It seems clear that at the start of the war the British Government had no plans for controlling colonial production or export of cocoa, or any other produce. Early in September 1939 the Ministry of Food, responsible for the British domestic market, drafted a 'Scheme for Control of Raw Cocoa' for consumption in Britain, noting that 'It is intended to prepare a separate scheme for the control of cocoa exports from West Africa to other markets'.[13] The memorandum proposed the appointment of a director of raw cocoa to act with an advisory committee, which would include representatives of the West African merchants and other interested parties in Britain. They would requisition all existing stocks of raw cocoa in Britain, buy all future imports in bulk on behalf of the food controller of the ministry, through the Cocoa Association in London, and sell to British manufacturers on a cost-plus basis.

This scheme, however, did not touch the two basic and closely related problems facing the West African merchants: the price they could get for the cocoa they had bought or were committed to buy, and where to sell cocoa for which the war had destroyed a market.

The initiative was taken by United Africa (UAC) as the largest exporter in the Gold Coast pool. In a letter of 11 September to C. L. M. Clauson of the Colonial Office, the secretary to the board of UAC, A. R. I. Mellor, argued strongly for the British government to do two things: to buy the whole main[14] West African cocoa crop for the coming season (from October 1939 to January 1940) and to pay £30 a ton fob as against the current £15. The general argument in support of these proposals was that, with a prospective crop of some 350,000 tons from the Gold Coast and Nigeria and the British market already saturated, some 95,000 tons which would normally have gone to Germany, Austria and Czechoslovakia would remain unsold, and sales to neutral countries would have to be limited to prevent re-export to enemy countries. The effect of this would be to depress the already low market price of £15 a ton to even lower levels. This in turn would have serious political effects in West Africa, probably leading to a renewed hold-up by producers and to a loss of foreign exchange, since the Americans and other neutrals would be able to buy cocoa at knock-down prices. Conversely an assured supply would provide 'a particularly concentrated and nourishing food' for British military and civilian consumers and would enable the government 'to release cocoa to neutrals at a reasonable price', so earning foreign exchange. As against these benefits the cost to the British Government 'would be an internal payment from the Empire point of view'. In his covering note, Mellor asked Clauson that 'perhaps, as you promised, you would look at [the memorandum], pull [it] to pieces, and then, re-fortified in the light of your criticism, it might go before the Food Defence Committee'.[15]

Moving as this appeal might be, it took two months before the British authorities brought the cocoa control into operation; even then only one of Mellor's two initial proposals was adopted. Government agreed to buy the whole of the 1939–40 crop, but on the basis of closing quotations on that date, which for the Gold Coast main crop was £15. 7s 4d, a far cry from Mellor's plea for £30; even that price was the result of unexpectedly strong American demand. During those two months, intensive bargaining took place between the four main parties involved, that is, the Ministry of Food, the Colonial Office, the Treasury and the merchants, through their Association of West African Merchants (AWAM). A leading role was probably played by the two UAC representatives on the Raw Cocoa Advisory Committee of the Ministry of Food, (Sir) Frank Samuel, a managing director, and C. E. Tansley, backed up by other members of AWAM (notably John Holt and John Cadbury). But it is clear that the decisive factor was that the Colonial Office was, throughout, in favour of government action which would avoid political trouble in West Africa.

Minor problems over foreign sales of cocoa, and in particular the danger that American buyers might force up the price, clearly stimulated official action. The American firm of Rockwood attempted to break into the west African cocoa market early in September, offering prices substantially higher than those the British Government was contemplating. O. G. R. Williams of the West African Department of the Colonial Office noted on 15 September that, after a meeting with Samuel and Cadbury that morning, he had checked with Sir Roy Wilson of the Bank of British West Africa, who had said that he was quite prepared to advance the money to enable Rockwood to buy cocoa there; while Sir John Caulcutt, of Barclays DCO, who had also been warned by UAC, said that 'he thought the best solution would be for HMG to buy the whole crop and sell what it would to [the] USA'. Williams 'told both Wilson and Caulcutt government were uneasy about possible high price which could not be maintained'.[16] The following day E. Melville, of the Economics Department of the Colonial Office, recorded his fear that if Rockwood offered a price based on the current US price, and the British Government purchased later at a lower price, 'this would raise political difficulties with the African producers'. UAC had 'reacted violently' to this threat of American intervention and was sending a delegation to Sir Henry Moore the next day.[17] Melville complained that it would be difficult to intervene until it was known that the government scheme was going to be adopted.[18] Five days later the governor of Nigeria cabled that Rockwood's agents there had applied for a licence to export 20,000 tons during the next 12 months and had been refused: 'United Africa Company have applied for direct shipment to New York in American ship now loading. Above agent protests strongly against issue of this licence if he is refused and alleges local firms wish to drive him out of market which is probably true',[19] to which the secretary of state replied by cable that 'I did not intend export licences to be withheld pending the government scheme for cocoa; I only wanted purchases of New Crop by Rockwoods at "inflated New York price" to be prevented if possible – you may issue licences'.[20] A couple of days later the governor of the Gold Coast cabled to the Colonial Office about a proposed UAC shipment of cocoa for Scandinavia on a Swedish ship.[21] Tansley explained to the office that this was a pre-war contract and asked for direction on future policy on Scandinavian shipments, assuming that a declaration of non re-export to Germany could be obtained.[22]

Such minor problems probably helped the Colonial Office to persuade the Ministry of Food and the Treasury that bulk purchase was necessary to avoid future difficulties of these kinds, above all to prevent British West African prices being raised to those current in New York. The decision-making process was stimulated by further memoranda to the Colonial Office from Mellor. On 27 September he wrote to Clauson:

As you know the Government can count on our warm co-operation as merchants in the Government scheme now under consideration for the purchase of the entire cocoa crop at a reasonable fixed price. We are quite convinced that the policy is sound, as in no other way will the African be assured that he can dispose of the whole of his crop and receive a reasonable price for it, and additionally there are in its favour the strongest arguments connected with the storage of food reserves and the provision of foreign currency . . ..

It is, of course, inevitable that there should be under existing conditions a wider margin than the usual schedule between the world price of Cocoa and the Coast price . . .. On the other hand, as you know, it has always been the policy of ourselves and other merchants with whom earlier we were associated, to give the African under normal conditions the full value of his cocoa on world markets. We are not now paying a price which present circumstances justify because you wish us to refrain from a policy which might prejudice the success of the plan now being studied and would, we agree, be most undesirable. But we may be misunderstood; Africans and government officials may misinterpret the low price if it is not explained that we are only 'refraining from our normal policy of raising the local price' in deference to your wishes.[23]

On 10 October, and on the ground that 'it appears to us if one can reasonably assume from their lack of activity that the Food Defence Committee are not very concerned to build up any additional cocoa reserves', Mellor returned to the fray with another memorandum for the Colonial Office to use in its pursuit of government action. Since, he said, 'the food situation now no longer appears to warrant any addition to the cocoa reserves', he dropped that aspect of his earlier argument and developed a negative case: 'it seems important . . . not to estimate the advantages which the scheme has to offer so much as to contrast these advantages with the very serious difficulties which will accrue should no such scheme be proceeded with'. The case he expounded was that the potential liability of government for an unsold cocoa surplus, should it buy the whole West African crop of perhaps 375,000 tons in 1939–40, would be no more than 125,000 tons, since the British, American and Scandinavian markets would absorb the rest. If the government bought the whole crop at an average of 10s a load (60lbs, that is, £20 a ton) at a West African port, sold the 100,000 tons already contracted for by the British Ministry of Food at 11s a load and sold 150,000 tons to the USA and neutrals at 12s a load (cheap to them, given the weak pound sterling) and valued the surplus at only 4s a load for future disposal, the loss to the Treasury would be only £700,000; and even this could be eliminated either by charging the UK consumer the foreign price of 12s or by paying only 9s at port to the producer. Moreover, the benefits of this to the colonial governments would be considerable. Political difficulties would be averted, Africans would have £7,000,000 purchasing power, and with import duties at 20 per cent, the colonial treasuries would recoup some £1,200,000. Finally the British Government would get £3,375,000 in foreign currencies. Conversely, if there was no plan for the purchase of the whole crop, and judging by events during 1914–18, the bottom would drop out of the cocoa market because with a predictable surplus of 125,000 tons, 'merchants, without any assurance that they would be able to dispose of any stocks that they might build up, could certainly not take this risk . . .'. Cocoa prices in West Africa would plummet, Africans would probably hold back their cocoa, and the Americans and others would be able to pick up the surplus at a give-away price. In short, only government purchase of the entire crop, even at a price much lower than that Mellor had been asking for a month earlier, could solve the problems caused by the war.[24]

Whether or not such arguments helped to strengthen the hands of the Colonial Office in dealing with the Treasury, preparation of the plan proceeded, and it was ready before 3 November. On that date the AWAM Cocoa Sub-committee sent its report on the plan to the

Colonial Office. It welcomed 'whole heartedly' the government proposal to buy all cocoa from British West Africa for the 1939–40
season. Established West African shippers would co-operate fully and
would invite 'established shippers with offices or responsible representation in England' to join them. Small shippers whom government did
not want to appoint as buying agents should get fixed tonnages based
on their 1938–9 crop year shipments, less any tonnage bought that
year before the control. Other shippers, of whom 15 were listed in the
Gold Coast and 12 in Nigeria (called 'non-shippers' by AWAM)
should be allowed quotas equivalent to the average percentage of total
crop shipped between 1936 and 1939, after deduction of the allocation
to the others mentioned.[25] By 7 November the Colonial Empire Cocoa
Control had been set up at the Ministry of Food, its members included
both Samuel and Tansley of UAC. The Cocoa Control came into
operation on 11 November.

In simple terms the control was to operate as follows. The UK
Ministry of Food fixed the buying price to be paid by the merchants
to the producers, with differentials for varying grades. The merchants
continued to buy and eventually to sell, but acting now as agents for
the control. They were given a commission and agreed expenses. For
1939–40 the buying price for grades I and II in the Gold Coast was
9s a load. The merchant firms were appointed buying agents for the
government and could claim approved expenses. They were given
buying quotas according to their previous purchases, divided into 'A'
(large) and 'B' (small) shippers. Cocoa Advisory Committees were set
up at Accra and Lagos to administer the system. The British
Government, initially through the Ministry of Food, took all risks and
was entitled to any profit it could make. What were the reactions of
the various interested parties to this decision? Four may be quoted,
one from a merchant firm, one from an African chief, with comments
by Colonial Office officies, and two from West African governors.

John Holt & Co at least were delighted at the outcome of
negotiations. On 15 November 1939 their Liverpool Administrative
Department sent a circular to all their district agents in Nigeria and
the Gold Coast as follows:

1 The hope we expressed in a confidential communication made
   to you some time ago has ... now been fulfilled and the
   Imperial Treasury has been persuaded by the Colonial Office
   to agree to the scheme in the interests of British West Africa.

The trade considers that, having regard to the heavy stocks of raw cocoa in the United Kingdom, France and America, and the difficulties of shipment and consumption for certain countries in war conditions, there was every reason to expect that of the British West African 1939/40 crop, at least 100,000 tons would be unsaleable, and that of the French West African crop, at least 30/40,000 tons. The position was very alarming and if it had been allowed to evolve [sic], naturally, cocoa, might have fallen to anything at all and the cocoa producing areas would have been ruined.

2 To save the Colonies from that, the Imperial Government has agreed to buy the whole of the 1939/40 British West African crop of cocoa. They will buy it through the merchants who will act for Government on commission. A cocoa-Director will be appointed (as a matter of fact it will be Mr John Cadbury) who, within the framework of the Ministry of Food, will oversee the details of buying and selling. Cocoa will be sold through the usual channels to such countries as can take it and will be allowed to take it, and the Ministry of Food will later have to decide what is to be done with any surplus of the crop left over. You will probably have gathered that the moves on the Gold Coast and the moratorium have not taken us by surprise and we knew all about what was going on. A small Committee of the Members has been in continuous collaboration with the Colonial Office for some little time . . .

4 We understand the Ministry of Food will own the cocoa though they will only pay us at the end of the season and we will do the finance. It will be sold under their directions and at their risk . . .

5 There will thus be no local speculation because there will be no market fluctuation . . .

6 To give you an indication as to how serious the position was, it was, until recently, quite problematical whether the Imperial Treasury would approve of this Government transaction. The UAC were so alarmed at the prospect before the cocoa trade that they told the pool that, unless the Government Control Scheme were [sic] launched quickly they, the UAC would have to move the abandonment of the cocoa agreement because they could not face the liability of having to buy their pool share of cocoa at their own risk. We had arrived at the

extraordinary position where the biggest shareholder in the cocoa pool was gravely disquieted because his pool share was too big.

7 A great deal has been said about the cocoa pool and what it did to markets, and how it exploited the African. It was, of course, all nonsense, but now that Government has had to step in to nurse the baby and now that cocoa has proved to be so much a drug on the market that the British taxpayer has had to come to the salvation of the cocoa areas, good use should be made of this propaganda point.

8 One of the things that is disturbing us is the question of storage ... We may expect to have to store cocoa on the coast for much longer periods than has been usual.

9 Another point is that this arrangement is for one season only. What is going to happen to the 1940/41 and subsequent crops, goodness only knows.[26]

Sir Ofori Atta, leader of the cocoa hold-up and a major cocoa dealer himself, was not so pleased. As early as 8 December, R. Harris, UAC's general manager in Accra, warned his London head office that the African chiefs would protest over details of the scheme; at the last meeting of the Accra Advisory Committee Ofori Atta had said it was like the old pool and Africans opposed quotas as they did the pool.[27] In May 1940 Atta duly proposed a motion in the Gold Coast Legislative Council in the following terms:

We suggest that if it is the intention of His Majesty's Government to purchase 1940–1 crop the Central Control Committee in England should not include representatives of the Companies or Firms buying cocoa in the Gold Coast and that the control of local purchases should be left in the hands of the Gold Coast Government assisted by a representative Committee who shall have power to make regulations for the control of such purchases.

I could not see the reason why His Majesty's Government, having offered so kindly to buy our entire crop, should tell us how we should sell or buy. I think that the only thing they could tell us and for us to do is not to ship cocoa to anywhere which will allow Germany to have access to it ... That is all that concerns His Majesty's Government but to say that A should buy cocoa so much B should buy cocoa so much C should not buy at all cannot be the concern of His Majesty's Government. And the reason why it has now become the chief concern of the Government is that the control is in the hands of people who are directly interested in the cocoa business of this country, and who naturally, human nature being what it is, would like to see that their firms get on better than any other. We suggest that it is most unfair.[28]

On this Melville of the Colonial Office minuted:

Another political point is the form of control in this country. The African community (ie the vocal part of it) takes no pains to disguise their view that the control is corrupt and is being run in the interests of the established shippers. This is a view which from personal experience I can say is entirely false and the expression of which ought not to be tolerated. Ofori Atta, the mouth-piece of the trading community, is not above suspicion. I have no doubt that he concentrates so much upon the exploitation of the African producer by the European firms because he regards this exploitation as being the preserve of the African middleman trader. I can see no possibility of running the control scheme on orderly lines unless the supervision of marketing policy is left in the hands of people who know something about the cocoa markets.[29]

Melville's colleague in the CO, O. G. R. Williams, minuted 'As regards to B shippers, they may be selfish rogues only anxious to exploit the African farmers, but the African probably resents much less being exploited by other Africans than by White men – at any rate less political capital can be made out of it'.[30]

Finally what did the governors of the two colonies concerned think about the scheme? Sir Bernard Bourdillon, governor of Nigeria since 1935 and arch-enemy of the big trading firms, was surprisingly moderate in a considered memorandum, probably written in April 1940. Reviewing the first season of state buying he gave the principle his blessing:

General: [sic] On the introduction of Control in November 1939 the scheme was well received: the price fixed was satisfactory, having regard to prices previously obtaining, and it was generally recognised that His Majesty's Government had acted in the interests of the Nigerian producer.

2 Fixed prices eliminated competition and speculation, and there was on this account some apprehension on the part of middlemen. There is little doubt that fixed prices tended to reduce the number of hands through which cocoa passed on its way from the producer to the exporter, and that a number of middlemen were eliminated from the trade. This was all to the good as the need for the reduction in the number of middlemen was generally recognised.

3 Prices were fixed at buying stations only, and no attempt was made to control transactions in the villages between the middleman and the farmer . . . It was considered that by means of propaganda by Administrative Officers and others and in view of the fact that middlemen were in competition with one another, the farmer would get in the country districts a fair price, and this in fact was the case during the period of purchase of the Main Crop.

But from this point Bourdillon became more critical, particularly of the way in which the quotas had been allocated to exporters and of the behaviour of the big firms. A first complaint was that the co-operative movement had been given no export quota, the only concession made by the Colonial Office being that the exporting firms should pay the co-operatives a premium of 12s 6d per ton on an assumed output of 5,059 tons, the previous year's total. This would have a discouraging effect on the movement.[31] Further, the impression had grown that, 'although the Cocoa Control Scheme was initiated with the sole view of protecting the West African producer, the influence of the exporting firms became so strong in implementing the scheme that the primary object was to some extent obscured, and the interests of the firms became paramount'. For example:

The marketing schedules provided generous allowance for overhead charges and a fixed profit of 1.5% on sales proceeds and thus safeguarded the firms' position and probably gave them a higher figure of profit than they enjoyed under marketing conditions obtaining from some time prior to the introduction of the Control Scheme. Moreover, from the general attitude of the firms' agents in Nigeria when discussing transport differentials to up-country buying stations, it appeared to be clear that they were determined to make further profit locally if possible. There was in fact little evidence in local discussions of any spirit of give and take.

Bourdillon was, however, certain that the government purchase scheme must be renewed for the following year. The economic and therefore also the fiscal effects of there being no market for cocoa would be disastrous, and the consequential risk of political upheaval 'serious'. But if the scheme was continued, Bourdillon wanted some changes: first, 'it might be advisable to reduce the local price, to reduce materially the firms' profit and reimbursements and to reduce or even remove the export duty'. That might reduce the cost to Britain, assuming the crop was unsaleable, by £300–400,000; second, the Calabar–Cameroon area quota should be separate from that for the western region; third, and probably most important in Bourdillon's eyes:

13 Control of purchases should be the function of local Control: the obligation of the shippers to buy up to the limit of their quota should be stressed and the local Controller should have powers to require any shipper to purchase any particular parcel of cocoa. In the event of refusal to purchase, the local Controller should have power to re-allocate quota [sic] to another shipper. Refusal to purchase has occurred on many occasions this season and Co-operative Societies being unable to sell their cocoa when offered. In fact, if it had not been for the co-operation of the United Africa Company Limited in always being willing to take any parcel which no other shipper would purchase, the situation would have been extremely difficult. It is suggested that if the United Africa Company Limited are overbought as a result of this helpful attitude, they should not be penalised.

Finally, shippers should make arrangements to reduce overlapping in the out-districts, and responsibility for storage as between shipper and government should be clarified.[32]

Writing at much the same time, Sir Arnold Hodson, governor of the Gold Coast, took a similar line:

5 As regards the reaction accorded to the scheme in the Gold Coast, it is, I think, necessary to have regard to two different aspects of the scheme. There can be no question that the guarantee of a fixed price, which was itself reasonable, has been a great boon to the African producer and has been generally recognised as such. Unfortunately the feeling which has arisen over the conditions laid down for Group 'B' shippers is very different. The fact that the arrangements proposed would lead to cases of hardship and would expose the scheme to criticism was pointed out during the earlier stages of the scheme . . .

6 The position of African shippers has been the subject of public criticism from the first announcement of the scheme, the main grounds being that whereas the African shippers have been made to carry out the recommendations of the Nowell Commission, the principle applied to shipping quotas in the scheme definitely prevents any further expansion and is not reconcilable with the Commission's recommendations. Although the fact has been pointed out on numerous occasions that the quota allotted to Group 'B' shippers was based on an exceptionally large crop and that the Group 'A' shippers would, in consequence, receive less tonnage than in the previous years, unless the crop again attained the exceptional dimensions of 1939–40 this argument has, I fear, not proved convincing to the African interests concerned. The working of this part of the scheme was the subject of unanimous criticism by all African members at the recent meeting of the Legislative Council and as soon as the transcript . . . is available, I propose to forward it to you. To sum up, therefore, it may be said that while the benefit to the producer is and has been widely recognised, much of its good effect has been lost through the feeling aroused in regard to the treatment of Group 'B' shippers.

7 [The scheme was very desirable and generous on the part of Britain. It was only a pity that the Group 'B' shippers were not given a larger quota, as he had frequently suggested]. Such an arrangement would have reduced proportionately the tonnage available for Group 'A' shippers but if even an additional 5,000 tons (ie a little more than the German shipments) had been earmarked for the Group 'B' shippers the reduction in the

tonnage handled by the Group 'A' shippers would have been only a little over 2%. The Nowell Commission . . . stated that over a period of years the merchant firms had not found the cocoa business a profitable one (from the large increase in their tonnage the African shippers presumably had) whereas under the scheme the firms have an assured remuneration together with the certain refund of all their expenses. In these conditions a small reduction in the tonnage handled by them would not seem to be an unreasonable contribution, particularly when it is remembered that any serious feeling against these firms will have a very direct effect on the profits which they expect to make on their other transactions . . . . I desire to record now my fervent hope that the scheme will be continued, but, if so, the attitude to be adopted towards the Group 'B' shippers will present a serious problem in view of the exacerbation of feeling and suspicion which has arisen.[33]

This is not the place to trace in detail the later development of this or any other scheme for state purchase and marketing of West African produce. But, since the original scheme was intended only as an emergency measure for the 1939–40 cocoa season, ending in September 1940, it is necessary to ask why it was continued for the following season, and in the event indefinitely, and what, if any, significant changes were made in the scheme in response to experience and criticism.

It was clear, when discussions took place in London in September 1940, that in the first place, since all interested parties liked the scheme, it would have to be maintained in one form or other for the duration of the Second World War. That being taken for granted, there were three main issues to debate arising from the previous season's experience: how much loss the British Treasury was prepared to sustain in future (it had lost £208,548 during the first year) and therefore what price should be offered to producers and what reward to merchants; who should run any similar scheme in future; and whether any change should be made in the quotas allocated to 'A' and 'B' shippers.

On the first point, and in the conditions of 1940, with heavy loss of merchant shipping, it had to be assumed that much of the next year's cocoa crop would have to be destroyed. (Given storage problems, it had already been necessary to destroy the mid-crop of 1940, which had involved a substantial loss to the Treasury.)[34] It was therefore decided that the main crop prices to be paid to the producer per ton should be reduced from the December 1939 levels of £15 17s 4d at Accra and £16 10s at Lagos to £13 1s 4d and £13 10s respectively.

Second, while the operations during 1939–40 had been run by the Ministry of Food, using an advisory committee, it was now decided to transfer control to the Colonial Office, which in turn was to set up a West African Cocoa Control Board (WACCB).[35] Its membership would consist of the parliamentary under-secretary for the colonies as *ex-officio* chairman, the head of the West African Department of the Colonial Office (*ex-officio* vice-chairman), and, initially, two experts drawn from the industry who were by then working for the Ministry of Food: John Cadbury and E. C. Tansley of UAC, who became marketing director.[36] The board was later expanded, when it became the West African Produce Control Board, to include two colonial officials nominated by the governments of Nigeria and the Gold Coast respectively. The WACCB now bought the total crop of cocoa in British, and some French territories and sold part of the crop to the Ministry of Food; for 1940–1 this was at the free-market price current in Britain at the time, in 1940, when that ministry was given a monopoly of domestic control. The balance could then be sold by the WACCB in foreign friendly markets at whatever price it could obtain, which proved to be substantially higher than that fixed in Britain. As a result, in future years the WACCB sold to the Ministry of Food at the average price received by it from all sales, which allowed British prices to creep up in parallel with international market prices. Significantly the Cocoa Control Advisory Committees in Accra and Lagos were not given the additional powers suggested by Bourdillon. They remained administrative and advisory, not decision-taking bodies.

It was the third question, the quotas to be allotted to the Group 'A' and Group 'B' shippers, that seems to have caused the greatest difficulty in September 1940. The key meeting of the WACCB was on 11–12 September and was attended by Melville as acting chairman, Cadbury, Tansley, two spokesmen for the Gold Coast Government and eight representatives of the Cocoa Committee of AWAM, headed by Frank Samuel of UAC.[37] Melville pointed out at the start that speed was essential since the new scheme had to start on 1 October. There was no disagreement over the prices to be paid, which had already been agreed with the West African governments. But once the topic turned to 'sharing of the crop', the debate became fierce.

It was common ground at the start that 'for reasons of administration . . . Group 'B' shippers would again have to be allocated a fixed
tonnage for which some priority of shipment over Group 'A' cocoa
would be given'. Melville then stated that a proposal had been made
that the 'B' quota originally set in 1939 of 28,500 tons should be
reinstated: 'He pointed out that, on political grounds, this would be
impossible. Indeed, it appeared certain that some increase in the
actual tonnage of 31,000 tons enjoyed by Group "B" shippers last
season would have to be conceded'. In this he was supported by R. O.
Ramage, who presented the Gold Coast Government's case for an
increase in the Group 'B' tonnage. Replying on behalf of AWAM,
Samuel

> urged the need for maintaining the principle, established in all
> Governmental schemes of dividing business on the basis of pre-
> war performance. He considered this basis was the only possible
> one in equity; he also suggested that it would be politically
> dangerous to make further concessions to 'B' shippers which
> could not be justified in principle; such action would merely
> encourage them in presenting Government with unreasonable
> demands both in the cocoa trade and in other fields.

This led to 'considerable discussion on the nature and origin of the
complaints against the quota system as it stood', Ramage stressing 'the
fact that the criticism was not confined to shipping interests or to a
group of "agitators" but was widely voiced throughout the whole
community'. Various compromises were suggested and rejected.
Samuel then suggested, on behalf of AWAM, a formula 'which he felt
would at least give the appearance of preserving the principle of past
performance as a basis for sharing the crop while making a substantive
concession to the 'B' shippers', and this was accepted in the following
form:

> During the 1939/40 [season] it was intended that Group 'B'
> shippers should receive a total quota of 28,500 tons which was
> their share of the last crop marketed before the war. This quota
> represented 9.5% of that crop. Owing to concessions granted to
> certain shippers and to other causes, the total tonnage actually
> allocated to Group 'B' shippers last season was 31,000 tons,
> equivalent to 13% of the crop of 240,000 tons. Let it be

recognised that the total share to be allocated to Group 'B' shippers in 1940/41 should be maintained at 13% of the crop. As the total crop cannot be known until the end of the season, let the average of the past five crops be taken for the purpose of fixing the tonnage to be allocated to group [sic] 'B' shippers.

This represented a considerable concession of principle. When it was worked out it was found that the average of the last five crops was 168,000 tons, which gave the Group 'B' shippers 34,840 tons. Samuel was anxious that this should be announced 'in such a way as not to imply that any concession in principle had been made. ... It was pointed out, however, that for local reasons it would be essential to emphasise the extent to which Group "B" shippers will profit by the revised basis of calculations'. Defeated on this, Samuel complained that in 1939–40:

there had been a tendency to allow merchants to take the blame for those parts of the scheme which were not acceptable to African opinion. He urged the need for revising this attitude in the handling of the new scheme. The fact that the scheme was a Government scheme should be made clear from the beginning. The local Governments should make themselves responsible for answering any criticisms and should be prepared to defend the merchants if those criticisms were directed against them.

The Gold Coast representatives accepted this and Melville promised 'to convey it to higher authority in the Colonial Office'. Samuel, however, insisted on discussing the point with the secretary of state.

Another concession made by AWAM was to extend to the Gold Coast the principle that, rather than allow the co-operative societies an export quota, they should be paid a premium of 12s 6d a ton on all co-operative cocoa sold locally, and that this should be paid at the start of the season. Based on the maximum past performance of the societies of 8,500 tons, this would be £5,312 10s. A figure of £3,500 was agreed after discussion for the co-operatives in Nigeria.

That left two questions: the shares of the individual 'A' shippers and the payments to be made to them. On the first matter, A. G. Leventis, which had obtained an increased quota of 1,000 tons in 1939–40 after protest to the local government, had their future quota slightly increased to take account of this. To meet Bourdillon's two points, separate quotas were fixed for western and eastern Nigeria, and the local government would have the authority 'to continue buying in a particular area should this be necessary to avoid hardship to producers'.

As to the remuneration the shippers were to be given, and in the light of complaints made by Samuel that this had been inadequate in some respects, it was suggested that, since the producer price was to be reduced, remuneration should be fixed at about 20 per cent below that of the previous year. The precise figures were decided by Melville and Samuel, after the main meeting, at 2s 6d per ton 'above the line', for head office expenses, and a commission of 7s 6d 'below the line', as in 1939–40.

What did British officials think of these decisions, which were to prove critical for the future of state marketing in West Africa? First, their reactions can be predicted from comments made in advance of the meeting on 11–12 September on the two main points being pressed by the West African governments: devolution of control over cocoa buying from London to the colonies, and larger quotas for 'B' shippers. On 5 September Melville, who would chair the meeting, gave his opinion on the first of these proposals, which was being pressed by the two visiting Gold Coast representatives. He decided against:

> On further consideration I think that this should be dropped and that instead the Gold Coast Government should make some contribution to the cost of the scheme eg by reducing export duty. This would not be possible in Nigeria for budgetary reasons. For the sale of the crop a special West African Control should be established independent of (although for reasons of convenience, housed in) the Ministry of Food.[38]

Melville had decided in advance on one major decision to be taken at the control board meeting: that the scheme should continue to be run from London and that the colonial governments should be mere agents of the central control.

On the question of quotas the Colonial Office seems also to have had little sympathy with Accra and Lagos though there was some difference of opinion as to how best to tackle it. O. G. R. Williams, writing on 10 September, noted that:

A good deal will, I think, depend on how generous an allocation of tonnage 'A' shippers can be persuaded to agree to our giving the 'B' shippers. The latter are not, I think, a very deserving class but they are politically vocal and if we can avoid increasing discontent and mistrust of HMG at the present time, it would be well worth a little injustice to the 'A' shippers. If the 'B' shippers are thoroughly disgruntled they may use the proposed reduction in price as a means of stirring up popular agitation among the producers.[39]

A much tougher line with the 'B' shippers was suggested by A. L. M. C.[40] On 11 September (presumably before the meeting) he wrote:

I hope that the concessions to the B shippers will be kept within the smallest possible dimensions for two reasons. The first is a natural objection to being blackmailed. The second is that I am much opposed to the creation, or rather the strengthening of a small capitalist class of Africans with incomes out of all proportion to the incomes of their fellow countrymen. Capitalists are, in my view, essential to society, but we have found by experience in this country that capitalists ought not to be too few or individually too rich; capital should be spread as widely as possible not concentrated in a few hands. The position in West Africa is approaching that in pre-war Russia with a very small relatively very rich class and a proletariat. We know what happened in Russia, and I do not want history to repeat itself. I agree that the British merchants ought to be squeezed a bit but this should be done by reducing their rate of profit not their scale of trade.[41]

In the event, as has been seen, these Colonial Office aims were largely realized. Control remained in London and minimal concessions were made to the 'B' shippers. Melville, writing after the meeting, also accepted the AWAM argument that the colonial governments must stop hiding from African criticism behind the skirts of the merchants:

The merchants, and Mr Samuel in particular laid stress in the discussions on the point that, now that a freely negotiated scheme was being put into operation, it was the responsibility of the Government to answer criticisms of the scheme and more positively to deny statements made in the local press and elsewhere that the scheme was a merchants' ramp. We must, I think, leave it to the Governor to decide how far he thinks he can muzzle the local press.[42]

That, of course, was only the beginning of the story, but it marks a convenient terminal point for this particular study. What, then, is the wider significance of the events of 1939–40 for the history of state marketing in British West Africa?

First, the genesis of the cocoa control lay not in deliberate policy by a British Government eager to take the opportunity offered by the war to put into operation some form of state control over private merchants. On the contrary, the government appears to have had no prior plan even to deal with the economic and political problems certain to result from restriction of export markets for African produce; the odds were that the market would be left to its own predictably disastrous future, as it had been in 1914. It was the merchants, facing serious financial losses on their existing stocks from 1938–9 and their long position for the main crop of 1939–40, who appear to have taken the initiative. Essentially they appealed to the British state to bail them out and to enable them to trade in cocoa at a reasonable profit, at least for the coming season.

This, in turn, raises the question of why the state responded to their appeal. The research behind this chapter does not justify any firm explanation, but it seems most probable that the merchants owed their success primarily to the Colonial Office, and that this department persuaded first the Ministry of Food and then, and with greater difficulty, the Treasury that the state should take responsibility for the effects of war on the cocoa trade. That, of course, leads to the consequential question of why the Colonial Office should have taken up the merchants' cause. A Marxist answer might be that in a bourgeois state the bureaucracy would naturally serve the interests of capital. But in the circumstances of 1939 this was inherently unlikely. The West African merchants had long been suspect in Colonial Office circles as 'big business' and they were then extremely unpopular with the colonial service in the aftermath of the cocoa hold-up. Rather, the immediate concern of the Colonial Office and its West African governors was to prevent the serious economic and political disorder in West Africa, and particularly the Gold Coast, that was the predictable result of a partial stop on cocoa sales and a consequential drop in cocoa prices. In addition they may already have had in mind the objective stated in the 1944 White paper: the need 'to break direct link between the producers' price and world market prices, the existence of which in the past has caused the local purchase prices to reflect every vagary of speculation on the world's produce markets'.[43] Either way, the colonial state acted primarily in its own interests, not that of British merchants.

Yet is is important that the view taken by the Colonial Office of the merchant firms and their needs, and also of the best interests of the West African colonies, changed substantially between 1939 and 1944. In 1939 the London attitude was different from that adopted in government circles in Accra and Lagos. The contrast had been obvious at the time of the cocoa hold-up and was evident in the events of 1939–40. Despite differences over policies, personal relations between the office and the AWAM firms, and in particular UAC, seem to have been affable, even warm. The office did not usually write as if it regarded the merchants as inveterate exploiters of African producers, and it was noticeably cool in its response to demands by leading African entrepreneurs such as Atta. In short, it seems very likely that the cocoa control came into existence, and the main exporting firms were given what from their point of view was a satisfactory deal, mainly because the Colonial Office of 1939–40 believed that there was a coincidence between the interests of the merchants and those of the imperial state and that officials believed that they could trust the British firms better than African entrepreneurs to run the new system of state buying. Or, to put it another way, the office thought rather differently from its governors in West Africa because it was relatively immune to the chameleon effect of direct exposure to African conditions and pressures.

That may explain the decisions of 1939 and 1940, but, to look ahead, why did this arrangement which, even in September 1940, was regarded as a temporary war-time contrivance, become a matter of long-term policy, so that state purchasing evolved into the system of marketing boards, which in turn have had such an immense impact on the economies of tropical Africa? Why, more specifically, did the White Paper of 1944 propose state purchase and marketing of all West African cocoa, leaving no apparent role for the merchants? A full answer lies beyond the scope of this essay, but four points can be made:

- It is clear that by 1944 the Colonial Office was convinced that state marketing had come to stay. One reason was sheer habit and experience: the system worked and provided an added dimension to the power of both the imperial and colonial state.

- The control had been extended in 1942 to include the òther main West African export commodities and had been renamed the West African Produce Control Board; so to end the marketing system involved much wider issues than merely cocoa.
- State marketing did indeed appear to provide a solution to the problem of market fluctuation and so reduce the probability of troubles of the kind experienced both in 1931 and in 1937–8. To an organization whose primary concern was to avoid political discontent in the colonies this was a critical factor.
- There were financial vested interests: state marketing was profitable to two British departments, the Colonial Office as controller of the marketing board, and the Ministry of Food as bulk buyer for the British domestic market at below world market prices. The interests of the second of these is obvious, let us concentrate on those of the Colonial Office and its colonial servants and look for evidence of a change of attitude to state marketing as a long-term policy and to the role of the merchant firms in the system.

By 1944 the WACC and its successor had proved that, by keeping producer prices low – justified by pointing to the dangers of inflation if prices were raised – and by speculating successfully in the American and other neutral or friendly markets, it could make money. By 1944 the board had built up a reserve of £3,676,253. This was a far cry from the losses made in the first year, and it clearly influenced Colonial Office thinking. On the one hand this sum could be used, as was claimed in 1944, to even out future fluctuations in world cocoa prices; on the other it constituted a convenient capital sum with which to fund permanent state marketing organizations in Nigeria and the Gold Coast, which were projected for October 1945 in the 1944 White Paper.[44] Since the lack of such capital had been one obstacle to the realization of the Nowell Commission's proposed association of producers, and assuming that some alternative type of statutory buying organization was now to be set up, the opportunity must have seemed too good to miss. Clearly to wind up the control would be to throw away very hard-won advantages and possibilities.

It was at this point, moreover, that the attitude of the Colonial Office to the future of economic life in West Africa came to coincide with that of the West African governments rather than with that of the merchants. Merchant interests had been served in 1939–40 and these were reasonably satisfied in general with the system as it had developed by 1944, though very critical of its detailed operation.[45] It was, after all, partly their scheme. The scheme proposed by the 1944 White Paper was not. How far the merchants were consulted over its drafting is uncertain; but it is probable that they were not told about it until the last moment, for it was only on 12 September that the Cocoa Sub-committee of AWAM was invited to the office to discuss the future marketing of cocoa.[46] The White Paper was issued the same month. It stated bluntly that:

> there should be established in the Gold Coast and Nigeria, as from the beginning of the 1945–46 cocoa season (ie in October 1945), organisations empowered by law to purchase the total production of cocoa, to prescribe the prices to be paid to the producers, and to be responsible for the disposal of the cocoa. These organisations would be established by, and be responsible to, the Colonial Governments, and would be required to act as trustees for the producers.[47]

From the standpoint of AWAM there were two main and very serious objections to this proposal: it appeared entirely to exclude private firms – the intention seemed to be to create a monopolistic governmental structure in which they would have no entrepreneurial role, or might at most be mere paid agents of the boards; and for the proposed system to be run entirely by the colonial governments would be much worse than the present system of control by London, since it left them exposed to the much-demonstrated hostility of the local colonial authorities.

AWAM therefore put up an alternative scheme which would have reduced the role of the state marketing boards to fixing a minimum price and buying residual parcels of cocoa if the merchants did not take up the whole crop.[48] In their resistance the merchants received fortuitous support from America; as the Ministry of Food told the Colonial Office in December:

> The President of the New York Cocoa Exchange has written a letter warning Americans of a British Government Cocoa Trust. 'The threat of a British State Monopoly' he says 'arouses in us a

burning sense of indignation. The implications of such a scheme extend far beyond the narrow frontiers of the chocolate industry'.[49]

Lord Halifax, British ambassador in Washington, also warned the Colonial Office that the State Department was very concerned about the White Paper and suggested that the best propaganda line might be that 'wartime control arrangements have been used not as justification for the new plan but as practical demonstration that [a] Government selling organisation can achieve local price stabilisation, which is the first objective of our policy'.[50] This US hostility to state monopoly of a crop for which the USA was the largest single market clearly worried the Colonial Office. In February 1945 the colonial secretary told the governors of Nigeria and the Gold Coast, to their fury, that he had 'come to conclusion that wisest course would be to postpone decision on marketing organisation . . .'.[51]

The result was a compromise, set out eventually in the White Paper of November 1946. The main and crucial difference from the proposals of 1944 was that, while the marketing boards would set the seasonal price payable to producers and would buy, ship and sell all cocoa abroad, the actual buying and transporting to the ports would be done by the merchants, as 'licensed buying agents'. Thus the merchants would retain important functions: to buy the cocoa at the minimum price or above; to bag, grade and store it; to transport it to the ports and place it on board ocean-going ships; and to finance the cocoa from the time of purchase to delivery on board ship. Their profit would come from the margin between the fixed buying price and the price fixed for sale fob to the marketing boards.[52] This was not what the merchants had wanted, which was essentially a return to pre-war competition but with the colonial state supporting the bottom of the cocoa market. But it was better than they had feared they would get a couple of years earlier. In fact the system worked quite well from their point of view, though increasingly not from that of the producers, until the merchants went out of produce buying in the late 1950s and early 1960s.

If this story has a moral it is that of the frying pan and the fire. In 1939 the merchants invoked the genie of the state to avoid certain loss on their existing cocoa commitments. They assumed that the system of quotas would preserve the pecking order of the pre-war market until the end of the war, when state intervention would have served its turn and could be discarded. But meantime the imperial and colonial states had found that this *ad hoc* system could be made to serve their longer-term purposes. Equally important, the wartime experience of collectivism and the rise of younger men seem to have affected Colonial Office attitudes to state intervention in economic life.[53] By 1944 the office had clearly moved a long way further to the left than its senior men had stood in 1939 and had come to accept most of the previously unacceptable nostrums of the West African governors. British West Africa was never again, at least before Nigeria abolished state marketing of cocoa in 1986, to have a competitive produce trade, and it is arguable that, in the longer term, it was African producers rather than British merchants who suffered most.

Notes

1. This essay is a preliminary by-product of research for a history of the United Africa Company (UAC) from 1929–87.
2. *Report on Cocoa Control in West Africa 1939–1943 and Statement on Future Policy*, Cmd 6554. September 1944.
3. Ibid., paras 1 and 3.
4. *Report of the Commission on the Marketing of West African Cocoa*, Cmd 5845, September 1938.
5. Ibid., para. 490.
6. Ibid., paras 490–506.
7. More democratic methods were ruled out because: 'These would certainly be inappropriate in the Gold Coast, where the ballot-box is not a commonplace of public life; and we do not envisage that either the question of initiating a scheme or matters involved in its operation should be put to the general vote of producers' (ibid., para. 519).
8. Ibid., paras 514–28.
9. Ibid., para. 540. But the commission recommended that in Nigeria the co-operatives should be used more extensively for cocoa (ibid., paras 554–7).
10. The New Zealand Primary Products Marketing Act 1936 was much admired in the later 1930s and, apart from its more democratic aspects, seems to have been the model for the West African Cocoa Commission Report. It was also much admired by (Sir) Keith Hancock; see his *Survey of British Commonwealth Affairs* (London 1942), Vol. II, Part 1, pp. 279–83. He reverted to this model when discussing the cocoa hold-up and the Nowell Report: ibid., part 2, p. 225, note 2.
11. *Statistical and Economic Review* 2 (1948), p. 22. The *Review* was published quarterly by United African Company (UAC) from 1948 to 1965 and contains much valuable and reliable factual and statistical material on West African trade.

12. Surprisingly there were then no American firms buying cocoa in West Africa; manufacturers bought on the New York cocoa exchange.
13. Ministry of Food memo, 22 September 1939, PRO CO 852/256/1.
14. There was also a 'light', 'mid-' or 'middle' crop between May and August which was normally of inferior quality and quantity.
15. CO 852/256/1; This reference I owe to J.-G. Deutsch.
16. Note by O. G. R. Williams, 15 September 1939, ibid.
17. Sir Henry Moore had been governor of Sierra Leone and colonial secretary in Kenya and was the first of three colonial governors who were brought back to the Colonial Office to serve a term as an assistant under-secretary, under a scheme introduced by Malcolm MacDonald as colonial secretary; the others were Sir Alan Burns and Sir William Battershill. See D. J. Morgan, *The Official History of Colonial Development*, (London 1980), Vol. 1, p. 67.
18. Draft note by Melville, 14 September 1939, CO 852/256/1
19. Ibid., 19 September 1939.
20. Ibid.
21. Ibid., 21 September 1939.
22. Tansley to CO, 22 September 1939, CO 852/261/4. He must have been told to apply for export licences, since on 13 October 1939 he told the CO that UAC had tabled to Accra to apply for licences for the balance of pre-war contracts for cocoa to be carried by a Swedish steamer in December 'quite definitely for normal consumption in Scandinavia', ibid.
23. CO 852/256/2.
24. Memorandum by Mellor dated 9 October 1939, enclosed in Mellor to Melville, 10 October 1939, ibid.
25. CO 852/256/2.
26. Holt Papers, Rhodes House MSS Afr, s825 535 (II); I owe this reference to J.-G. Deutsch.
27. CO 852/256/4. This is a carbon copy which must have been sent to the CO by UAC.
28. Governor Gold Coast to CO, No. 272, 3 May 1940, CO 852/319/3.
29. Minute 15 June 1940, CO 852/319/3.
30. Minute 19 June 1940, ibid.
31. This was a general complaint in Lagos government circles; see, for example, Wolley (of the Nigerian secretariat) to Melville 15 December 1939, on the minutes of a meeting of the Cocoa Control Scheme Advisory Committee:

> We were . . . astonished to read the comments of Messrs Iredale and Samuel [both representing AWAM] in the Minutes of the 15th November, which apparently went unchallenged, to the effect the co-operative societies here were merely a collection of middlemen who controlled little of the crop, and that a lot of the cocoa marketed by them originated from non-members. The firms have told us more than once, and in connection with the Cocoa Commission report that they are in full sympathy with the movement, but the above

comments seem to indicate that their sympathy, if it really exists, is worth nothing. (CO 852/256/4)

John Cadbury, then a member of the Cocoa Control Board in London, was unimpressed by Bourdillon's argument:

> The fundamental reason for drawing up the scheme on the basis it was finally agreed was that it was realised that any scheme of the kind might have far-reaching repercussions on the cocoa trade, particularly the various types of individuals concerned. It was the endeavour to introduce a scheme which, when it ceased to operate, would leave the relations between the various parties concerned as near to the position in which they were when the scheme commenced as it was possible to do. It was therefore impossible to use the scheme as an opportunity for pushing any one section of the trade at the expense of others. The suggestion that the Nigerian co-operative societies should have received the enemy purchases [what would have been bought by German firms] would have definitely upset the balance between the various interests, and this would have been contrary to the ideas of the scheme. (Note by Cadbury, 7 May 1940, CO 852/319/3).

32. CO 852/319/3. This was rare praise from Bourdillon for UAC.
33. Hodson to CO, 11 April 1940, copy in CO 852/319/3.
34. See *Gold Coast Gazette Extraordinary*, No. 38, 30 May 1940. The crop was bought in the same way as the main crop, but Group 'A' shippers received no commission (though they did get expenses); Group 'B' shippers received the previous 2.5 per cent.
35. The following outline is based on *Report on Cocoa Control*, Cmd 6554, passim.
36. An undated Colonial Office memorandum, probably by Melville, in suggesting the creation of this board, proposed that it should include J. Cadbury and someone from the Nowell Commission. It continued: 'The effective work will of course be done by Mr Tansley, who has so competently run the selling side of the present scheme. It is proposed to give him some such title as Secretary of the West African Control Board, again for political reasons. Mr Tansley has agreed to disassociate himself entirely from the United Africa Company, an action which will be welcomed in West Africa.' In the margin O. G. R. Williams commented: 'if believed' (CO 852/319/3). The evidence suggests that Tansley did indeed act entirely as a public servant, and this was remarked on by a number of people on both the governmental and commercial sides.
37. The following account is taken from the minutes of the WACCB for 11/12 September 1940, CO 852/319/7.
38. CO 852/319/3.
39. Ibid.
40. I have been unable to find anyone with these initials in the *Colonial and Dominions Office Handbook* for 1940; unless they are G. L. M. Clauson's.
41. CO 852/319/3.

42. Memo by Melville, 19 September 1940, ibid.
43. *Report*, para. 34.
44. Ibid., para. 35.
45. See, for example, notes on a meeting of Gold Coast 'A' shippers on 31 May 1944 at which, as it was retailed to the Colonial Office, Samuel reported that on a recent visit there he had found that 'Conditions were chaotic. The existing agreements regarding brokerages were entirely disregarded and buying had become a scramble – everyone being out to buy the greatest quantity possible' (CO 852/595/4).
46. UAC board meeting 12 September 1944, minute 2320, UAC Archive, 8632.
47. Cmd 6554, para. 35.
48. This was summarized in Samuel (as chairman of AWAM) to CO 21 December 1944, CO 852/596/1.
49. Ministry of Food memo, 14 December 1944, MAF 83/1639.
50. CO 852/596/2.
51. Secretary of State to Richards and Burns tel, 27 Feb. 1945, ibid.
52. *Statement on Future Marketing of West African Cocoa*, Cmd 6950 November 1946, paras 16–20.
53. There is a note by G. H. Creasey, then head of the Colonial Development and Social Services Department of the CO, on Halifax's letter of 28 January 1945 to the effect that there was a danger in postponing the plan for state purchasing on the ground that British public and parliamentary opinion were turning against state interference. The office, ironically in view of the forthcoming Labour triumph, may well have felt the need to act fast before war-time collectivism became out of fashion and politically unacceptable.

9

THE EWE QUESTION 1945–56
French and British Reactions to Nationalism in West Africa

John Kent

The Ewe people, inhabiting the southern parts of the Gold Coast and French and British Togoland, appear to provide a good illustration of how historical models of decolonization can be reconciled with the early stages of the transfer of power in West Africa. Initial moves towards the 'decolonization' of Togoland,[1] described by one historian as a possible prelude to the later process when larger territories and more significant nationalist movements demanded self-government and independence, seemed important for a number of reasons.[2] In the first place, the Ewes, on superficial examination at least, appear to be a single group building a political movement aimed at securing the right of such ethnic nationalities to self-determination. This was given added significance in 1946 when Togoland, a former mandate, became a trust territory of the new United Nations (UN), thereby obliging France and Britain to advance its inhabitants towards self-government in accordance with the freely expressed wishes of the people concerned. Such policies were already being formulated within the British, if not the French, Colonial Office, but the provision of UN machinery to oversee the process forced the colonial powers to operate in front of a critical audience on an international stage where Ewe representatives also received performing rights. Thus one sees that well-known combination of progressive colonial policies, international pressures and effective nationalist movements determining the nature and timing of the end of colonial rule.[3]

In addition, it is sometimes assumed that the British reacted more positively to the developing situation in Togoland than the French, because of their commitment to self-government within a loosely organized and largely uncontrollable commonwealth. The French, on the other hand, with their commitment to the more unitary and centrally controlled structure embodied in the Union Française, were averse to the kind of policies pursued by the British but forced to follow on behind, thereby undermining the union as the decolonization of British Togo reached its climax in 1956.[4]

These two scenarios contain important elements of truth, but a closer examination of French and British policies reveals a much more complex process. Colonial policy was frequently subordinated to the requirements of foreign policy, and reactions to events within Togoland were influenced by British, and particularly French, fears of jeopardizing the continuance of their imperial roles within Africa. In addition, an examination of the reactions of the respective colonial governments reveals not only policy differences, but the extent to which responses were conditioned by the different structures and administrative practices of colonial rule.

The Ewes were one of a number of West African ethnic groups in Togoland which had been divided by the drawing and redrawing of frontiers following the German conquest of 1884. The position of the Ewes as a divided nation had been raised at the 31st and 35th sessions of the Permanent Mandates Commission in 1934 and 1938 and formed part of the grievances of the TOGOBUND, an inter-war organization demanding the unification of Togoland and a return to German rule. Traditionally interpreted as embryonic nationalists, such political movements were conditioned by prospects of social and economic advancement which were closely tied to the linguistic skills demanded by the administering authorities. German-speaking Ewes in British Togo, administered from the Gold Coast, were clearly at a disadvantage after the First World War in their competition for jobs within trading firms, the colonial bureaucracy and the Ewe Presbyterian Church. Such factors explain the ease by which Ewe immigrants from the Gold Coast, well practised in English, were able to secure a dominant position in such organizations, arousing considerable resentment after the Second World War.[5] In fact these, and other inter-Ewe rivalries, primarily related to which authority should rule rather than to straightforward opposition to colonialism, were to be a significant factor in French and British responses to Ewe nationalism.

Grievances about administrative boundaries were increased by the Second World War, which in theory brought the complete closure of the frontiers between French and British Togo and the Gold Coast and French Togo from 1940–42. Even when the frontiers were reopened in 1943 there were many restrictions on the cross-frontier movement of people, produce, currency and consumer goods. In the Gold Coast, Governor Hodson and, later, Governor Burns received petitions from Ewe chiefs calling for a unified Ewe state or a united Togoland under British administration, and if that were not possible the removal of import and export restrictions between the French and British zones.[6] It thus looked, at least to Governor Burns, that Ewe grievances had economic roots in the hardships stemming from wartime restrictions and frontier controls.[7] The British authorities were initially sympathetic to the demands, and Burns proposed the incorporation of the Gold Coast and Togo Ewe populations in one administrative district.[8] In the end no administrative changes were made until 1947, and the Gold Coast Constitution of 1946 did not apply to southern British Togo, but an Anglo-French report on the Ewe movement the following year described the attitude of the British colonial authorities as one of toleration.[9]

By the end of 1946 the movement for a united Eweland[10] had gained in strength and coherence, established cross-border links with French Ewes and was sending petitions to the UN. Daniel Chapman, a Gold Coast Ewe, had founded the *Ewe News Letter* in May 1945, and the Ewe Unionist Association based in Accra provided an organizational framework by 1946. The movement then joined forces with its French counterpart at the All-Ewe Convention, which called for an examination of the problems of Eweland by the Trusteeship Council. In June, the All-Ewe Conference, from then on the focal point of the campaign, resolved to reject any trusteeship agreement which did not provide for Ewe unification, and to press for the whole of Eweland to be brought under British administration. The British authorities then began to accept that the movement was not simply inspired by economic grievances but had political aims.[11]

A rival political movement founded in 1943 was to emerge in 1948 with support from those British Ewes in Togo fearful of domination by Gold Coast Ewes. Their social and economic grievances were compounded by political fears after the Watson Report of 1948 excluded Togo from its constitutional recommendations. The Togo-land Union, later the Togoland Congress, was an effective southern Togo rival to the All-Ewe Conference in 1948, although support for it waned in the early 1950s. Its political demands for seats in the central Legislative Council and a separate regional council for southern Togo reflected fears of absorption into the eastern province of Gold Coast Colony.[12] As a result the nationalism of the Togoland Union was geared to the unification of the two Togos rather than the creation of a unified Ewe state.[13] These differences in the south of Togo added to the fundamental division between the northern and southern peoples of the Gold Coast and British Togo and weakened the nationalist opposition to colonialism. In the north not only did traditional chiefs fear domination by educated élites but a unified Togoland would have divided the ethnic groups straddling the Gold Coast–British Togo frontier.

In the French territory initial support for the Ewe unification movement came from members of the *Comité de L'Unité Togolaise* (CUT), a political party founded in 1941 by members of the *grande bourgeoisie* of Lomé and the southern towns, and dominated by Sylvanus Olympio. As in the British territory there were economic factors influencing the CUT's support for a united Eweland under British administration. In French Togo there was a tax on business turnover and disputes occurred over the allocation of scarce consumer goods to leading trading houses. Wartime shortages, as elsewhere in French West Africa, had been much worse than in neighbouring British territories and the Free French administration attempted, at the end of the war, to impose controls over merchants responsible for supplies and distribution.[14] Most of these were in fact British traders or agents and Olympio, the representative of the United Africa Company (UAC) in Lomé, had received a British education. Clearly these economic problems had political implications, made acute by the French decision in 1945 to give Togo representation in the Constituent Assembly but on a combined basis with Dahomey.[15] At a meeting in May with the French high commissioner in Lomé, African representatives made clear their desire to see French Togo placed under the control of the future UN. Four months later a statement was issued by the notables of the four southern towns rejecting membership of the French Constituent Assembly, which contained an ominous Anglo-Saxon phrase:

Conformément au principe du Trusteeship applicable au Togo, les Togolais évolués qui aspirent naturellement et légitimement au 'self-government' se refusent toute prise de position concernant la députation avant la connaissance et l'etude approfondie du systeme du Trusteeship.[16]

In their increasing determination to prevent integration into the French Union, which was what the French intended to do with their former mandates, the merchants of the CUT were prepared to support any movement which increased their chances of avoiding such a fate; the All-Ewe Conference and the UN both offered opportunities to strengthen their position. Moreover those traditional chiefs in the southern districts who were in close contact with merchant élites were prepared to sign petitions to the UN supporting a united Eweland under British administration and thereby boost the credibility of the French Togo nationalists. Over the next few years the latter were to find it remarkably easy to be taken seriously as nationalist movements, as opposed to sectional interest groups, amongst the corridors of the UN.

In these circumstances, with the *Union Française* being challenged, the authorities in Lomé did not react with the tolerance that was later attributed to the British, and steps were taken to suppress the unification movement. Chief Quem Dessow of Anecho was threatened with imprisonment or deportation if he continued to associate himself with cables to the UN. Herbert Kporta, a teacher who had drafted a telegram, was forced to flee to the Gold Coast in 1946. The French also approached Chief Lawson in an unsuccessful attempt to persuade him to order his sub-chief to send a cable to the UN calling for the unification of Eweland under French Trusteeship.[17]

The fact that all the early demands for Ewe unification requested British trusteeship was obviously embarrassing for the French, but their repressive reactions were influenced by other factors, which made it more difficult to co-ordinate responses with the British. In 1945 there was a significant African exodus from French Togo to the neighbouring British territory. This was explained by the administration in Lomé in terms of the attractions of the British army, the need for labour at the US camp in Accra and the compulsory agricultural production imposed by the French.[18] But the Gold Coast press was producing a mass of anti-French articles which many French officials and administrators felt was encouraged by the British authorities. In the wake of Mers-el-Kebir, the wartime supply controls imposed by the British and the Americans and the expulsion of the Free French from the Levant, it was easy to see the nationalist campaigns as encouraged by the British in order to undermine France's African empire. Right-wing former Vichy officials who remained in positions of authority in Africa and Paris, and whose influence would have been increased as the Cold War developed and the *épuration* receded, must have been particularly prone to such feelings. Noutary, who was an ardent Free Frenchman, described Olympio not as an African nationalist but as an agent of Anglo-American finance working for the integration of French Togo into the Anglo-Saxon Empire.[19]

Some Frenchmen tended to see agents of British imperialism whenever organizations or individuals adopted hostile attitudes to the *Union Française* in any part of West Africa;[20] this reinforced the view that African nationalism was limited to a small number of isolated anti-French individuals rather than certain sectors of society in southern Togo whose complaints deserved attention. The fact that the Ministry of Overseas France adopted such views was also assisted by the structure of French colonial rule. Central direction from Paris was the only channel open for colonial policy-making in Africa, and French governors were often keen to give the impression that instructions emanating from the capital were being implemented successfully. With inspectors visiting French colonies to compile reports, the French system had a built-in tendency for governors to point to the success of metropolitan policy rather than to consult over reactions to new developments in Africa or take policy initiatives themselves. As a result it is not surprising to discover that Henri Laurentie, the director of political affairs in the Ministry of Overseas France, informed the British in 1946 that there was no Ewe problem; he argued that the campaign was confined to a small number of *évolués*, and complained about the nefarious campaign in the Gold Coast press.[21]

The Ministry of Overseas France's desire in the immediate post-war years was to minimalize the significance of the Ewes as far as possible. The *Union Française* was seen as providing a political future for the former mandate of French Togo, and it was hoped that improvements in the economic condition of the territory would lead the population away from the influence wielded by the southern élites, whose activities appeared to be supported by the British. Help would be given by the authorities to those groups prepared to support French rule or to reject the ideas of the élites, and the colonial government therefore encouraged the formation of the *Parti Togolais du Progrès* (PTP) in 1946.

Composed largely of *fonctionnaires* with a vested interest in French rule, the PTP obviously faced difficulties in becoming a mass party, especially with the limited franchise that was in place in the immediate post-war years. In the rural areas the French planned to establish *Conseils de Circonscription* (District Councils) with the chiefs assisted by a council of members elected every four years. As advisory bodies they had no executive power, but the French administration saw them as a way of providing a voice for small peasant producers in opposition to the southern chiefs and the commercial houses.[22]

In the years before 1950, the PTP was a source of disappointment to the French, and the Ministry of Overseas France accused its leaders of failing to understand the need to build up support and present a coherent programme attractive to those prepared to oppose the notables of Lomé and the southern towns. They therefore asked the authorities in Togo whether a new party was required or whether the PTP would eventually fit the bill, because they definitely needed a party which would not disturb their political and administrative freedom and which could present a progressive programme. The worry was that so long as the PTP contained the majority of traditional chiefs they would not be able to attract support from the masses.[23]

The policy of the Ministry of Overseas France therefore was to ignore or suppress the agitation of 'unrepresentative' Ewe nationalists seeking to change international frontiers and encourage the kind of mass-based nationalism which would support a commitment to the *Union Française* and counter the demands of those aiming to secure a different destiny for French Togo. It was a policy they were to pursue throughout the period despite the events in the Gold Coast and British Togo. The problem for the Ministry of Overseas France, and one which forced them to develop additional policies as a very brittle icing on the cake of the French union, was the UN. There, once the mandates became trust territories, the Quai d'Orsay had to work with the British Foreign Office to prevent the good name of France being tarred by international criticism over the Togo question. The result was increasing pressure for the Ministry of Overseas France to work with the British Colonial Office and co-ordinate a response to the

Ewes' protests and petitions, despite the very different French and British reactions to the Ewes' initial demands for unification.

The Colonial Office, with its desire to maintain Britain's international reputation as a liberal colonial power, and with a post-war commitment to a new partnership with Africans, took the complaints from Togoland very seriously. Far from deciding rigidly upon a policy and looking to produce African nationalists to support it, the British were convinced from the start that concessions would have to be made in an effort to deal with Ewe grievances. It was not, however, simply a question of responding to, or channelling, the political demands of African movements in preparation for self-government and independence. In the case of Togo, gaining independence as part of the Gold Coast did not simply result from Ewe demands supported by the UN, nor from any completion of the Colonial Office's efforts at nation building. From start to finish the process was conditioned and constrained by the requirements of British foreign policy and the importance of maintaining good relations with France.

A draft cabinet paper in the summer of 1946 made it clear that there was a conflict between supporting the Ewes' demands for frontier changes and the preservation of good relations with the French. In the Colonial Office a series of options was considered as a possible response to the Ewe positions, but the paper's conclusion supported the maintenance of existing frontiers along with a commitment to have the complaints investigated.[24] As the Colonial Office became aware of the French desire to dismiss the Ewe movement, the official responsible for the draft, J. S. Bennett, became more committed to a positive British response which was likely to alienate the French, including an enquiry directed by the Trusteeship Council. The Ewes would then be free to express their grievances in line with Britain's claim to be a colonial power having great regard for the wishes and interests of dependent peoples whether technically under trusteeship or not.[25]

On the other hand there was a view in the office that the importance of the Ewe problem was being exaggerated. It was also felt that there was a possibility of 'allowing the Ewe question to endanger the prospects of an Anglo-French alliance to which our foreign policy has been closely directed during the last two years and the achievement of which is calculated to have effects on the internal politics of France, which as I understand it, are considered by HMG to be of major importance.'[26] Such views were much more satisfactory for the

Foreign Office which felt that the Ewes were a small matter in comparison with the maintenance of good Anglo-French relations.[27]

But the Colonial Office also realized that because of the UN it could not fall in with French wishes and treat the matter as one of little or no consequence. In the words of one official, to do so would 'raise such a hornet's nest around our ears that I shudder to think what the results might be'.[28] There had to be a response which would show the Ewes that both colonial powers were prepared to take their views seriously, but one which avoided proposals unacceptable to the French.[29] At this point the Colonial Office was hoping to satisfy both the Ewes and the French in order to proceed to a solution which would be acceptable to the UN. They were soon to abandon hopes of finding a solution to satisfy the Ewes and concentrate on actions which would avoid major ructions with the French or the UN. As Noutary's successor noted, it became a quest to get 'something done' in order to prove themselves to the Trusteeship Council, 'mais sans avoir manifestement le désir de réaliser gros efforts'. Ironically[30] for the British, the more impossible it became to find a solution to the problem the more important it was to be seen trying to manufacture one.

What this entailed prior to 1950 was a Joint Consultative Commission of colonial service officers, including the governors of French Togo and the Gold Coast, which also contained four African representatives. It followed an enquiry, conducted by one French and one British officer, which was not empowered to carry out on-the-spot investigations, and which came out against unification while noting the problems posed by the frontier.[31] Anglo-French efforts were therefore geared towards preserving the political and territorial status quo and alleviating the economic difficulties arising from the existence of frontier restrictions. The aim, quite clearly, was to satisfy the short-term French desire to sweep the political dimension of the problem under the carpet while attempting to get something done.

Unfortunately the policy of establishing a Consultative Commission to deal with the Ewe problem by tackling economic grievances was wrecked by the 1949 Visiting Mission of the Trusteeship Council, which found that the unification campaign in the two Togos and in the Keta district of the Gold Coast had assumed the character of a popular nationalist movement.[32] The British were now convinced that 'something would have to be done' to deal with the political aspects of the problem and pre-empt any calls for the direct involvement of the UN. The problem was finding a form of action which, in the short term, would go some way to satisfying the Trusteeship Council while proving acceptable to the French. With the Ministry of Overseas France, to the increasing irritation of the Quai d'Orsay, refusing to face up to the political dimensions of the problem, this did not seem an easy task.[33] In 1948 the Quai had hinted that with the British involving Togo representatives in the government of the Gold Coast similar policies in AOF would be easier to sell at the UN than the idea of involving Africans in metropolitan politics. The Ministry of Overseas France insisted, however, that the two African Trust Territories 'font constitutionellement partie intégrante de la République Française',[34] a position which while technically incorrect,[35] appeared to rule out constitutional changes incompatible with the French Union. In these circumstances it was only with great difficulty that the Colonial Office managed to persuade their French counterparts of the need for a new initiative in the wake of the Visiting Mission's report.[36]

By 1950 the British had definitely decided that no solution was likely to satisfy Ewe grievances without provoking other similar complaints, and, even if it were, no change of frontiers would prove acceptable to the French because that was certain to mean the loss of French territory. With Togoland independence thus ruled out, in the long term the only thing that could be done with British Togo was to incorporate it into the Gold Coast. This was the solution favoured by the head of the African division in the Colonial Office, Andrew Cohen, who also came up with a possible answer to the short-term problem. His idea was to enlarge the Consultative Commission by incorporating representatives from throughout Togoland in the hope that they would squabble amongst themselves. Representatives from the north would oppose Ewe unification while those from the south would be divided over whether the Gold Coast Ewes should or should not be included. In this way the UN would become convinced that no nationalist solution based on self-determination would be possible, and the ground could therefore be prepared for the integration of British Togo into the Gold Coast without any redrawing of international boundaries. It would also allow sufficient time for the inhabitants of Togo to see the new Gold Coast constitution of 1951 in operation and in Cohen's view, once the magnitude of the advance towards self-government was appreciated, incorporation into the Gold Coast would prove irresistible.[37]

During the next two years these British solutions to the problem of Ewe nationalism faced a number of difficulties, some of which were connected with French attitudes. In the first place the British were unable initially to tell the French of their wish to incorporate British Togo into the Gold Coast. This was not because they feared adverse reactions to a policy of self-government at odds with the French union, but because they realized the incorporation of British Togo would be interpreted as part of yet another perfidious Anglo-Saxon plot to destroy the French Empire.[38] What was of particular concern to the French was the 1951 Gold Coast Constitution; it was assumed in Paris that the constitution would attract British Togo to the Gold Coast with the corollary that French Togo would follow suit, especially as Olympio was suspected of being in the pay of British Intelligence. In Whitehall such fears were seen as the major obstacle to developing a joint Anglo-French policy on Togoland, and it was noted that some French officials 'including their senior people, have deep-rooted suspicions of British intentions which they have never attempted to conceal'.[39] The one long-term bright spot for the Colonial Office was that the Quai attributed the unhappy state of affairs in AOF to the stupidity of the Ministry of Overseas France in refusing to consider genuine self-government.[40]

In the short term, although the Ministry of Overseas France agreed to go ahead with Cohen's idea of extending the Consultative Commission to 30 representatives from French and 17 from British Togo, the Colonial Office's plan immediately backfired. The elections were on a much extended franchise in French Togo and the administration managed to influence them to the extent that an anti-unification majority was inevitable by the first stage of the electoral process, which caused the CUT to withdraw from the six (of 14) southern seats they were likely to win.[41] Sadly, amidst a series of complaints about the conduct of French elections most representatives from British Togo then decided to boycott the commission; so instead of producing squabbling Africans, the first meeting was dominated by representatives from French Togo who, according to Arden-Clarke, spoke like 'a troop of well drilled parrots' against unification or any change of administering authority.[42]

The governor of the Gold Coast could find no evidence of anything improper in the way the French conducted the elections, but the British received various reports indicating that pressure was exerted by the administration to help produce the right result.[43] One, from an African source, referred to a circle commander who instructed voters to come to his office to vote in public. There they were faced with a walk between two ranks of policemen and had to choose a blue or white ticket; it was clear that the former represented a vote for Britain, the latter a vote for France.[44] Pressure on voters and African representatives was central to the French policy of producing the right kind of nationalists, and the British, rightly or wrongly, perceived it as a feature prevalent throughout French West Africa.

In the Dakar consulate, the British colonial attaché reported on French electoral practices after a tour through AOF in 1951 and early 1952. Pirie found that the French added Africans to the electoral role who were not legally qualified to vote, started up political parties with government funds and bought off African agitators; if that failed the latter were sometimes deported to other parts of the federation. One junior French service officer told of asking an African how he had voted and of receiving the reply of 'for the commandant'. French circle commanders were obviously making it quite clear how they expected their native charges to vote.[45] In Togo the British view of the 1950 Consultative Commission elections was that the large-scale nature of the assistance and encouragement given to pro-government parties meant it was a result of orders from the central government in Lomé rather than from individual officers.[46]

French actions in helping to secure an anti-unificationist majority in the 1950 elections were in accord with their general approach to the influencing of nationalist opinion, but they also reflected the tactics of the Ministry of Overseas France and the Togo authorities in dealing with the Ewe problem. Unlike the British, they saw dealing with anti-French nationalism in Togo as the only response that was necessary; now that the electorate had rejected unification they felt nothing more needed to be done because this was the only issue on which the election had been held. It was therefore simply a question of telling the UN that that was the end of the Ewe unification movement.[47] The British, however, realized that the problem had ultimately to be resolved in the UN because the Trusteeship Council had to endorse whatever final solution was arrived at. Therefore for them, while petitions continued to arrive at the UN, the vote in French Togo served only to justify maintaining the status quo until some other remedy for the petitioners' grievances could be found. The British also realized that integration would be acceptable to the UN only if it meant uniting British Togo with an independent Gold Coast; their Gold Coast and Togoland strategies had therefore to be co-ordinated. Whatever the wishes of the inhabitants of Togoland this was the only solution which would be acceptable to international opinion while preserving good Anglo-French relations. For the British, the nationalist question centred on how best to ensure that support for such a policy was secured in both Africa and the UN.

There then began a great battle by the British, the Quai and the French representative on the Trusteeship Council, Henri Laurentie, to convince the Ministry of Overseas France that the problem had to be dealt with at the UN; and that with the enlarged Consultative Commission proving unworkable because of the boycott, yet another initiative would be required. The danger, so the British argued, was that as the commission had failed to provide a solution the UN would regard the Ewe problem as re-opened, with the possibility of a UN plebiscite or even UN administration of Togoland. The idea that emerged in 1951, after consultation with the Americans and a crisis in allied relations at the UN, was a joint council, which had clear political overtones.[48] The British never expected it to achieve anything but hoped it would buy time until a majority of the inhabitants of British Togo could be guaranteed to support integration into the Gold Coast.[49]

Fortunately, in 1951 both the Ministry of Overseas France and the UN went along with the idea, but unfortunately the latter showed too much enthusiasm for it; it saw in a joint council the makings of a legislative body for the whole of Togoland, and the Trusteeship Council wanted it elected on a basis of universal suffrage. The British were now heading towards dangerous waters because if the progress of Togoland towards self-government was made along these lines the French would certainly be alienated. Their concern increased when in 1952 the All-Ewe Conference began to support Togoland unification as the first step towards a unified Eweland, a policy which Olympio had apparently been urging on Nkrumah with some success.[50] Since the 1951 election Nkrumah and the CPP had been part of the Gold Coast government, and on assuming ministerial office had initially refused to meet all Ewe Conference representatives on the grounds that Ewe unification could not usefully be discussed until full self-government was achieved.[51] But by 1952 the British believed that as a result of a talk with Olympio, Nkrumah was now prepared to support the unification of the two Togos in order then to incorporate the whole of Togoland into the Gold Coast.[52]

This was obviously the worst possible outcome from the French point of view and also bad for the British who, in 1951, had looked to the CPP as a useful weapon in arousing support for the integration of British Togoland into the Gold Coast; if African nationalists supported this there would be no need to upset the French by telling them it was British policy. Luckily the urgency of this need was removed in 1952 when the suspicions and distrust harboured in the Ministry of Overseas France began to decline. In Europe there were talks between the two ministers responsible for colonial affairs, Lyttleton and Pflimlin, and the British ambassador was instructed to impress upon the French that Britain had no intention of annexing French Togo to the Gold Coast. In Africa, Nkrumah and the CPP declined to take part in the elections for the new Togoland Joint Council, a step which would also have reduced French fears of the incorporation of a united Togoland into a self-governing Gold Coast.[53]

The British were therefore able to inform the French of their ultimate goal without too great a fear of the reactions in Paris. From now on there was a common Anglo-French policy on the integration of British Togo into the Gold Coast. The main reason for this French acceptance of the Colonial Office's policy appears, from the British archives, to have been the realization in the Ministry of Overseas France that this was the only way to prevent French Togo being lost to the French Union. To go for Togoland unification would have led to the whole territory being lost, because a unified Togoland would prefer self-government or integration into the Gold Coast to incorporation into the *Union Française*. In other words, from the Ministry of Overseas France's point of view, far from seeing self-government and independence for the Gold Coast and British Togo as heralding the demise of the *Union Française*, it was the only way to save it. The common policy of division and integration was thus the way to preserve good Anglo-French relations and allow each to pursue its own colonial policies.

An important consideration was the timing of the transfer of power in the Gold Coast, for the British had to ensure that support for integration was formally confirmed by a plebiscite before the Gold Coast became independent. The Joint Council, which also proved unworkable, was not revived after 1954, but elections of that year in the Gold Coast also involved British Togo where the issue was one of unification versus integration. The nationalists supporting the unification of Togo were opposed by the nationalists of the CPP arguing for integration, and of the six seats in Southern Togo the CPP won three with one going to an independent. This was a key victory because the electoral rejection of unification would carry weight in the UN where the two colonial powers were having trouble convincing the Arabs and the Indians of the benefits of integration. The Togoland Union had told the 1952 Visiting Mission of their desire for a UN trusteeship followed by independence within five years, and the anti-colonial elements in the UN were reluctant to abandon French Togo to its non-independent fate. In these circumstances the British remained keen to use Nkrumah's nationalists to support integration because they felt they themselves could not afford to be seen to do so.[54]

The problem was that Nkrumah's nationalists were not effective enough in parts of Southern Togo, and the British would certainly have preferred a greater endorsement than that given in the 1954 Gold Coast election. Another drawback was Nkrumah's lingering desire to obtain French Togo as well; and the CPP leader may have been subjected to a certain amount of pressure to abandon his campaign for unification followed by integration. One lever was the Volta River project which the British felt might not go ahead if British Togo was not satisfactorily integrated into the Gold Coast. At all events, Nkrumah's co-operation was secured, a fact which when leaked in the form of a secret government document proved embarrassing for the British and the CPP.

The end of colonial rule in British Togo and the Gold Coast had to be achieved as part and parcel of the same Anglo-French operation. This meant that while the British could put pressure on Nkrumah to co-operate in the implementation of the combined operation they were also committed to ensuring that Nkrumah acquired British Togo in return for abandoning French Togo. In the run up to Togo's independence the British were therefore bargaining with CPP nationalism as part of a strategy devised, not in response to nationalist pressures in Togo, but because of the specific need to get rid of the territory without embarrassing the French or bringing direct UN interference into the affairs of Togoland; failure, the Colonial Office believed would affect the Gold Coast's position, if not the timetable for independence, very seriously.[55]

The culmination of the strategy was in the 1956 plebiscite approved by the Trusteeship Council in 1955. Ironically the authorities in the Gold Coast felt an important boost would be given to the integration campaign if it was made clear that there was no possibility of Britain continuing to administer British Togo in the event of integration being rejected. A speech by Sir Charles Arden-Clarke in 1955 emphasized the determination of the Gold Coast government to abandon its responsibility for the trust territory, thereby making the election more a straight choice between independence as part of the Gold Coast or administration by some other authority.[56] What in fact Arden-Clarke was keen to overcome was the short-term attraction for some Togo nationalists of continuing under British administration, in other words, decolonization with a vengeance. Arden-Clarke's tactics gave priority to the securing of an independent Gold Coast/British Togo in a way which would retain the good will of the nationalists in the CPP by doing everything possible to ensure the Gold Coast acquired British Togo. From Arden-Clarke's perspective, if the French had to be appeased so did Nkrumah.

It was then that a threat to this policy appeared in the person of the British Colonial Secretary, Lennox-Boyd, who refused to rule out the continuation of British rule in part or all of Togo if integration were rejected;[57] this was rightly perceived by those on the spot as encouraging the unificationists who were eager in the short term to continue under British rule, and therefore to risk alienating Nkrumah if the Gold Coast achieved independence without British Togo. Whether or not the uncertainty over British Togo's future if integration should be rejected influenced the plebiscite, the combined efforts of the nationalists and the administration failed to prevent a unificationist victory in Southern Togo by 54,785 to 43,976. It was only the 4 to 1 integrationist majority in the north (48,793 to 12,619) which enabled the British to say that what in effect was a policy of unite with the Gold Coast and decolonize had been a success.[58] What is significant in terms of reactions to nationalism was that the British shift from divide and rule (or divide to preserve the status quo) to unite and decolonize was implemented from 1952 onwards not because of the situation in Togoland but because of a French acceptance of the policy. Similarly the French acceptance was conditioned not by the African dimension, but by declining fears of British imperialism and a realization that integration provided the best chance of preserving French Togo as part of the *Union Française*. From the beginning to the end of the period the latter aim appears, from the British records, to have been the French priority, although there was clearly a conflict over the fundamentals of colonial policy represented by the *Union Française* and over the modifications needed in order to secure its acceptance by Africans. In Paris those outside the Ministry of Overseas France clearly had doubts by the beginning of the 1950s as to whether the union would prove a viable long-term proposition; these doubts were also shared by some officials in Dakar who realized that Africans would sooner or later seek power and responsibility in AOF rather than Paris.[59] It was partly to try and reconcile these views with the continuation of the union that moves towards greater internal self-government were made by the French in the mid-1950s. Jacquinot, Minister of Overseas France from August 1951 to February 1952 and January 1953 to June 1954 was a believer in greater decentralization, which was certainly not the view of some of his leading officials. His commitment to strengthening territorial assemblies[60] was accompanied by a desire to strengthen the Assembly of the French Union, and the policy of a centralized *Union Française* combined with local decentralization was spelled out to the British in 1954 by his successor at the Ministry of Overseas France, Robert Buron. The French minister made it clear that 'this decentralization, and the granting of a very widespread local franchise, are not, as with the British, symptomatic of a loose association but on the contrary the direct counterpart of a tendency towards closer integration with the mother country'.[61] By 1955, yet another new minister, P. H. Teitgen, was looking to achieve administrative decentralization and a federal structure within the union. Faced with the hostility and inertia of the French parliament, Teitgen was exploring the possibility of an enabling law which eventually became the *loi cadre* and was passed by the French parliament in June 1956.[62]

These moves, seen by some as necessary to preserve the union in a reformed guise, coincided not only with the plebiscite in British Togo but with the discussions over the position of the French overseas territories in the European Economic Community (EEC). On this issue, leading members of Mollet's government saw the creation of the EEC on Euro-African lines as the only way to save what could be saved of the *Union Française*.[63] In France, therefore, policy towards Togo and the reforms brought by the *loi cadre* have to be considered in the general context of adapting the union in order to maintain France's global role and preserve the ties between the mother country and colonies. Models of decolonization based on reactions to nationalism and independence are not sufficient.

In particular, the idea that the French were forced to contemplate new moves to self-government in 1956 in response to the effect of

British policy on French Togo is too facile. The reaction of the authorities in Lomé to Togo nationalism had produced a situation in which the opponents of the union achieved no electoral successes from 1950 to 1955. Moreover from 1952 the agreement with the British provided an opportunity to work for a resolution of the Ewe question which would preserve French Togo as part of the *Union Française*; it was a policy of separate political development designed to serve long-term imperial goals. What the French were faced with in 1956 was the need to get broader support in Togo for the union in order to convince the UN that the territory's future lay within it. The ideal opportunity seemed to stem from the Togo Territorial Assembly's resolution of 1955 in favour of terminating the trusteeship agreement and incorporating the territory into the *Union Française*. The French were keen to exploit this favourable situation. But as the Colonial Office pointed out, if the intention to hold a French plebiscite was announced before the one in British Togo was held, the whole Ewe question would be back in the melting-pot and the UN might refuse to ratify the British plebiscite pending the results in French Togo.[64] Worst of all, it would strengthen the unificationists' position by enhancing the prospects of both parts of Togo remaining under trusteeship until a united Togoland was ready for self-government. The fact that such an eventuality would have been totally unacceptable to the French and the Gold Coast authorities explains why the announcement of a French plebiscite was delayed until July 1956, after the referendum in British Togo had been held and endorsed by the Trusteeship Council.

Thus the July 1956 announcement of a plebiscite did not reflect a sudden change of policy by the French,[65] but the post-1952 co-ordination of Anglo-French plans for Togoland. The rapid and dramatic nature of the public shift stemmed from the early 1956 need to oppose any simultaneous plebiscite, and the subsequent French fear that with the Gold Coast independent and the restraining hand of Britain removed, pressure on French Ewes to secede and join the Gold Coast would be increased.[66] Throughout the period it was this fear of secession that conditioned French policy more than the need to follow in the self-government footsteps of the British because of nationalist pressures.

In turn this embodied a commitment to the maintenance of the *Union Française* whether on Euro-African or exclusively French lines, and with or without some form of decentralization and local autonomy present in it. The need was to rebuild and retain a French imperial presence in Africa, and this general requirement, still based on the union, dominated the approach to the Ewe question and relations both with African nationalists and the British. The attitudes of the African groups were just one factor which had to be considered within the combined international and local context. In general terms the moves by the Ministry of Overseas France in the mid-1950s towards greater decentralization and partial self-government[67] stemmed from perceptions of both African and international requirements; but it is hard to detect any sign that the demands of Togo nationalists produced any specific changes in the attitudes of French colonial policy-makers or the timing of their initiatives. The Ministry of Overseas France was initially much more concerned with the threat of British imperialism than the threat of African nationalism and later prepared, however inexplicably, to see self-government and co-operation with the British as a means of preserving rather than undermining the *Union Française*.[68] In general terms the moves towards autonomy within a reformed, but clearly identifiable union may have reflected the well-known combination of international opinion, African demands and internal bureaucratic pressures on the Ministry of Overseas France; but they do not explain why or when specific policies were adopted in Togo, with integration being preferred to unification.

Togo was important because the French saw its loss as extremely damaging for the empire; and both the supporters and opponents of more decentralization and self-government within the *Union Française* had to find the best way to prevent such an eventuality. This dictated French policy, and explains the post-1952 moves towards co-operation with Britain over Togoland's ultimate future; it also explains the timing of French initiatives (and the lack of them) in 1955 and 1956. In the post-1952 period when British and French policy towards the Ewes was geared to a long-term mutually acceptable strategy, French tactics developed from the need to appease the UN and co-operate with Britain's policy of integrating British Togo into the Gold Coast rather than from nationalist pressures. The post-war reaction of the Togo authorities to nationalism was based on distinguishing between those groups in favour of the *Union Française* and those opposed to it, and the administration consistently endeavoured to help the former to electoral success; it was a question of inducing the Africans to support the policies and therefore in marked contrast to policy making in response to African demands. Unfortunately, despite its apparent success, this proved insufficient to satisfy the UN, requiring a plebiscite in 1956 to gauge the extent of mass support for the pro-*Union Française* African leaders.

The British, too, sought collaborators in Togo who would support their policies, but were less inflexible than the French and more prepared to adapt policies to attract African support. Indeed one initial reaction in the Colonial Office emphasized the importance of this principle, although others were more aware of the foreign-policy restraints on its application. Moreover, as the Colonial Office soon realized, there were no nationalists whose policies could be adopted without arousing the opposition of others. This indicates an important aspect of the relationship between the colonial authorities and Togo nationalists with the latter forming a number of competing parties whose differences could be exploited to ensure that priorities rather than principles were secured. The process was a complex one in which priorities in London and Africa were not always the same, and in which care had to be taken lest the securing of one goal jeopardised more important ones. For Britain the goodwill of Nkrumah, the timing of Gold Coast independence, UN support, meaningful responses to Ewe protests and good Anglo-French relations were difficult balls for colonial policy-makers to keep in play.

In such circumstances the need to stay in the imperial game and preserve British influence dictated priorities, and reacting to Togo nationalism was not one of them. If alienating Nkrumah would have been a major setback, a break with the French or allowing direct interference by the UN would have meant certain defeat. It was these international considerations, not reactions to nationalism, that conditioned the nature and timing of British initiatives in Togo and which, with French co-operation, produced the shift from dividing and ruling to uniting and decolonizing in the post-1952 period.

Notes

1. 'Togoland' will be used to refer to the two mandated, later trust, territories administered by the French and British. 'Togo' will apply to either the French or British parts of Togoland.
2. M. Michel, 'Le Togo dans les Relations Internationales au Lendemain de la Guerre: Prodrome de la Décolonisation ou "Petite Mésentente Cordiale?" 1945–1951' in *Les Chemins de la Décolonisation de l'Empire*

Colonial Français 1936–56. Colloque organisé par l'Institut d'Histoire du Temps Présent sous la direction de C.-R. Ageron (Paris 1986).

3. A good analysis can be found in A. N. Porter and A. J. Stockwell (eds), *British Imperial Policy and Decolonisation: Vol. I 1939–51* (London 1987).

4. E. Mortimer, *France and the Africans* (London 1969) p. 203; John D. Hargreaves, *Decolonisation in Africa* (London 1989) pp. 142–4.

5. *West Africa* magazine, Feb. 1951.

6. CO 537/2037, Memorandum on Ewe Petitions Aug. 1947 Appendix 'History of the Ewe petitions'.

7. FO 371/60112, A. H. Poynton to T. R. O. Mangin, 28 Sept. 1946.

8. This would not of course have incorporated all the Ewes under British rule because many were dispersed away from the areas in which Ewes predominated. Nor would it have solved the problems of the Ewes in French Togo. The Ewes accounted for 33 per cent of the population in French Togo, according to figures given by J. S. Coleman, 'Togoland' *International Conciliation* 509 (1956). According to the 1948 census there were 113,000 Ewes in British Togo and 391,000 in the Gold Coast, 93,000 of whom lived outside the area of Ewe concentration.

9. FO 371/49295: Sir A. Burns to G. Creasy, 9 Dec. 1944; FO 371/67718 Memorandum by T. A. Mead and M. Maillet, July 1947.

10. 'Eweland' was defined on the east and west as an area between the Mono and Volta rivers. On the north, the boundary was ill-defined in the north of southern British Togo where Ewe clans (*dukomewos*) mingled with other ethnic groups and those who had close affinities with the Ewes. These groups separated the southern Ewe-dominated areas from the northern parts of Togo and the Gold Coast inhabited by distinctive ethnic groups which had not yet benefited from the economic and educational advances made in the south.

11. FO 371/60112: copy of despatch from T. R. O. Mangin, 8 Oct. 1946.

12. CO 96/811/31651: Petition from Togoland Union to the UN, 1 April 1949.

13. In economic terms a single Togoland state under British administration would have the same effect regarding the removal of frontier controls as a united Eweland, for there were no barriers between Togo and the Gold Coast. In political terms it was quite different as not only would there be many non-Ewe people incorporated in the north, but the Gold Coast Ewes would be excluded. For the French Ewes, both options could be, and were, supported as a way of escaping from French rule.

14. Archives Nationales Section Outre Mer (ANSOM) Aff. Pol. 3279, Rapport sur la politique d'ensemble du Territoire du Fev au Mai 1944, ANSOM, Aff. Pol. 3297. Noutary (high commissioner, Togo) à Monsieur le Ministre France Outre Mer, 2 May 1947.

15. This decision was later reversed and Togo given its own representative.

16. FO 371/60112: copy of a letter from the president of the Council of Notables (Lomé) to the high commissoner of Togo.

17. Ibid, Gold Coast Policy Report, 20 May 1946.

18. ANSOM, Aff. Pol. 362, 'Bulletin de Renseignements 30 Aug. 1945 'Activités Britanniques au Togo'.

19. ANSOM, Aff. Pol. 3297, unsigned, undated minute.
20. See, for example, the article in *Le Figaro* about the Dakar Communications Conference of 1947 in CO 936/33/1 and British assessments of
some French attitudes in FO 371/95757: Minute by C. P. Hope, 17 Nov.
1951, and FO 371/88498: Minute by C. M. le Quesne, 9 Jan. 1951.
21. FO 371/60112: H. Laurentie to A. J. Dawe, 22 July 1946.
22. ANSOM, Aff. Pol. 3297, Note pour le Ministre, 19 Sept. 1947.
23. ANSOM, Aff. Pol. 3316/5, Ministère de la France Outre Mer à M le
Commissaire de la République au Togo, May 1948.
24. FO 371/60112: J. S. Bennett to A. Rumbold, 11 July 1946.
25. CO 537/2037: Minute by J. S. Bennett, 1 Feb. 1947.
26. Ibid., minute by K. E. Robinson, 25 Feb. 1947.
27. FO 371/60112: Minute by O. Harvey, 12 Aug. 1946.
28. Ibid., A. H. Poynton to T. R. O. Mangin, 28 Sept. 1946.
29. CO 537/2037: Minute by A. Campbell, 25 June 1947.
30. ANSOM, Aff. Pol. 3316/5, Cedile à Ministre de la France Outre Mer,
29 April 1948. (Report on visit to the Gold Coast).
31. The French refused to consider an on-the-spot investigation, although
the authorities in the Gold Coast believed that such an enquiry was
necessary and desirable.
32. CO 537/5713: Report of the 1949 Visiting Mission, 17 Feb. 1950.
33. When the Visiting Mission was in Togo the French had tried to argue
that the political problem was one of '10 persons'. CO 96/810/31614/14:
Note of meeting between Anglo-French Working Party and Visiting
Mission, Dec. 1949.
34. ANSOM, Aff. Pol. 3316/5: Le Ministre des Affaires Étrangères à M le
Ministre de la France Outre Mer, 6 Feb. 1948; ANSOM, Aff. Pol. 3316/
4: Delavignette (Director of Political Affairs MOF) au Ministre des
Affaires Étrangères, 11 March 1949.
35. Associated territories were not included in the French Republic. See L.
Rolland and P. Lampue, *Précis de droit des Pays d'Outre Mer* (Paris 1949),
p. 108. I am grateful to Professor John D. Hargreaves for pointing this
out and providing the reference.
36. CO 537/5816: Record of Anglo-French Discussions, 10–11 March
1950.
37. Ibid., A. B. Cohen to Sir C. Arden-Clarke (Governor of the Gold Coast),
22 Feb. 1950.
38. For the nature and extent of French suspicions of British imperialism in
West Africa during this period see John Kent, 'Les Relations Franco-
Britanniques et L'Avenir du Togo 1945–55', *Relations Internationales*
(forthcoming). Even H. Laurentie, a notable anglophile, was threatening
a frank French government statement that the British representatives in
Southern Togo had annexationist tendencies *vis-à-vis* French Togo. CO
537/5818: Sir G. Jebb (Paris) to Foreign Office, 28 Nov. 1950.
39. CO 537/7179: Draft letter to Washington Embassy, April 1951.
40. CO 537/5818: Memorandum by C. P. Hope (FO), 12 June 1951
(recording a conversation with M. Gaucher of the French Embassy).

41. The electoral system used in French Togo was not the same as that in operation for the Territorial Assembly election.

42. CO 537/5818: Sir C. Arden-Clarke to A. B. Cohen, 15 Nov. 1950. The governor of the Gold Coast later commented that the French 'presumably as a result of their own practices seem unable to believe that we allowed our representatives to speak freely' (Sir C. Arden-Clarke to A. B. Cohen, 4 Jan. 1951).

43. CO 537/7178: Sir C. Arden-Clarke to A. B. Cohen, 4 Jan. 1951.

44. CO 537/7179: W. A. C. Mathieson to A. N. Galsworthy, 2 May 1951, reporting a conversation with S. G. Antor, a supporter of Togoland rather than Ewe unification.

45. CO 936/89: Report by D. G. Pirie on West African Tour, Nov. 1951–Feb. 1952.

46. CO 537/7178: Note on the elections for the Standing Consultative Commission in Togo, Oct. 1950.

47. CO 537/5818: Sir C. Arden-Clarke to the secretary of state, 26 Sept. 1950.

48. For the details, see John Kent 'Les Relations . . .', op. cit.

49. CO 554/663: Sir J. Martin to C. P. Hope (FO), 12 Dec. 1951 and CO 537/7180: T. B. Williamson to Sir C. Arden-Clarke, 2 Oct. 1951.

50. CO 554/664: Minute by M. G. Smith, 31 July 1952.

51. CO 537/7179: Sir C. Arden-Clarke to L. H. Gorsuch, 6 April 1951.

52. CO 554/664: Minute by M. G. Smith, 31 July 1952.

53. CO 537/7180: Minute by T. B. Williamson, 2 Oct. 1951; CO 537/7179: Foreign Office to Sir O. Harvey, 7 April 1951.

54. CO 554/1032: Conclusions and Recommendations of 1952 Visiting Mission; secretary of state to Sir C. Arden-Clarke (Secret and Personal), 11 Jan. 1954.

55. CO 554/664: secretary of state to Sir C. Arden-Clarke (Secret and Personal), 9 Jan. 1953. For information on the leak of the most 'Most Secret Document' see CO 554/666: Extracts from Gold Coast Weekly Intelligence Report no. 11, 8 Aug. 1953, and C. E. Welch *Dream of Unity: Pan Africanism and Political Unification in West Africa* (Ithaca 1966), pp. 105–6; CO 554/1037: H. T. Bourdillon to Sir C. Arden-Clarke, 13 Jan. 1955.

56. This speech aroused the wrath of the colonial secretary Lennox-Boyd who, like the die-hard Tory imperialists, could not bear to contemplate part of the British Empire passing to the UN or to the French. See John Kent, 'Les Relations . . .', op. cit.

57. For the Cabinet discussion, see CAB 128/29: CM (55), 40th, 10 Nov. 1955.

58. For the results of the referendum, see C. E. Welch, op. cit., pp. 121–6; CO 554/1040.

59. CO 537/4611: Report by A. B. Cohen on a visit to AOF, June 1949.

60. Marchés Coloniaux, 13 May 1954, cited in J. R. de Benoist, *L'Afrique Occidentale Française de 1944 à 1960*, (Dakar 1982), p. 161.

61. FO 371/108109: Record of Anglo-French Ministerial Meeting, Oct. 1954. His statement came when a new statute for Togo was being

considered which he hoped would allow the inhabitants of the more advanced territories to '*participer à la gestion des territoires*'. J. R. de Benoist, op. cit., p. 182.

62. J. R. de Benoist, op. cit., pp. 162–3.
63. Pierre Guillen, 'L'Avenir de l'Union Française dans la Négociation des Traités de Rome', *Relations Internationales 57* (1989), p. 104.
64. CO 936/332: Brief for Lennox-Boyd on Anglo-French official discussions, Nov. 1955.
65. Welch, noting initial French opposition to a plebiscite, explains the shift solely by suggesting the French hoped to eliminate the power of the UN to intervene in Togo affairs (C. E. Welch, op. cit., cited in note 55, p. 127).
66. CO 936/316: Record of Anglo-French-Belgian talks on colonial questions at the UN, 1–2 Oct. 1956.
67. The British were quick to point out that the powers given to the new French Togo Assembly did not cover customs, the administration of justice and some aspects of labour and higher education, and therefore fell short of full self-government (CO 554/1042: Minute by J. E. Marnham, 3 Oct. 1956).
68. Bernard Cornut-Gentille, high commissioner of AOF from Sept. 1951 to July 1956, was one who did see the contradiction between local autonomy and the centralized assimilationist *Union Française*. Cornut-Gentille became the first, and last, minister of overseas France in the Fifth Republic.

10

HABITS OF MIND AND FORCES OF HISTORY: France, Britain and the Decolonization of Africa

John D. Hargreaves

Throughout the post-war decade, as during earlier periods, contrasts between the objectives and methods of French and British colonial rule in Africa seemed self-evident. For Kenneth Robinson, the starting-point of the academic career to which he turned on leaving the Colonial Office in 1948, was 'an assumption, more general then than it is now, that there were significant differences between the colonialisms of the different powers and that these differences might be expected to have long-term consequences'.[1] That there were differences and long-term consequences is undeniable. After a quarter-century many observers might still agree with Michael Crowder 'that when one crosses from Nigeria into Dahomey or Niger, or from Gambia to Senegal, the main impression one has is that of crossing the twenty miles of water that separate England from France.'[2] Academic studies are beginning to amplify that impression in precise detail.[3]

Yet historical perspective, as Kenneth Robinson's formulation concedes, sometimes reveals powerful similarities of structure and direction beneath the colourful contrasts. Had the makers of post-war policy not shared some sense of common objectives, as well as of common constraints, Kenneth himself could hardly have established such close relationships with French contemporaries like Paul-Marc Henry or Charles-André Julien. As John Kent has demonstrated, attempts to concert common policies at the time came to little, but essentially because of differing priorities of international politics: the French were primarily anxious 'to restore their imperial prestige and influence'[4] against American challenges which their partners took less seriously, and to retain metropolitan control over the process of colonial reform. Yet their persistence with such conversations reflected a strong sense of common purpose within a common predicament. If 'decolonization' was never a phrase much favoured by officials, by the later 1940s reformers in both Paris and London – if not in every African Government House – had become committed to reforms on such a scale that charges of colonialism would lose their credibility, among Africans as well as internationally. Both governments were still hoping to retain long-term benefits from their colonial relationships, as sources of strength in those same economic and political crises which had made reform unavoidable, and in the longer-term re-establishment of an international balance of power; but some at least had begun to appreciate that economic benefits formerly derived from the possession of colonial authority might actually become impediments to modernization of the metropolitan economy.

As they came to deal with the realities of post-war Africa, France and Britain encountered many experiences in parallel. In the Gold Coast in 1948 and the Ivory Coast in 1950, popular movements based among the Akan compelled each government in turn to collaborate with African partners formerly judged unacceptable. In Madagascar and Kenya insurrections with deep but essentially local roots were with difficulty brought under military control. At Suez in 1956 both countries shared a bitter lesson in the limitations of their military power. And eventually every African dependency of the two powers north of the Zambezi, except Jibuti, achieved sovereign independence within the nine years 1956–65. Perhaps indeed the most striking divergence between French and British policies in Africa came after, not before, this apparently climactic period.[5]

But academics viewing processes of government from outside can easily exaggerate the importance of policy. If the course of historical change is set by forces which even powerful statesmen and prescient counsellors can deflect only marginally, the institutions and cultural climate within which change is actually experienced by living persons may be influenced by behaviour at much humbler levels. Kenneth Robinson himself has made the point with lapidary precision: 'habits of mind are important even if "policies" are not'.[6] Building on his own autobiographical reflections, this essay will explore some lasting residues of the differing styles in which Frenchmen and British undertook the liquidation of their colonial empires.

The exercise of authority

Despite the extensive literature comparing administrative structures in the African empires of France and Britain, the cultural and intellectual assumptions of the men who devised and operated them are harder to define. Those few who, like Kenneth Robinson, have had opportunities to observe district officers at work in both empires are wisely cautious of generalization. On the French side particularly, there were important generational changes, as recruitment broadened and training methods changed; men of very different background and temperament co-existed within the colonial service.[7] On her brief reconnaissances into Chad in 1932, Margery Perham was struck by the contrast between the cultured and cosmopolitan Governor de Coppet and his unshaven and unhelpful *chef de Cabinet*.[8] The literature does not facilitate systematic comparison; perhaps we have enough published memoirs by British DCs to support some tentative generalization, but there appear to be only two comparable books by French colonial administrators – of different generations, and in one case self-consciously atypical – together with some semi-autobiographical writings by Robert Delavignette.[9]

One possible starting point is the education of the rulers of empire. French officials, appointed to administer the system of public law codified by Napoleon were traditionally trained in law and jurisprudence, and these subjects remained the basis of the curriculum for colonial administrators.[10] But while French law faculties provided the bases from which wider studies in the social sciences developed, the cutting edge of these disciplines does not seem to have penetrated the *Ecole Coloniale* to any great extent. Into the 1920s its dominant spirit was that of Paul Dislère (1840–1928), a dry bureaucrat whose overseas experience in Indo-China went back to the Second Empire; his main concern seems to have been that students should know what French law prescribed so that they could faithfully apply it in the colonies. Deschamps, while admitting the value for reference of Arthur Girault's *Traité de legislation coloniale* which served as the course Bible, remembered with contempt boringly detailed expositions of the content of laws and decrees, and theoretical expositions of 'colonial policy' by Louis Vignon.[11] For some alumni at least this training may have

encouraged pedantic zeal to follow metropolitan bureaucratic procedures, as well as laws: habits of mind still observable in the public
service of some independent states.

These aridities were redeemed by contributions from gifted teachers with field experience, like Maurice Delafosse, pioneer in the
search to understand African cultures, and later Robert Delavignette,
who emphasized the need to balance 'a double concept: what is legal,
and what is humanly feasible for the natives'.[12] Once in the field,
graduates of the 'Colo' struck their own balances; most of them, as
Deschamps puts it, seem to have 'managed very well without the
Bible'.[13] His own memoirs, like those of Méker, suggest that legal
training often counted for less than a rough administrative ethos of
benevolent despotism; the 'kings of the bush' were not inspired by
Girault but by Kipling, who was no less popular in France than in
Britain.

Many members of the British Colonial Service held broadly comparable values. Their university education, like that of Whitehall
officials, was more likely to have centred on Classics, History or (later)
Modern Greats than on Law, and some effects of this at the level of
policy-making will be considered later. But many of the young athletes
recruited by Sir Ralph Furse were more interested in the practice
than in the theory of political justice; like their French counterparts
they managed, with varying degrees of actual indiscipline, to evade the
constraints of bureaucratic hiearchy in order to concentrate on what
they perceived as important practical needs of the local communities
they had been appointed to serve. Broadly humanist ideals of just and
disinterested government, with projects for material improvement
pursued by the more active, provided French and British administrators with some common habits of mind; this shared culture of the
bush may have out-weighed the divisive influences of national culture
and education.

In so far as these working administrators ever considered their
ultimate purposes, there is clearly some truth in the generalization
that while the British hoped to see Africans governing themselves in
accordance with their own 'traditions' or national character, the
French retained the assimilationist ideal of creating Africans in their
own image. Although until the Second World War this was too distant
a goal to have direct effects on policy, their constitutional thought
centred on the notion of French citizenship, as a means of conferring
on Africans rights and liberties which Frenchmen enjoyed by birth.

The British were more chary of following precedents from the Roman Empire: Palmerston's celebrated evocation of the rights of the *Civis Britannicus* had created complications. It was simpler to deal with British *subjects*, whose rights were regulated by local legislation (and were to undergo much redefinition during the liquidation of the empire).

But the French too encountered problems in translating universalist ideals into laws acceptable to their own legislators. Although in 1945 almost 100,000 Senegalese enjoyed French citizenship, this was the result of grudgingly recognized historical accident rather than successful policy; other Africans could achieve this status only by demonstrating their personal qualifications. Although the Brazzaville conference envisaged a much broader extension of citizenship as the key which would release France's African subjects from colonial status, when it came to implementing this intention in the constitution of 1946 the new provisions were marked by considerable confusion and 'slap-dash draftsmanship'.[14] Nor, of course, was it only the question of citizenship which created anomalies. There is a curious paradox here. While British policy makers, happier in their common-law tradition than with legal codes, tended to regard self-government as an evolutionary and educational process of 'nation-building' rather than a fixed institutional structure,[15] they seem to have applied greater legal expertise to devising transitional constitutions for the diverse territories of the British empire than went into the constitution of the new *Union Française*. The generosity which inspired French ideals of assimilation was never reflected in the half-hearted attempts to apply them in legislation, except perhaps in Réunion and the Caribbean.

It was, however, often assumed that their assimilationist temperament made Frenchmen readier than the British to cultivate personal relationships with their subjects. Ormsby-Gore returned from West Africa in 1926 convinced that: 'The Englishman has naturally an instinctive dislike of "assimilation". We like to keep our life distinct from that of other races whether European or not . . . In these matters we are apparently by nature the exact opposite of the French.'[16] But the latter dictum does not appear to have been based on direct observation; perhaps it was a reflection of British prejudice about the marital customs of French officials. Had Ormsby-Gore visited Senegal it is doubtful whether he would have found more evidence of cultural assimilation than what he had seen, and disliked, in Freetown. When Kenneth Robinson toured French West Africa in 1950 he was struck by the extent to which French officials kept their own life, and that of their official visitor, apart from contact with African *évolués*.[17] Indeed, he might have recalled how, three years earlier, French officials had been embarrassed to discover that the British delegation to a conference in Dakar on medical co-operation included legislative councillors from the Gold Coast and Nigeria, C. W. Tachie Menson and T. A. Odutola. While hastily nominating token Africans to their own delegation, they resented this ideological intrusion into a conference designed for white 'technicians' and initially allocated the two Africans accommodation which the British delegation refused to accept as satisfactory.[18]

Frenchmen would resist the charge that such behaviour was evidence of racism. They claimed to judge the merits of Africans by their achievements: participation in medical debates required real medical knowledge. Assimilation was a privilege to be earned, after rigorous examination. African deputies, duly elected, could share the rights of other deputies; university graduates, but not holders of diplomas *bons pour l'Orient*, had earned their place in the republic of letters; black artists were welcome in Montparnasse for their art's sake. But this rigour, if appreciated by those who had arrived, could produce astonishing insensitivity towards the feelings of Africans still travelling hopefully. It is hard to imagine British officials submitting, to a constitutional committee with African members, a document recommending a *politique de domination*.[19]

Did British habits of mind conduce to greater cross-cultural trust and respect? It can hardly be said that British élites were particularly flexible in adjusting professional and educational standards to local conditions, or, at least before the Second World War, in recognizing regional variations of standard English, even within the United Kingdom. But social attitudes had certainly changed since Ormsby-Gore pronounced his doctrine; if 'collaboration' had not yet become an academic theory, its extended practice was clearly necessary. The nomination of African councillors to what was intended to be a technical working conference might, on the principles developed by Lord Hailey, be regarded as an educational exercise in practical administration but it also seems symptomatic of new attitudes among younger officials. Where Indirect Rulers had seen the utility of working through established African institutions, the new generation was prepared to enter into a wider range of personal relationships. Initially these often retained a strong paternalist flavour; but paternalism is not necessarily the decolonizer's most deadly sin. There are many ways to play the role of a father, and every unhappy family heaps its own reproaches on the parents, whether in French or English.

There seems no easy way to measure and compare changes in relations between officials and Africans in the two empires during the 1940s and 1950s. Once they had decided that old colonial attitudes were obsolete, officials in both empires began to treat Africans differently, if often in rather self-consciously patronizing ways, whose awkwardness was more obvious to foreigners than to themselves. Robert Montagne, on a brief study tour in Nigeria in 1947, felt British officials were shocked by his familiarities: 'It is true that we as Latins shake hands more easily with a notable, talk more naturally with the man in the street, and join naturally in the life of the people'. Yet even while noting Nigerians' complaints about the remoteness of their rulers, Montagne did not find these wholly confirmed by his own observations.[20] In the new political climate, British officials of a new generation began cautiously to cultivate personal relations with nationalist politicians and other educated Africans, initially perhaps as matters of duty, which for many became valued sources of pleasure and enlightenment. Stiff and mutually embarrassing invitations to tea were followed by family visits, and sometimes by the development of genuine friendships (which might have much significance when the pace of political change accelerated).

It is difficult to draw comparisons with contemporary French habits. Memory suggests that the degree of inter-racial meeting achieved by the Freetown dinner clubs of the early 1950s, on a pattern established in Lagos before the war, surprised many French visitors; yet an enterprising *commandant de cercle* was promoting inter-racial clubs, at Bougouni in 1947, at Sikasso in 1952, in much less sophisticated settings.[21] But even when such *foyers* can be identified, it is difficult to tell how far they managed to escape an atmosphere of condescension or patronage. Until power was transferred, friendship could be a delicate relationship; like Fielding and Aziz, Europeans and Africans continued to 'swerve apart', whatever the cultural assumptions underlying their relationship.

Administrators, political parties and self-government

One apparently sharp contrast between the habits of mind of French and British colonial administrators can be identified in attitudes to party politics. During his visits to AOF Kenneth Robinson noted how frequently French public servants, from governors down, were identified with political parties, to which they were accustomed to look for help in their careers.[22] Those British officials who did have party sympathies avoided advertising them; but Deschamps, while attached to the Colonial Ministry in 1930–2, regularly attended the SFIO *section* in the 14th *arrondissement*, bringing along Governor Brunot to support his advocacy of a progressive colonial policy. Still more surprising to British readers is his membership of a trade union of colonial British administrators, which he mockingly calls *le syndicat des rois*, affiliated to the CGT; and his natural assumption that, on appointment by Vicy to govern the Ivory Coast, he should bring in socialist friends, as well as *camarades de promotion*, to sustain his position.[23]

Yet those shaping British colonial policy were more insulated from party politics in theory than in practice. Since the 1920s ex-governors like Sydney Olivier and Colonial Office officials like J. F. N. Green had been advising the Labour Party on colonial affairs, and such contacts increased after the Fabian Colonial Bureau assumed the role of advising the Labour leadership. Commissions of enquiry, the time-honoured institution for impartial trouble-shooting, were sometimes chosen with regard to political sympathies; it would be interesting to know how three Scottish Fabians of limited African experience were selected to report on the Accra riots of 1948. But party connections were usually indirect, and the Watson Commission was able to operate more independently than the seven deputies whom the National Assembly charged to enquire into the 'incidents' which threatened French authority in the Ivory Coast in 1950. Selected to ensure party balance – with a secretary from the very party allegedly implicated in the incidents – the Damas Commission compiled some 2,000 pages of fascinating evidence, but never managed to deliver its promised analysis.[24] In fact, as Lord Hailey noted, it was usually the Colonial Inspectorate which, less obtrusively, discharged the functions of British commissions of enquiry; in the Ivory Coast case it seems to have been the report of Ruffel and Demery which stimulated the Pleven ministry to turn to Houphouet in order to restore Ivoirians' confidence in their rulers.[25]

Perhaps the most important effect of the partisan activities of French officials, and of the sizeable French population resident in Senegal, was to provide African citizens with 'a political initiation' into party organization. Sometimes the zeal of these Frenchmen might lead them to push their African comrades into the background, though a recent study suggests that Guèye's Senegalese socialists managed to retain a considerable degree of initiative during the pre-war offensive of the SF10.[26] This acceptance of the legitimacy of party, if only for the privileged group of citizens, contrasts with the attitude of most British administrators, habituated to regard political parties as more likely to prejudice than to promote good government, at least until African political society had become sufficiently mature. During the period of decolonization the French, while in emergency prepared to repress ruthlessly, as in the case of the *Mouvement de Rénovation Malgache* in 1947, thus found it easier to deal with African tribunes by incorporating them within metropolitan party alignments, or by creating *partis d'administration* under official patronage.

There is an intellectual background to this divergence of practice. As suggested above, many British post-war policy makers were educated, like Kenneth Robinson, in History or in Politics, Philosophy and Economics, disciplines which fostered evolutionary views of political development. While French academics approached political parties through the sort of descriptive analysis promoted by Maurice Duverger, in Britain the dominant influence of the 1940s was that of Lewis Namier. His studies of British political development led to conclusions rather reassuring to the conscience of colonial rulers: that until the political factions in Parliament became based in 'an electorate thinking in terms of nation-wide parties' they would be unable to mount compelling challenges to the executive. A governor skilled in managing the 'Court party' and the 'independent country gentlemen' should be able to keep his colony's politicians under reasonable control.[27] Time would have to pass before nationalist parties could grow to maturity; enlightened rulers could offer political education, but it would be futile to intervene directly in the formation of such parties. Edgar Parry's desire to help the growth in Sierra Leone of 'a TU and Labour movement . . . with its hooks well into both sides of Transport House' was politely discouraged by Fabian nation-builders.[28] This British reluctance to become involved in West African political movements, either to guide or to control them, was regarded with surprise by French observers;[29] but it becomes more understandable on the assumption of the late 1940s that the social and political conditions for a final transfer of power could only be attained after a period of prolonged 'nation-building'. As late as October 1949 the

British government could assume that 'the absence of an established and well-tried party system' in the Gold Coast would still prevent the electorate imposing their candidate for leadership upon the governor.[30]

More broadly, Frenchmen trained in legalistic habits of mind found difficulty in understanding a British approach to decolonization which, in the 1940s, still laid less emphasis on ingenious constitutional structures than on large experiments in political education. (The golden age of constitutional mathematics would come later, during the decolonization of eastern Africa.) The French pretence that the commitment in the UN Charter 'to develop self-government' could only be translated as '*de développer leur capacité de s'administrer eux-mêmes*' may seem disingenuous, or it may reflect concern to discourage the claims of Algerian settlers or American intruders. *Autonomie* was, after all, a perfectly familiar concept, used in their own contemporary discussions. But the broader strategy of nation-building, as a diverse course of practical instruction directed by a tutelary Colonial Office, was less easily translated into French, even by those who were making their own attempts to promote community education and to guide the development of trade unions and co-operative societies. British emphasis on local government as the major organ of political education was puzzling to centralizing Jacobins who regarded municipal consti-tutions as privileges to be conferred only when suitable conditions already existed. Maurice Méker, commending the *commune-mixte* of Sikasso as '*une excellente école de gestion administrative et financière*' may seem to echo a distinctive British attitude; but he is not really looking towards the English pattern of elected local authorities governing their communities with relatively little control or direction from the centre.[31]

British devotion to this ideal of local government, as embodied in the famous despatch of 1947, may indeed have proved inhibiting. Although the Coussey Committee, two years later, deliberately rejected French or American models in favour of 'the more developed democratic form of local government in the United Kingdom',[32] doubts soon arose, even in the Colonial Office, about attempts to transfer this model to African societies once they had begun to move rapidly towards transfers of power at the centre. 'I do not know much about the French metropolitan system,' Sir Charles Jeffries admitted in 1952, 'but it may well be that it offers a better model for Colonial territories than the British.' Certainly, a recent thesis on Sierra Leone confirms the impression that the district councils there failed to provide 'an organized machine for carrying on the administration of the country', but rather had the effect 'of demoralizing the administrative service and involving the chiefs in party politics'.[33] Perhaps the habit of mind which had retarded the entry of Africans into the central administrative service in order to encourage apprenticeships in elected local government did not really assist the British ideal of nation-building from below?

By the 1950s the post-war trend towards increasing consultation and co-operation among Europeans interested in the developing world was making national habits of mind less significant. Although the long-term consequences of past decisions and attitudes were still being worked out there was increasing recognition that more powerful historical forces were determining the pace, if not the style, of the transfer of power. The end of the decade saw far-reaching re-appraisals of the role of European states in their former empires, which were notably radical under the Fifth Republic. Though differences of style persisted, in co-operation no less than in colonial government, these now took new forms. De Gaulle's readiness after 1950 to replace the abortive structures of the *communauté institutionelle* by a flexible system, based on personal contacts and bilateral agreements, showed that he at least was not the prisoner of out-dated habits of mind.[34]

Notes

1. Kenneth Robinson, 'Colonialism French style, 1945–55: a backward glance', *Journal of Imperial and Commonwealth History* XII (1983), p. 30.
2. Michael Crowder, *Colonial West Africa: Collected Essays* (London: Cass, 1978 (1965)), p. 314.
3. See, for example, A. I. Asiwaju, *Western Yorubaland under European Rule, 1889–1945* (London: Longman, 1976); W. F. Miles, 'Partitioned royalty: the evolution of Hausa chiefs in Nigeria and Niger', *Journal of Modern African Studies* 25 (1987), pp. 233–58.
4. John Kent, 'Anglo-French colonial co-operation, 1939–49', *Journal of Imperial and Commonwealth History* XVII (1988), p. 63.
5. I have developed this theme in a paper to the 1988 Oxford colloquium on Francophone Africa since Independence: 'Decolonization: French and British styles' (forthcoming).
6. Kenneth Robinson, op. cit., 'Colonialism . . .', p. 38.
7. W. B. Cohen, *Rulers of Empire: the French Colonial Service in Africa* (Stanford 1971).
8. M. Perham, *West African Passage* (London 1983), Ch. 7.
9. H. Deschamps, *Roi de la Brousse* (Paris 1975); M. Méker, *Le Temps*

Colonial (Dakar 1980); W. B. Cohen (ed.), *Robert Delavignette on the French Empire: Selected Writings* (Chicago 1977). We may now add the diary for 1945–6 of the young *chef de sub-division* of Oumé (Cote d'Ivoire) : R. Gauthereau, *Journal d'un Colonialiste* (Paris 1986).

10. Cohen, op. cit., *Rulers of Empire, pp. 34–5, 45*. See also C. J. Friedrich, 'The continental tradition of training administrators in law and jurisprudence', *Journal of Modern History* XI (1939), pp. 129–48.

11. Deschamps, op. cit., *Roi de la Brousse*, pp. 95–9.

12. 'L'école coloniale' [1937]: in Cohen, op. cit., *Delavignette*, p. 42.

13. Deschamps, op. cit., *Roi de la Brousse*, pp. 121–5.

14. Kenneth Robinson, *The Public Law of Overseas France since the War* (Oxford Institute of Colonial Studies: Reprint Series, nd), p. 15. For a summary of the constitution, see the standard work by L. Rolland and P. Lampué, *Précis de droit des pays d'Outre-Mer* (Paris 1949), esp. pp. 85–6.

15. The classic statement by A. Creech Jones of 'Labour's colonial policy' (Fabian Colonial Bureau, 1947) devotes one sentence to 'constitution-making', but is immediately followed by a list of constitutional White Papers.

16. W. G. A. Ormsby-Gore, *Report . . . on his Visit to West Africa during the Year 1926*, Cmd 2744, p. 23.

17. Robinson, op. cit., 'Colonialism . . .', p. 25.

18. PRO, CO 936/33/1, Locker to Creech Jones, Conf. 9 June 1947: minutes by J. K. Thompson, K. E. Robinson.

19. S. M. Apithy, *Au Service du mon Pays* (Paris 1956), p. 14.

20. Rhodes House, Oxford: Perham Papers Mss 406/1.

21. Alan Burns, *Colonial Civil Servant* (London 1949), p. 107; Méker, op. cit., *Le temps colonial*, pp. 162–5, 189–91.

22. Robinson, op. cit., 'Colonialism . . .', p. 29.

23. Deschamps, op. cit., *Roi de la Brousse*, pp. 129–30, 179, 237.

24. Assemblee nationale, Session de 1950 No. 11348. Rapport fait au nom de la Commission chargée d'enquêter sur les incidents survenus en Côte d'Ivoire par M. Damas (reprinted Abijan 1975).

25. ANSOM, AP 2255/6, Rapport Ruffel-Demery, 29 April 1950; cf Hailey, *An African Survey: revised 1956* (London 1957), pp. 330–31.

26. G. W. Johnson, 'African political activity in French West Africa', J. F. Ajayi and M. Crowder, *History of West Africa II* (2nd edn, London 1987) pp. 627–9; see also Daphne N. Topouzis 'Popular Front, war, and Fourth Republic politics in Senegal' (Ph.D. thesis, University of London 1989), Ch. 2.

27. See especially his Romanes Lecture of 1952: Lewis Namier, *Crossroads of Power* (London 1962), p. 20, 'Monarchy and the party system'.

28. Fabian Colonial Bureau Papers, Rhodes House, Oxford; Brit. Emp s 365 86/2, fo 125–8. Parry to Hinden, 24 Nov. 1946; Hinden to Parry, 24 Dec. 1946.

29. ANSOM, AP 3416/5 Report on Political Parties BWA, 22 July 1946.

30. Creech Jones to Arden-Clarke, 14 Oct. 1949 (Colonial No. 250, London 1949), para. 30. For an extraordinarily stringent definition of these

conditions, see [Watson] *Report of the Committee of Enquiry into Disturbances in the Gold Coast* (Colonial No. 231, 1948), para. 115.

31. Méker, op. cit., *Le temps colonial*, p. 188.
32. Gold Coast. Report to His Excellency the Governor on Constitutional Reform, 1949 (Colonial No. 248, London 1949).
33. Memo by Jeffries, 14 January 1952, in A. N. Porter and A. J. Stockwell (eds) *British Imperial Policy and Decolonization 1938–64*, Vol. II (Basingstoke 1989), pp. 139–40. The thesis referred to is that of A. M. Lavalie, 'The transfer of power in Sierra Leone. British colonial policy, nationalism and independence, 1945–61' (Ph.D. dissertation, University of London 1989).
34. I am grateful to Roy Bridges for his comments on a draft of this chapter.

11

SHAPING THE POST-IMPERIAL STATE: Nehru's letters to chief ministers

W. H. Morris-Jones

Since history abounds in paradox, it should not be unexpected that the post-imperial state is at once a reflection of and a reaction against the preceding imperial state. The founding fathers, who then normally became the first rulers, of new successor states sought both to bring down and to re-build, both to replace and to reproduce. The past regime was anathema but at the same time a model worthy in some respects of preservation or imitation. The rulers certainly were to be changed but the rules of ruling might be carried over.

When the new rulers addressed their public, they were usually clear as to what the change of regime would mean for their people: at least in the rhetoric, the status of the people was to be transformed and those who had been subjects of alien rule would become citizens of their country. Their 'tryst with destiny' meant that they, through their own countrymen as leaders, would become, at only one remove, controllers of their own destinies. Even within South Asia, the first of the decolonized regions, the extent to which this expectation was to be realized, for example through adult franchise and free and regular elections, varied appreciably.[1]

If the changed status of the people was clear at least in principle, could the same be said of the status of the state? One matter was surely evident: the new state would cease to be, in terms of international law, a dependency; it would acquire sovereign status and in that respect be at last on a par formally with others in the world of states. This would initially be a matter of great satisfaction to the new inheritors of ruling authority and perhaps of some pride even to the new citizens. Soon, however, the aura of external sovereignty would begin to pall as inequalities of power became more manifest. But if status equality in external relations was in practical implications uncertain and often disappointing, it was at least conceptually clear. That was rather more than could be said of the status of the state in its internal aspect.

Stateness

It is more than 20 years since this latter subject was raised in its most general form in a seminal article by J. P. Nettl, 'The state as a conceptual variable'.[2] Initially focusing on Western countries, Nettl suggested that the concept of state, as well as the very term, was in so much more established use in France and Germany than in Britain and the USA that it was appropriate to describe the first pair as instances of 'high stateness', the latter as cases of 'low stateness'. This historically formed distinction related essentially to contrasts between 'an autonomous collectivity', that is, coherently consolidated institutions (in, say, France) and the more loosely connected political institutions of Britain (monarchy, crown, parliament, civil service, law courts, local governments) and USA (president, congress, supreme court, as well as the separate states of the federal polity). Nettl added that while federalism connoted low stateness, fears of federal tendencies or other claims to autonomy, or indeed any obstacles to smooth state-formation, had historically often promoted or supported a thrust towards high stateness. He also pointed out that autonomy among the professions, especially the law, was regularly associated with low stateness whereas in high stateness France judges and prosecutors were state servants. Nettl was careful to insist that while high stateness means a state that stands tall, this does not entail that such a state has to be loved; he reckoned that the commonly negative attitudes towards the state in Italy are a paradoxical part of high stateness in that country.

Thus far it would appear that measurements of levels of stateness might possibly be based on content-analyses of the written and spoken word revealing the occurrence of the term 'state' but more essentially on assessments of the positions on a coherence–autonomy scale of different countries' political institutions. Nettl went on to add two further points of relevance to this chapter. He suggested that high stateness meant most especially 'the institutionalisation of power' as opposed to the personalization; from this it seemed to follow that a coherent structure, if it were built around and dependent on one leader figure, would scarcely qualify for high stateness; second, in the few remarks which Nettl made on non-Western countries, he held that on the whole in the new states the salience of the idea of the nation was so marked that the concept of the state remained undeveloped. In this connection he observed that 'new and developing nations have sought self-definition, integration and even domestic viability by emphasising their international role and . . . status'. Somewhat surprisingly, he did not believe that this attempt could succeed; the salience of the new state in its external relations would not yield high stateness internally because the main consequences of prominence in international roles would be a cult of 'personalismo', itself the very denial of high stateness.

More recently and with special reference to the state in Asia, Subrata Mitra has sought to develop further Nettl's scarcely elaborated criteria for assessing levels of stateness.[3] While endorsing Nettl's criterion of the institutionalization of power, Mitra suggests that degrees of stateness tend to match with levels of public order and with the strength of 'a shared citizen identity as a unique and exclusive bonding principle'. The latter criterion certainly seems to be a useful extension of the 'coherence' emphasis. The former criterion of public order is less straightforward. On the one hand, regimes of low stateness do not appear to be especially associated with lack of public order; on the other, it would appear that a condition of disorder may indicate low stateness either in the sense of ineffective administration or, alternatively, as an expression of social strains so severe as to produce disorder even, despite a satisfactory administrative system.

It is surprising that neither of the two authors who have wrestled with the matter of stateness have considered that differences in the levels and in the very scope of state activity must have a significant bearing on the question of stateness. As we have just noted, Nettl does indeed consider the case of states which seek energetically to pursue an active international role, only to reject any positive influence from this on their level of stateness. Likewise Mitra, more attentive to the internal role of the state, focuses on public order and citizenship identity (on which states may indeed be active) without considering the relevance for stateness of other directions, economic for example, of state activity.

In what follows here, the meaning of stateness will therefore be extended. It seems appropriate to take account generally of levels of state activity if only for the reason that high levels will tend to enhance the salience of the state in the consciousness of citizens. Whether salience carries with it approval is, of course, a separate issue.

The stateness of Britain's Indian empire had contained from its very nature a nice ambiguity, for there were two loci for its expression and registration: the rule was exercised in India but had its source in Britain. Its stateness in Britain was essentially vicarious and reflected, somewhat spasmodic, generally positive but with negative patches early and late within the period; its stateness in India was at least more continuous. But even there it was emphatic in some respects but restricted in others. The bureaucratic pyramid – representative institutions were a relatively late addition – which extended from the viceroy downwards through presidencies and districts to villages was certainly an encompassing, coherent and well-articulated whole, easily recognized and readily respected. But one-third of the country was run as a separate operation of 500 variegated, separate princely states only slightly tied to the pyramid. Or again, it could seem that even the two-thirds which was British-ruled, though only with a great army of civilian and military Indian collaborators, was only minimally governed. The society was to be protected from external attack and internal disorder, and its own internal disputes were to be settled by regularized procedures, but it was not to be interfered with in its native customs except for the putting down, often at the insistence of reforming Indians, of certain practices now seen as abhorrent. The state was expressly protector and arbiter, not much more. Yet that same state presided over a near-transformation of society through revolutions centred around railways, canals and schools.[4]

The paradoxes which characterized the imperial state tended to disappear with the transfer of power, but only to be replaced by others in the new independent India. In order to explore these a little further, yet in a way manageable within a single essay, it may not be inappropriate to focus on the concerns and perceptions of India's nationalist leader who became the country's first prime minister and held the position until his death 17 long years later: Jawaharlal Nehru.

The 'fortnightlies'

A convenient approach to Nehru's view of the travails and triumphs of the Indian state under his guidance can be found through his *Letters to Chief Ministers, 1947–1964.*[5] This extraordinary collection had a fittingly extraordinary beginning. It appears from the first letter, dated 15 October 1947, that Nehru had already 'about the middle of August', that is, at the moment of the transfer of power and the traumatic partition of the country, suggested that his chief ministers (of the units of the federal polity) should write to him every fortnight and that he would reply. Evidently this did not work: 'Neither of us has been able to keep to this programme . . . We have all of us, I fear, been somewhat overwhelmed by the pressure of events'. He therefore decided that he would initiate 'the fortnightly exchange': 'I intend to write to you on the 1st and 15th of each month'.

It is very unlikely that Nehru's zeal and enthusiasm was shared by the chief ministers; certainly there are few references to letters sent by them. The PM's output of these letters was surely extraordinary – the 281 letters of the period 1947–57 cover nearly 2,400 pages – and perhaps without comparable parallel.[6] It is not surprising that on a few occasions he explained a gap in the regular supply of letters by referring to his being 'depressed' or 'not in the mood'. That these were true and sincere descriptions is not to be doubted; at the same time it appears that he is also making a point, namely that the cause of his depression is distress about the behaviour or attitudes of followers, including some addressees, who are not quite following. There was probably the same double aspect to his more public contemplation of resignation in October 1954, already qualified as it was by not wishing 'to take any step in a hurry' and thinking of it not as permanent but 'at least for sometime'. These moments apart, the routine was as regular as he could manage; the letters were normally dictated late in the night at the end of a busy day.

During the whole of his period as prime minister Nehru was also minister of external affairs, as well as congress president for several years and no doubt the holder of other less taxing positions. For what reasons, then, did he invent and carry through the extra task of 'the fortnightlies'? He was certainly a more than conscientious man, dedicated rather, driven. He was also, despite phases of self-doubt, a man with no low opinion of himself. He had, after all, been trusted by Gandhi. As he looked around at his colleagues, he could, not unreasonably, have seen himself not merely as hugely popular[7] but also as endowed with a wider vision and a more reflective aspect of mind. Furthermore he was, almost unstoppably, articulate in speech and on paper; unlike even those of his fellows who read widely when in prison, Nehru also used those periods for incessant writing.

Beyond these features, Nehru was a preacher–teacher. As a preacher he was a man with messages to deliver. As is well known, these were essentially four, two for India and two for the wider world. His secularism stemmed not only from an absence of religious convictions and a distaste for religious devotions but from a real horror of religion as a source of social exclusivity and fanaticism. This distanced him only somewhat from Gandhi but much more profoundly from very many of his colleagues. His socialism, despite the occasional hackneyed phrase, was far from doctrinaire; it connoted state planning and some state ownership and its goal was the lessening of social inequalities, but these were strenuously to be reconciled with democratic procedures and respect for civil liberties. The message of nationalism was that this was the natural way of the world but that there was unfinished business on the agenda; empires had blocked the way but India had now opened it; until the process of national statehood was complete there would have to be legitimate struggle, as non-violent as possible. The message of avoidance of war was that, while in relations between nation-states conflict of interest might be inescapable, the utter and ultimate horror of war could be averted by a combination of patient direct negotiations and the use of international organs of mediation. The preacher proclaimed the messages but it was the teacher in Nehru who had to explain the implications for policy-making. This had to be done continuously with respect to the all-India and world scenes. The chief ministers had their work cut out to govern the large areas for which they were responsible, but they had to be supplied with information relating to an understanding of even wider contexts, otherwise coherence would be lost and dissonance would replace harmony. Nehru was the conductor of a symphony orchestra and the players had to grasp his reading of each theme in the music before them.

Thus the very institution of 'the fortnightlies' bears directly on the matter of stateness through the emphasis on securing an all-India coherence of perspectives and goals. In the very first of the letters Nehru explains their purpose: he hopes

by this means to keep in touch with important developments in your province [later, of course, termed state] and also to keep you informed not merely of the more significant developments in the centre but also of events in other provinces which have repercussions over the rest of India ... it is more than ordinarily incumbent on us to keep in close touch with each other, so that we can put forth concerted efforts to overcome the grave dangers facing us

Naturally, this formulation is silent as to Nehru's concern that his addressees should additionally share his own perceptions, hopes and preferences, a concern which was unconcealed from the start and already well understood by all concerned. Nehru, in any case, addressed the nation from several arenas, that is, parliament, congress meetings and other public occasions, and in fact often referred in his letters to his speeches; the importance of the letters was precisely that they were not public but private, albeit rather one-sided conversations, with all the urgency of intimacy on problems of policy in governance, on matters of state.[8]

Internal matters

In exploring the letters for our present purpose of assessing levels of stateness in the new India, it will be convenient to attend to internal matters first and India's external relations later. It is also appropriate at once to suggest that what appears most manifest throughout is the contrast between Nehru's aspirations for high stateness and the actual conditions of low stateness with which he found himself confronted, a riot, so to speak, of autonomies of different kinds. We will focus, within the internal matters, first on the battle against the obstacles to stateness before reviewing some of the positive moves in the direction of enhanced stateness.

Since the letters began only two months after the partition migrations and killings, Nehru at once addresses the legacy of bitter hatred, among Hindus and Sikhs, especially the refugees, and alarmed fear, among remaining Muslims:

I know there is a certain amount of feeling in the country ... that the Central Government has been weak and following a policy of appeasement towards Muslims. This, of course, is complete nonsense ... We have a Muslim minority so large in numbers that they cannot, even if they want to, go anywhere else. They have got to live in India ... we have got to deal with this minority

in a civilised manner. We must give them security . . . [otherwise]
we shall have a festering sore which will eventually poison the
whole body politic

and also lose India valuable international goodwill. The communal
disturbances in Punjab threatened, if they spread into the North
Indian heartland, 'complete chaos in the country and the destruction
of all constitutional government', but 'we have overcome this danger
. . . we have turned the corner'. Nevertheless, 'unceasing vigilance is
still necessary', and soon Nehru was giving warnings about the
mobilization of Hindu fanaticism in the drilled and armed RSS
(Rashtriya Swayamsevak Sangh) and the failure of some state governments to use existing powers against their intimidating demon-
strations: 'I do not wish to interfere with your discretion but . . .
acquiescence in defiance is likely to have grave consequences'. Indeed
within a month of that warning Gandhi had been assassinated by men
under RSS influence. Gandhi's pleas for communal harmony had
continually to be repeated by Nehru. In early 1950, when a wave of
Hindu migrants entered from East Pakistan to Calcutta and sparked
off the killing of Muslims in that city, Nehru was pleased to be able to
sign a modest agreement with Pakistan's Prime Minster Liaquat Ali
Khan, only to find two of his cabinet ministers resigning in protest
and demanding instead that populations should be exchanged. Nehru
confessed, as he could well have done several times during his rule: 'I
have been more troubled by communalism than by any other matter
in India'. This was a matter not of sentiment alone but also of the
state: 'our loose-knit society with inner walls of olden days could not
survive in the present times'; unity and strength would come from
'breaking down barriers'.

Divisions in Indian society did not stem from communalism alone.
Fissiparous tendencies came in several shapes, and always the result
of 'thinking in terms of some smaller group at the expense of the
larger community'; hence 'provincialism, communalism, casteism,
faction, etc'. He felt 'deep sorrow' in late 1954 when the 'intensely
communal' Akali Dal scored a crushing victory in elections within the
Sikh community: 'we cannot accept any policy which weakens the
state and tends towards separation'. Much earlier he had detected the
restiveness of linguistic minorities in several states: 'Assam has some
trouble with the Bengalis, Bengal with the Gurkhas'; 'eventually some
readjustment [of boundaries] will be necessary', but not 'at this stage'.

Within six years the Telegu-speakers had won a new state of Andhra through the division of Madras and Nehru had set up the States Reorganisation Commission to make recommendations for the whole country. When its 'Pandora's box' was opened, passions flared and Nehru wondered if this was a 'relic' of 'a tribal age' now having its 'final spurt before the ghost was laid'. It was not quite final and Nehru acknowledged that 'the emotional integration of India still remains the most important need of our country'; 'we seem to live on the verge of violence, often crossing that borderline'.[9]

Social features were not the sole obstacle in the way of raising stateness. Nehru had also to pay attention to deficiencies in the machinery of government.[10] Here he focused mainly on the bureaucracy. His attitude to the top officials, members of the (inherited) Indian Civil Service and the (new) Indian Administrative Service (IAS), was ambivalent. At times he expressed distrust and disrespect towards those who had been trained to serve the British raj, and it was Patel who ensured with determination the guarantees of the services' status.[11] Yet he surely realized that they constituted the keystone of the administrative arch and as such were precious to the sustenance of the state. Additionally he should have appreciated that they, by serving not only at the centre but also at state and even district levels, were essential integrators of the system. In the very first of the fortnightlies he acknowledged indirectly their importance when he warned that the services had to be 'preserved against the communal virus' and added that 'fortunately' there had been few 'lapses'. Later there came more general complaints. He was justified in saying that states composed of formerly princely areas suffered from 'low standards of administration', and perhaps in condemning all state-level machinery as 'archaic', 'inefficient' and lop-sided in that revenue and law and order functions predominated over 'nation-building activities'. But although he talked big about 'overhauling the machinery', he could give no effective lead.[12] In his occasional despair on these matters, he sometimes slipped into approving pictures of the imperial past; 'it would be most unfortunate if we lose the legacy of efficient administration'; 'the whole structure of British administration was built up on the District Officer' who must not be interfered with by local politicians; and the British, 'in spite of numerous failings' were at least not tempted to make bad appointments through provincial or other favouritism.

Political interference and favouritism could easily relate to another feature which adversely affected stateness through the machinery of administration: corruption. Nehru worried a great deal about this: it 'must be tackled efficiently or we shall sink in this morass'. He set an early example by promptly accepting the resignation of his finance minister who had ordered the withdrawal of income tax cases against certain industrialists; 'even *bona fide* errors cannot be tolerated . . . we must have the highest standards of public conduct'. He thought that often 'the smaller people are caught and punished . . . while the big sinners escape' and he had to remind his premiers that the Preventive Detention Act had been amended to be used against hoarders and black marketeers; authorities were using it readily for public order offences but 'we have not shown the same earnestness in dealing with these other anti-social activities'. At the same time Nehru warned against the 'tendency to repeat every rumour . . . and float all kinds of vague and unjustified allegations'; indeed, 'continuous condemnation actually leads to a feeling of lethargy and produces the very atmosphere in which corruption, etc flourish'.

Among the internal problems which created difficulties in the way of enhancing India's stateness were two which were neither social nor administrative but more strictly political. The first of these was the Communist Party (CPI); dealing with it sometimes posed problems for Nehru in view of his strong attachment to the preservation of civil liberties. When the CPI organized a crippling strike in Calcutta, the West Bengal government banned the party in that state without consulting Delhi. Nehru did not countermand the ban – after all, 'the business of the State' was 'threatened' – but he did not approve; he advocated instead the arrest of individuals, and made it plain that he wished state governments in future to consult before banning. When the CPI later engaged for a period in virtually guerilla warfare in certain regions, Nehru sanctioned bans. The two principles to which he tried to hold with respect to both CPI and RSS were: that terrorists could properly be denied civil liberty but legitimate political activity had to be allowed; and that powers of arrest and detention of individuals should be preferred, in all but extreme cases, to the banning of organizations. Nehru robustly chastised some state governments which aimed to curb high courts in the matter of writs of habeas corpus. The defence of the state was vital but did not require that individual rights be destroyed. The line was often difficult to draw but Nehru sometimes wrote as if he thought some colleagues were too power-happy: 'it is always unsafe to weaken on principles'; 'repression has never crushed an idea or solved a problem'.

The second source of difficulty was also a political party, none other than Congress itself. Although, as already indicated, congress affairs did not occupy much space in the letters, there were occasions when Nehru did feel obliged to draw attention to the way in which its failings were damaging to matters of state. Initially Nehru was satisfied and even comforted that Congress, even after the withdrawal from it of the socialists, his ideological brothers, was still 'the one major cementing factor' which ensured the 'unity and stability of India'. Soon enough, however, Nehru was sounding warning notes. Having admitted early on that some party members were 'attracted' to the 'fascist and Nazi modes of thought and practice' found in the RSS, it is not surprising that he should begin to detect and condemn 'factionalism' and 'groupism' in the Congress. Such developments simply incapacitated the party, rendering it unable to perform its mediating role between government and people. 'Government as such cannot function in the way the Congress should function'; 'repression becomes inevitable when a challenge to the State is made', but that necessity is reached because 'there is not sufficient work being done by Congressmen'; they should, as they did in the past, move among the people with 'a personal and human touch ... explaining the situation and pointing out our difficulties'. For example, sympathetic action by 50 unions aggravated the damage done by the 60-day textile strike in Bombay and exposed 'the gulf' between workers and government; 'normally it would have been the function of congress to bridge the gulf'. It must have been nearly the last straw for Nehru when he felt obliged to quote from a report of visitors from the American Congress on yet another gulf, that between the Congress Party and Congress governments in some states:

> The extent of popular participation and control of government varies widely. The main pressure groups are landed interests, commercial groups and language groups. . . . As a result the State Governments have tended to be conservative in character, some-times resisting the implementation of reform measures included in the platform of the ruling Congress Party.

That quote serves nicely to move our discussion on from the obstacles to stateness to the positive stateness-enhancing measures initiated by Nehru. He knew that India confronted depressing economic conditions and that the country's 'political prestige cannot last long without strong economic foundations'. How to achieve those was the problem. India entered independence with food shortages which were not substantially remedied during Nehru's years: October 1947: 'there seems no end to our dependence on overseas sources for our food supplies'; November 1957: 'our future depends on food production ... extreme effort is essential'. The Grow More Food Campaign, started in the British days of 1942, had failed, so it was revived only to fail again. There was no shortage of orders, relating to control of food prices and movements, procurement and rationing, or of advice, on crop diversification away from wheat and rice and matching changes in food habits, or of ideas – Nehru suggested that school and college students should go out to help make compost – but the precious foreign exchange continued to drain away on cereal imports. Pointedly, Nehru wrote to inform the premiers that the International Bank reckoned that the provinces were not co-operating with the centre's plans: 'these are objective views of disinterested parties and should have weight with you'. But he had to continue to be appalled at 'mountains of sweets' alongside 'common people lacking necessities'.

Food production could, of course, be related to the pattern of agricultural holdings. Congress was already committed to the abolition of *zamindari* (rent-receiving) rights, but the process of complex legislation and lengthy litigation took years and required amendment of the constitution. In any case this 'peasants' charter' as such did not affect actual holdings, did not yield any 'land to the tiller'. Nehru, thinking aloud, may not have realized that he was releasing a bombshell when he wrote:

> It is clear that in the long run the improvement of agriculture demands large-scale economic units. .... Immediately and without any difficulty, reclaimed land should either be run as big State farms or on a co-operative basis. Even in regard to smaller peasant holdings, attempts should be made, wherever possible, to introduce some form of co-operative organisation. It is not good enough to say that this is against our age-long habits and might give rise to trouble.

But these ideas did create trouble, sufficient to drive some congressmen, alarmed by such socialist talk and raising the banner of property rights, to leave the party and form another.

Nehru gave reassurances that coercion was not contemplated, that co-operative farming would be a voluntary business; this only meant that such developments were few. He encouraged states towards legislation to place ceilings on landholdings in order to release land for those with uneconomic plots or no land at all; Congress legislators were as unenthusiastic about this form of social justice as they were about co-operative consolidation of holdings. Instead, Nehru became a helpless spectator watching the emergence of rather different co-operatives which brought together well-to-do farmers with an interest in cheaper inputs and higher prices for produce. Ever resilient, Nehru switched attention and enthusiasm to the US-aided Community Development Programme and National Extension Service. Starting with 55 project areas, it was designed to achieve not much less than a transformation of village life through the efforts of villagers themselves encouraged by trained personnel. Under dynamic direction the programme extended to cover half the 500,000 villages of India, acquired its own ministry and created its own parallel bureaucracy of development administrators. Change did occur, and when to development was added grassroots democracy in the form of a three-tier structure of elected bodies reaching down from district to village, Nehru was buoyant: 'Thus we give a wide and firm foundation to the State and to the intricate working of its creative and productive apparatus at the ground level'.

Those were good seeds to sow and, indeed, democracy and development might have been expected to help each other's growth. But the social soil of rural India had been neglected for too long to produce dramatic results. Those came too late for Nehru to see, but in some measure they came because Nehru had insisted that development and democracy alike depended on what he possessed: 'faith in our people'. Fortunately for Nehru, nothing was quite so recalcitrant as agriculture; other sectors of the economy and its overall management yielded more easily a role to direction by the state. From early on, 'planning' had for Nehru acquired the character of a *mantra*, a magic and sacred word that brought spiritual power. He inserted the 'establishment of a Planning Commission' in an early report of a Congress Economic Programme Committee but proceeded cautiously and quietly to its actual creation outside the constitution and by simple resolution rather than by law. Though strictly advisory, it became decisively influential and its Five Year Plans became frameworks of goals towards which centre and states had to strive. Its priorities were reported to a National Development Council on which the states were represented but Nehru was chairman of both commission and council. Even when operating at this grand level, Nehru was tormented by problems of popular participation:

> the people have to feel that they are partners in the great enterprise of running the State machine . . . sharers in both the benefits and obligations . . . that the plan has been evolved with their co-operation and that they are responsible for its success . . . If these *panchayats* [the lower-level elected local bodies] could be drawn into the network of planning and its implementation, that would bring the plan to the doorstep of the villager.

Stranger than this vague dream is the fact that much later something like this did begin to happen.[13]

Less innovatory than the planning machinery was the whole field of state control and state ownership. The former was not much more than an extension of wartime economic controls introduced by the imperial administration. Price control in respect of food and cotton cloth were vital to check inflation and rescue the poor from real distress; whenever business interests, disingenuously arguing that controls produced corruption, succeeded in scaring the government into decontrol, the outcome was such price rises as to bring control back promptly.[14] State ownership was a well-established part of the congress creed and it could be said that there had already been a fair amount of pragmatic rather than doctrinal public enterprise in British India. There was, therefore, little controversy about 'the nationalisation of key industries', especially since Nehru made it clear that 'the resources of the State are limited' and therefore 'we should concentrate on the State owning and controlling new key industries, public utilities and the like, rather than acquiring old ones'. Within the pragmatic Nehru there was always an idealist and ideologue trying to break out. Thus: 'Democracy means a progressive economic equality . . . a society where there are no great differences and where opportunity comes to all. Any vested interests and vested privileges do not fit with such a plan. . . . The pattern of society to be aimed at should be socialistic . . . where the State owns or controls the means of production . . . at all the strategic points'. These words would not bring his fellow-socialists back to Congress and the rightists were anyway going to leave on seeming to discern the advent of collective farms; but at least the words made him feel better, and therefore able to continue to cajole and harass his colleagues and perhaps to keep alive hopes out there in the lower reaches.

External relations

In now passing from India's internal situation to her external relations, it is to be noted at once that comments on the former from foreign visitors were passed promptly on to his readers. For example, in 1949 'even the hard-headed businessmen of the International Bank told me of their surprise at the enthusiasm and high-class ability that they came across. All these foreigners go back with the conviction that India is a great State'. He was moved to add: 'There is ... a fundamental soundness and stability in India, a vitality which must have its way. ... India is the only State in all these vast regions of Eastern, South-Eastern and Western Asia which can be looked upon not only as a firmly established State but also one that is advancing towards greater strength, both political and economic'. It has in fairness to be said that such glowing portrayals were usually followed by confessions of 'embarrassment' and an extra weight of enhanced responsibility.[15]

In the letters, a great deal of space was given to foreign affairs, even more than could be expected from his holding of that portfolio and his own longstanding interest in international relations. Some of the explanation is no doubt to be found in his teacher–preacher role; he wished to educate and inspire his colleagues towards knowledge and a view of a world beyond India. It is equally certain that he wanted the expected growing salience and perhaps glory of India-in-the-world to reflect back through his readers in the form of enhanced purposefulness and pride in their country. Problems in plenty at home would not thereby be solved but they might be more firmly tackled. Admittedly there was little to support such hopes in the first years. Independent India began its life with just two external relations: the one with the UK was dying gently, though the Commonwealth link helped and provided India with its first international conference; the one with Pakistan was fraught with bitter hostility and actual warfare in Kashmir for over a year.

However, Nehru wasted little time in widening India's reciprocal diplomatic relations. Indeed this occasioned one of Nehru's angry letters when he reacted sharply to newspaper criticism of lavish expenditure on embassies: to ask another country to represent India 'would not be in keeping not only with our dignity and status but also with any external policy we wish to pursue'; waste was surely to be avoided but costs could not be cut further because 'Embassies represent the state'. Nor did Nehru waste time in forming an Indian picture of the world, indeed of India's place in the world. His first 'fortnightly' of 15 October 1947 was devoid of international affairs but there were few others like that. The second letter (2 November) came after the Pakistan raiders had entered Kashmir; domestic affairs were now intertwined with India's first and most uneasy international relation. From then on, the world opens up by stages and along essentially four dimensions: India as the post-imperial state in a global, though initially Asian, process of decolonization; India as a non-aligned state in a world of Cold War confrontation; India in relation to the new Communist China; and India alongside its own smaller neighbours.

Bandung

The decolonization theme appears quite soon and Indonesia, 'the gallant young Republic, fighting for its freedom against the Dutch' was soon prominently in Nehru's view. Already he had sponsored Indonesia's membership of ECAFE and was pressing the UK and USA, 'with some results', to prevent 'further Dutch aggression'. More striking was the 'great success' of the Asian Conference on Indonesia called in Delhi which 'enhanced the prestige of India all over the world' and constituted 'a turning point in history'; 'the countries of Asia will come closer together and India will play a leading part' not, Nehru hastened to say, in anything that could be called a bloc, simply a linking of anti-imperialist new states. Such large expectations were scarcely fulfilled and it was six years – during which the French had failed to take Nehru's advice to withdraw gracefully from Indo-China – before another impetus was given to the emergence of the decolonized through the summoning of the Asian–African Conference in Bandung in 1955. Before the conference he was sure that it would be another 'historic event' and that it would reflect 'the new resurgent spirit of Asia' as well as 'a coming together of the countries of Asia and Africa'. But the preparations were not free from trouble and the outcome for Nehru fell a little flat. He had nothing to say about the black African representatives (still awaiting independence)[16] but a great deal to say about the 'aggressive' representatives of 'pure

American doctrine', Turkey, Pakistan, Iraq, Lebanon and Iran which made it difficult even for Nehru to find words to suggest any positive outcome. Perhaps an even greater damper on Nehru's enthusiasm was that, as he acknowledged, 'Chou-En-lai [Zhou Enlai] attracted the most attention' and 'created a very good impression'. 'It was not India's purpose . . . to seek the limelight', Nehru wrote, only 'to work quietly'. Happily encouraged by U Nu, he found this solace: 'the two most important countries at Bandung were China and India'. It may have been a useful trial run for the later Non-Aligned Movement.

The Bandung experience underlined what Nehru had known from the start: the decolonzation process was born into a world divided by the Cold War. When Nehru was about to visit the USA in 1949, he wrote that he hoped for economic help not 'as beggars' but 'on terms of mutual advantage'. For India, too, had 'much to give. . . . It is well recognised today all over the world that the future of Asia will be powerfully determined by the future of India, more and more the pivot of Asia'. He was 'greatly affected by the warmth of the welcome' he received, so much so that he was moved to add that although he had felt 'out of place' and 'critical', nevertheless 'calling them materialistic . . . was a very partial truth . . . the US and Soviet Russia . . . both have very great achievements to their credit'. In his address at Columbia University he had explained India's policy of 'detachment' from power blocs and a few years later he was able to write that it was 'our earnest wish' to apply a 'touch of healing to a tortured world'. The Baghdad Pact and, more especially, American military aid to Pakistan placed a strain on any equality of 'detachment'; the Cold War was now making its entry into the Third World and the sub-continent. The visit by Nehru to the Soviet Union and Eastern Europe and the return visit of Bulganin and Khrushchev to India were a kind of response, though not unconnected also with fresh leadership in the Kremlin. Nevertheless, 'the one broad result' according to Nehru 'has been to raise India's prestige and status in the world'; how high that prestige would now be, given that he had even earlier declared that 'there is no escaping the destiny that must pursue India'! Perhaps, however, it would be a little more difficult to sustain a previous claim that 'we remain that principal link between the rival blocs'.

It may be that Nehru was not the only statesman who failed to foresee the outcome of the onward march of Mao armies. But even when he was envisaging communist rule confined to North China or Mao forming a coalition government, he did think about repercussions on communist movements in neighbouring areas and he did mildly say that 'the future of Tibet may become a subject for argument'. At the same time he was able to extract something positive from the shifting scene: 'the precarious balance of power is affected and . . . India, rather suddenly and inevitably, becomes the most important country of Asia, apart from the Soviet North . . . all eyes are turned upon her'. But fantasy and realism often took it in turns to focus Nehru's vision and soon he wrote: 'We would like Tibet to be autonomous and have direct dealings with us . . . but it is clear that we cannot bring any effective pressure to change the course of events'. A year later, Mao's first ambassador arrived in Delhi and met Tibetan representatives who were already there; Nehru wanted 'to help a peaceful settlement between China and Tibet' and while he thought it 'some success at least' to have received a note from Beijing recognizing China's duty to use peaceful methods, it was wise of him to add that 'we must not imagine that the danger is over'. Indeed, little more than a month later Chinese forces had moved into Tibet, 'an act of discourtesy' which 'has hurt us considerably'. This 'involves no particular danger to India' because of the difficult terrain and 'the great Himalayan barrier' but 'we shall keep proper watch on our extended frontiers', albeit with a cut in defence expenditure. Soon Nehru was distinguishing between India's 'vital' interests and others, and Tibet was now not vital, the couple of tiny Indian garrisons there being readily surrendered. But 'our frontier with Tibet, the Mac-Mahon line, is our fixed and definite border and we are not prepared to consider any change in it'. However, China is now 'a great power . . . and our neighbour', so Nehru went out of his way to receive Zhou when he indicated abruptly that he would like to call in at Delhi on his way home from Geneva. But even on Nehru's own careful accounts of their meeting, as well as of a second one in Beijing, it is clear that Nehru was wary and equally clear that when Nehru talked of misleading Chinese maps of their frontiers Zhou was dismissive.

Nehru's China anxieties spilled over at times to some of India's smaller neighbours: appropriately, in one letter, a paragraph on Tibet is immediately followed by, 'We are concerned with some of our border countries or States. Bhutan and Sikkim may be considered as definite parts of India. Nepal is not. But it is too intimately related to India for us to view with unconcern what happens there internally or externally'. The phrase about Bhutan and Sikkim was ill-considered; it was much later made true of Sikkim but not of Bhutan, which managed its affairs so cannily as to get India's support for its UN membership as well as Indian aid. On Nepal Nehru was right: 'with the development of the Chinese situation', the antiquated regime should undertake 'major domestic reforms'. When changes eventually came about through internal revolt, which India tried, unsuccessfully, not to assist, India before long found that reforms internally did not remove the danger of Nepal playing the Chinese card. Nehru responded to Zhou's great curiosity about Nepal by saying that Delhi and Katmandu had agreed that foreign policies were to be co-ordinated and 'in line with each other'. He added that India 'did not approve of foreign intervention in Nepal in any way', but he was to be disappointed. With Ceylon and Burma India's relations were focused on the position of the Indian communities. This was touchy ground; in a phrase only subsequently made odious, Nehru said of both: 'We are the big brother and we have to proceed a little gently so as not to create barriers in the way of future co-operation'. Burma's non-cooperation was speedy, Ceylon's more drawn out.

A substantial success

The letters are the work of one man, but one who was centrally placed and in charge of the new Indian state from its inception. Also, although the style is conversational, the subject matter is business of the state. On the other hand, it is true that these are not necessarily the man's private thoughts. They are targeted to a particular audience and designed to convey information and explanation in relation to policy decisions. Acknowledging that his addressees may in some respects hold views quite different from his own, the letters aim also to persuade. And persuasion often includes rather exaggerated expressions of both delight and disappointment.

On the whole the merits of the letters outweigh their limitations. They portray well not only the condition of low stateness manifest at the birth of the new state but also the continuing battle that the leader, with his evident aspirations for high stateness, had continuously to conduct. Nehru's use of the term state was not frequent – the excerpts are in that respect obviously distorted – but frequent enough to distinguish his attitude, despite his English conditioning, from the British and Indians alike. It is fair to conclude that in this mission he succeeded, to use a phrase of his, 'not in full measure, but substantially'. On only one of the criteria discussed earlier may there be a question: was his drive towards the institutionalization of power marred by tendencies towards personal power? The view taken here is that the danger was averted by Nehru's marked respect for the institutions within which he had to work.

Notes

1. India, independent in 1947, had completed its constitution-making by 1949; it held its first elections on the basis of adult franchise in 1952. Pakistan encountered difficulties with both processes: constitutions have been hard to make and harder to keep, while the exercise of direct adult franchise has been infrequent. Sri Lanka had adult franchise 17 years before its independence, except for the Indian Tamil estate workers who were disfranchised, in 1931 partially, in 1948 completely.
2. *World Politics* 20 (1968).
3. S. K. Mitra, 'Between transaction and transcendence: the state and the institutionalisation of power in India' in S. K. Mitra (ed.) *The Post-Colonial State in Asia* (1990).
4. See Ashis Nandy, 'Images of the Indian state' (M. S. Mehta Memorial Lecture, 1986).
5. Published under the general editorship of G. Parthasarathi and as a project of the Jawaharlal Nehru Memorial Fund by the Government of India in five volumes: I, 1947–1949 (1985); II, 1950–1952 (1986); III 1952–1954 (1987); IV 1954–1957 (1988). The last volume was not published in time to be seen before this chapter had to go to press. Originally there were to be six volumes taking the letters up to Nehru's death in May 1964. The decision to make Vol. V the last one was taken during 1989. The present author has no information as to the basis on which the latter years have been compressed into one volume. All excerpts given below are from vols I–IV, and it has not been thought necessary to multiply footnotes with precise page references.
6. Victorian statesmen no doubt performed prodigious feats of letter-writing but here we have an institutionalized practice linking the prime minister to a set of office-holders at, in principle, regular intervals. It should be added that while the letters were always addressed to the chief ministers, copies were widely circulated to cabinet colleagues, 'senior officials throughout the country' and Indian diplomatic representatives overseas. (The letters were marked 'Secret' and Nehru was very angry when on one occasion there was a leak to the press). The intervals between letters in practice varied considerably and tended to increase over time, through pressure of work, more frequent overseas visits and tours within India, but were punctiliously accompanied by explanatory apologies. Only occasionally did Nehru ask Patel as deputy prime minister to substitute for him; when Patel died at the end of 1950 the office was unused and the gaps unfilled. It may be worth mentioning that the *Letters* distinguish between 'the fortnightlies' and 'special' letters, the latter normally shorter,

addressed to a particular urgent matter and calling for action; also that gaps caused by visits and tours were often more than compensated for by extensive 'enclosures' covering these experiences and despatched on his return.

7. Nehru's appeal to huge urban crowds was obvious. A further aspect, however, has been brought to light lately in a fascinating paper, 'Image de Nehru dans l'Inde rurale: naissance d'une tradition populaire' presented by J. L. Chambard of L'Ecole des Hautes Etudes en Sciences Sociales at a UNESCO seminar. In the Madhya Pradesh village which he has studied since 1957, Chambard was able to record a song in honour of Nehru still being sung by the village women. The verses refer to the wavy hair of his youth, the tragedy of his wife's death caused by cheap food, as part of nationalist austerity, and his building of canals (the word from which the name Nehru is derived) to bring fertile land to the people! Veritably, Nehru as a folk-hero prince!

8. The value of the letters should not, however, obscure their limitations as a source. For example, the constitution-making process during 1947–9 is hardly referred to; the proceedings were amply reported and the basic principles were settled early. Congress affairs are seldom substantively discussed; party matters were for party debate.

9. Nehru was sometimes too alarmist. A meeting of now-powerless princes was called to complain about loss of their privileges. After saying 'this has no great importance' Nehru nevertheless went on to roar 'it is a bad sign and we have to make it clear that no individual can challenge the authority of the State'.

10. As regards the broad constitutional structure, Nehru had little to say, surprisingly perhaps since he was one of the key constitution-framers. The constitution which served during 1947–9 was the (quasi-federal?) adapted 1935 Government of India Act. It is at first glance odd that when the new republican constitution came into force in 1950 with its explicit and fairly full-blown federal provisions on centre-state relations, Nehru passed no comment on those in his letters. Indeed he moved fairly promptly from 'the pageantry' of Republic Day to the imminent creation of a Planning Commission, an institution to which the states would have to 'give their full co-operation' and perhaps even replicate at state level. However, this may mean not that Nehru did not respect federalism but rather that among Congress Party colleagues informal relations might be expected to prevail.

11. See David Potter, *India's Political Administrators, 1919–1983* (1986), especially chs. 3 and 4. Professor Potter has remarked that it appears that Nehru, normally very happy to give a talk, never bothered to meet any of the annual batches of IAS entrants.

12. On one matter, however, he issued orders very quickly: the intelligence service had to be totally rebuilt. It had failed totally during the partition riots, being experienced 'chiefly in tracking Congressmen'. Its incompetence was further exposed a few months later when it failed to learn of the conspiracy to kill Gandhi.

13. It has to be added, however, that it did not long continue, nor was it the

only part of the Nehruvian structure which became ill-maintained or even dismantled subsequently.

14. There were a couple of forms of state interference to which Nehru was quite strongly opposed. When some congress governments in the states were moved by quasi-Gandhian sentiments towards introducing prohibition on alcohol and race-meetings, Nehru questioned their wisdom and indicated that the central government could not make up for the revenue they were losing.

15. The obverse of using foreign praise to boost internal morale was also evident: Nehru very frequently concluded his admonishing analysis of some internal failure by adding that this would 'worsen our bad press abroad' or 'lose us international good-will'. (This is not to say that Nehru always accepted a 'bad press abroad' as justified; on Kashmir and Hyderabad, in particular, he found foreign comment wilfully ignorant and unfair.

16. Nehru's interest in Africa was marginal and also slanted, being focused on colonial misdeeds and the position of Indian communities. Writing on the position of the latter in Kenya in 1952, he felt able to say 'Africans look up to them in their dire hour of peril'!

12

INDIA'S NINTH GENERAL ELECTION

Dennis Austin and Anirudha Gupta

A cause for wonder

Facts before theories. And the facts themselves spoke wonders. This was India's ninth general election since independence. For two months, seven nationally recognized parties, ranging from extreme-right, Hindu revivalism, to extreme-left, revolutionary Marxism, covered the sub-continent with their flags, symbols, money and agents to woo almost 500 million electors. The lowering of the age limit from 21 to 18 had added 5 million new names to the register. There were 15,500 candidates for 526 parliamentary (*Lok Sabha*) constituencies. In addition, elections were held for 1,547 regional assembly seats in Uttar Pradesh, Karnataka, Goa and Sikkim. Around 300,000 government officials manned 6 million polling stations with the assistance of 150 companies of the central police forces.

The cost of administering the elections was well over Rs150 crore (c. £60 million). For each contestant, the Election Commission imposed a ceiling of Rs1.5 lakhs (£6,000) on the cost of canvassing; but that did not rule out additional funding from parties, relatives and other sources. The result was that candidates were free to spend whatever they could get their hands on. The opposition parties accused Rajiv Gandhi's Congress[1] of giving each of its candidates a handsome gift of Rs10 million (£400,000) and five party jeeps; Congress of course denied the charge, and accused the opposition of having its own private sources of funds from which to purchase votes. But such accusations apart, the contest was an astonishing demonstration of India's administrative competence in support of a form of liberal parliamentary democracy that has no equal in the world in size and complexity.

Phrases such as 'the world's largest democracy' roll off the tongue and, repeated too often, lose their force. But that is what India has become, a continental society whose numbers of electors, not its population but its electorate, are twice the total population of the USA, whose number actually voting is larger than that of the whole population of the former USSR, and whose conduct of a political democracy spans as great a variety of language, religion, race and culture as can be found anywhere in the world. And India holds together democratically. Threats of secession have receded, the Latin American record of military intervention is absent. An astonishing record. In the fragmented, nationally divided world of the late-twentieth century, small is neither beautiful nor sensible. The need is for politics as an agent for putting together not for breaking apart, and India's achievement is precisely that: holding together, democratically, a very large portion of the globe, and a sixth of its population.

Themes

Not everything in the Indian garden of politics is lovely, although for a time the heat and dust of the campaign, stirred up by party leaders with their freshly painted jeeps, chariots, elephants and camels, blotted out the main issues. No one, not even the astrologers, knew which way the electoral wind would blow. The only certainty was the division between Rajiv Gandhi's Congress Party and V. P. Singh's *Janata Dal* (JD), in loose association with the Hindu conservative Bharatiya Janata Party (BJP) and the Communist Party Marxist (CPM). But as the election moved forward, the issues became clearer.

Corruption

In the days of the East India Company, criminals were blown from the muzzle of a gun; now it was hoped that Congress would be destroyed by a Swedish-made howitzer. The scandal over alleged commissions and bribes arose from contracts for the purchase of the Bofors gun from Sweden. The inept way in which the government

handled the issue by its lies, prevarication and contradictory statements, involving critical comments from its own auditor-general and
the retired army chief of staff, deepened the suspicion that Rajiv
Gandhi was involved in one way or another. Public criticism was kept
alive by generous reference to the heroes and villains of the Indian
epics. The *Mahabharata* tale of the wicked Duryodhana who, by fraud
and cunning, banished his five Pandava cousins was used to malign
the image of the prime minister; so was the popular story, a television
as well as a religious epic, of Rama, who banished his wife, Sita,
merely because of rumours against her. An anti-Congress, anti-
corruption 'wave', to use local terminology, now began to assume
formidable shape.

Rajiv Gandhi took upon himself the main burden of refutation. To
begin with, he acted coolly, neither contradicting nor confirming the
allegations which were daily manufactured; he sought instead to
equate Congress rule with unity and stability. 'My heart bleeds for
India', ran a series of full-length advertisements in over 2,000
newspapers, 'if it falls into the clutches of opposition parties'. That
was much too negative a stance even for his own supporters, and Rajiv
was forced to wake up to the fact that a sequence of opinion polls,
plus his own intelligence bureau, showed that Congress was falling
behind, particularly in the Hindi-speaking states of Uttar Pradesh
(UP), Bihar, Rajasthan and Madhya Pradesh. There were also
disquieting reports that two of the important constituents of Congress
support, that is, the Muslims and the Harijans, were deserting the
prime minister. What was he to do?

Communal factors

'We have to choose between two basic approaches', wrote Jawaharlal
Nehru to his chief ministers on 17 May 1950. 'One may be called the
general Congress approach representing the Congress viewpoint in
regard to communal matters during the last 40 years or more, and the
other is the communal approach which is ideologically represented by
the Hindu Mahasabha and like organisations. There are variations
and gradations between the two. But the choice is ultimately between
the two'. His grandson was less forthright. He attempted, covertly, to
play the Hindu card.

And already tempers were inflamed. The Muslims, heavily concentrated in the northern belt, now number over 90 million. In the run-

up to the elections, many of them were killed in communal rioting in Bhagalpur, a town in Bihar. (The incident was all the more gruesome because of the assistance of the local provincial constabulary which was said to have encouraged rioters to loot and demolish Muslim houses). Similar riots occurred in a number of Congress-ruled states. 'Why should this be', Muslims began to ask, 'when we have traditionally supported the ruling party in return for protection?'

There were hopes that the government would at least stand by its publicly announced commitment that it would not allow the Vishwa Hindu Parishad (VHP), a fanatical Hindu organization, to lay the foundations for a new temple within the court of a mosque in Ayodhya (UP). For years, the VHP had claimed that the mosque, the Babri Masjid, stood on the spot where Lord Rama was born in 3,000 (or 30,000) BC. The VHP carried bricks for the temple from all parts of India and abroad, including, it was said, one from China, while Congress and the central government maintained a posture of fair-dealing. Together with the courts, they held that the site was a disputed one. So the Muslims believed that no *Shila Puja* (brick ceremony) would take place. But on 9 November the bricks were laid, accompanied by the chanting of mantras, blowing of conch shells and the clash of cymbals to herald the dawn of a new Hindu Era. And the government turned about-face. It declared that the disputed territory was in fact 'undisputed'. On this assumption, the VHP was free to perform its ceremonies.

The Muslim community was incensed. Its leaders, of all hues and sects, rebelled. The Imam of the Great Delhi Jama Masjid ordered his followers to vote against Congress and for the JD. Rajiv Gandhi must have come close to panic. Fearing he had lost the Muslim vote, he overplayed his Hindu card and proclaimed, at a village significantly close to Ayodhya, that Congress, when re-elected, would build Ram Raja, the Kingdom of Rama. The fanatics who wanted their temple to Rama had nothing, it seemed, to fear from a party which promised them His Kingdom.

A different communal problem came not from religion but from caste. The scheduled castes, notably the Harijans, were also beginning to desert Congress in favour of a new association, the Bahujan Samaj Party (BSP), founded by a charismatic leader, Kansi Ram. It professed support for scheduled castes, tribes and backward classes, and Mr Ram urged voters to end 'slum-landlordism'. The language was unfamiliar to the upper castes. Despite constitutional guarantees and legal assurances, Harijans are still not free; they can neither draw water from the wells nor enter the temples used by higher-caste families. Many live in terror of village life, their claim on land brutally suppressed, their women molested. During the run-up to the election the number of violent clashes between castes in Bihar and UP mounted daily. The sense that lower-cast opinion was turning away from Congress was correctly assessed. When the final results were announced, it was seen that Harijans had succeeded in getting 3 BSP candidates elected to the *Lok Sabha*, and 13 to the state assembly in Uttar Pradesh.

Organizational failings

If Congress was divided over secularism and communal loyalties, it was also beset with factional disputes. Many members who sought election on the Congress ticket were soured when their case was either not considered or rejected. The younger would-be candidates who had enthusiastically supported the lowering of the franchise were particularly aggrieved. If all the sitting MPs were chosen to stand again, what chance was there for the new generation? In many constituencies the party machine was ineffective, its members either unwilling or unable to mobilize its supporters, and Rajiv's own campaign was almost grounded in Gujarat, Bihar and the eastern state of Orissa. Congress, which had once mediated disputes between the states and the centre, between castes, regions, communal groups, divisions between north and south and between left and right, which had used the resources of the state to harmonize and not inflame tempers, that Congress had lost the 'Nehru touch'. Indira Gandhi had sought to concentrate power, Rajiv Gandhi had failed to manage even the politics of the centre.

Violence

There were more outbreaks of violence during the 1989 election than in any of India's previous contests. The first two days of polling brought 42 deaths and 500 injured; there were endless accounts of intimidation, ballot-rigging and 'booth capturing' by organized gangs of thugs in the pay of party agents. Violence distorted the outcome in a number of areas and the Electoral Commission ordered fresh elections in 930 polling booths in 90 parliamentary constituencies.

There was widespread disorder even in Rajiv Gandhi's constituency of Amethi and, under pressure from the opposition, the commission ordered a second poll to be conducted in 96 of its stations. The last two days of voting (24 and 26 November) saw a drop in the political temperature; even so, 23 more deaths were reported and the threat of further violence hung heavily in the air. In Fatehpur constituency an unidentified attacker fired a single shot at V. P. Singh – and missed – and charges of malpractice were brought by each side against the other up until the last hour of the election. The threat of violence was not only in the brutality of particular events but in its extension into politics via agents of the major parties which recruited thugs and *goondas* to murder their opponents.[2]

A contrast in fortunes

After the election, peace descended but the suspense continued. Unlike 1977 and 1984 there was no clear swing – in Indian parlance no discernible 'wave' – either to Congress or to the opposition. In the 1977 election the shaky coalition of the Janata's landslide victory, with a tally of seats three times that of the Congress total, had been a massive vote of non-confidence in Mrs Gandhi's style of government. Three years later, she returned to power, not because her party had enlarged its customary 40 per cent share of the vote but because petty squabbles had split the anti-Congress vote. By 1984 Mrs Gandhi's position was again uncertain but the bullets which killed her on 31 October carried both her party and her son to power with an unprecedented three-quarters of the seats in the *Lok Sabha*. Voters were moved not only by sympathy but by the government's call for a strong response against terrorist violence in the Punjab, separatist movements in the north-east, and agitation for 'Gorkha land'. Rajiv was then appointed as prime minister, with all the pomp and ceremony of dynastic rule.

But the wave of sympathy ebbed, despite constant exposure through the government-controlled media, too large an exposure, perhaps, as charges of corruption mounted against the prime minister. In addition, Rajiv Gandhi's own brand of absolutism alienated old congressmen. The octogenarian Kamlapathi Tripathi, who had been a close associate of Jawaharlal Nehru and Indira Gandhi, openly complained that Congress was losing its national character. Similarly, K. C. Panth, Rajiv's defence minister who refused the party's nomination for the

Nainital seat in UP, sent an open letter to the prime minister saying that there had been 'a revival of state bossism [and] of the interference of inexperienced non-political coteries in political decision-taking'. Once again, as under Indira Gandhi, the federal division of power was tilted in favour of the centre at the expense of local bases of control in the states.

A few days before the election dates were announced, a strong rumour circulated that a syndicate of Congress leaders, including those in UP, Madhya Pradesh and Maharashtra, was planning to oust Rajiv Gandhi. Such stories may have been deliberately planted but they had the effect of causing Rajiv to bring forward the elections by almost a month. The announcement surprised not only the opposition but Congress itself and contributed to the disarray in its ranks.

The actual campaign failed to enthuse electors. In some constituencies, Muslims declared they would not vote, ostensibly because they were resentful of Congress attitudes, in practice because they could find no acceptable alternative. In some states, however, polling was quite heavy, about 60 per cent for example of registered voters in the south (132 seats). Voting was surprisingly high too in Punjab (c. 65 per cent). But in the northern states of Uttar Pradesh and Bihar (139 seats) only half of the electorate turned out to vote. (Final figures now available confirm the low vote – 58 per cent.)

Results

Because voting was delayed in Fatehpur (by unexpected rains) and in Amethi (by re-polling), the electoral fate of the two arch rivals, Gandhi and Singh, was determined after most of the results had come in. Rajiv Gandhi trounced Rajmohan (Mahatma Gandhi's grandson) by over 220,000 votes; V. P. Singh defeated the son of Lal Bahadur Shastri, who had succeeded Nehru as prime minister in 1964–5, by a margin of over 120,000 votes.

Other battles involved sons, grandsons, cousins and in-laws in the true spirit of the *Mahabharata* war. In Rajasthan, Haryana's chief minister, Devi Lal, staked his personal honour on defeating his brother-in-law, B. R. Jhakar, speaker of the outgoing *Lok Sabha*. In Madhya Pradesh every member of the royal family of Gwalior entered the fray. The queen mother and her daughter were JD candidates, the son, Maharajah Sindhia, stood for Congress, all in different constituencies; all three were elected. The issue was not Congress versus its opponents, but equitable obeisance to the royal house of the Sindhias! But the Maharajah of Jaipur was less fortunate. His stepmother, Maharani Gayatri Devi, backed his rival BJP candidate, and the Maharajah was beaten decisively.

In the larger all-India contest, these family feuds were subsumed in the broader, party conflict. And two obvious trends were evident: south Congress; north anti-Congress. Throughout the south, voters expressed their frustration over the performance of their non-Congress governments to such an extent that, in one sweep, all opposition candidates from left to right were brushed aside. Of the 129 southern seats, Congress captured 106: 27 of the 28 in Karnataka, 24 out of 39 in Tamil Nadu, 39 out of 42 in Andhra Pradesh, 14 out of 20 in Kerala; it also won 2 seats in the Union Territories.

History had repeated itself. In 1977 when Mrs Gandhi lost all but 2 seats in the north, she won an astonishing 124 out of 132 southern seats. Now, in 1989, the pattern was similar. Rajiv Gandhi lost the north and won the south. The extent of the Congress defeat in the north, east and west can be demonstrated by comparing the 1989 results with those of 1984 (see Table 12.1).

Assessment

The clearest indication was the desire for change. The electorate wanted a non-Congress government at the centre. The north voted for change, but, it is argued, the pro-Congress south also wanted a different set of rulers in their own areas. All the southern states, Kerala, Tamil Nadu, Karnataka and Andhra, had been under opposition and/or regional-party rule since 1980. Because voters in the south were more involved in local issues they were less concerned about issues of corruption and communalism which convulsed the north; hence the anti-state but pro-Congress vote.

So it is argued, and there is a good deal of truth in the interpretation. In the two assembly elections, at state level, in Karnataka and Andhra Pradesh the verdict went massively against both the JD and the Telegu Desam under Chief Minister T. Rama Rao. Congress took two-thirds of the seats in Karnataka and an absolute majority in Andhra Pradesh. In the northern state of UP, however, Congress with 92 seats trailed far behind the JD which not only emerged as the single largest party (263 seats) but one well posed to form the next state government. Similarly in Sikkim, the Himalayan enclave annexed in 1974, Nara

Table 12.1: Congress (I) performance in north, east and western states in 1984

States	Total Seats	1984	1989
Bihar	54	48	4
Delhi	7	7	2
Gujarat	26	24	3
Haryana	10	10	4
Himachal Pradesh	4	4	1
Madhya Pradesh	40	40	8
Maharashtra	48	43	28
Orissa	21	20	3
Rajasthan	25	25	0
Sikkim	1	1	0
Tripura	2	2	2
Uttar Pradesh (UP)	85	83	14
West Bengal	42	16	4
Total	366	323	73

The overall picture in 1989 was as follows: total *Lok Sabha* (544); seats contested (526); no contests were held for 12 seats in Assam; polling in the remaining 6 was countermanded.

Congress I	193
JD	142
BJP	86
Communist Party (Marxist)	32
CPI	12
Telegu Desam	2
DMK	0
BSP	3
Others	56

Bhandari's Sikkim Sangram party annihilated the Congress by winning all 32 assembly places, as well as the single *Lok Sabha* seat.

The results 'reflected a call of change'. But Congress is still there as the largest single party in the *Lok Sabha*, as it has been since 1947. For over 40 years the party kept a dynasty in power. Except for two brief periods of interregnum, the Congress and India were ruled autocratically by three generations of the Nehru family. And if one asks whether the 1989 results were an unambiguous judgement against dynastic rule, the answer must be 'no', or, perhaps, 'not yet'.

The failed aspects of Rajiv Gandhi's rule are clear. There was not only the Bofors scandal but a number of tactical errors, not least the decision, that is, Rajiv Gandhi's decision, to bring the election date forward. He also claimed primacy over the party throughout the election campaign. It was he, with close advisers, who selected the party's candidates and their constituencies. And he aroused the worst fears of the minorities by yielding to majority sentiment in the Ram-Babri-Masjid dispute. His 'eagerness simultaneously to appease Hindu and Muslim fundamentalists', commented the *Times of India*, more sympathetic than most to the prime minister, 'unleashed a wave of hostility in both communities. The alienation of the Muslims will undoubtedly rank as the most grievous lapse of the Rajiv Gandhi government' (28 November 1989).

In more ways than one, therefore, the defeat of Congress was a demonstration of the failure of Rajiv Gandhi as its leader. A vote against the party was a vote against him. Yet the diminished number of Congress MPs did not hesitate to elect him unanimously as leader. Why?

Paradoxically, Congress reverses in the northern states, and its sweep of the seats in the south, strengthened Gandhi's position in the party. The old Congress bosses belonged mainly to the Hindi-speaking regions; they may or may not have been planning Gandhi's overthrow, but they were now forced to humble themselves in the light of their own defeat. Those elected from the south, on the other hand, profess a fawning respect for Rajiv. They live far from the centre and are uninterested, and uninvolved, in northern party feuds. The former prime minister's hope, therefore, must be that he can stage a return to office as dramatically as his mother did in 1980.

In the meantime, in good parliamentary tradition Rajiv tendered his resignation and announced that he would not try and form a new government. The non-Congress parties then struggled to put together a majority. Cohabitation between the JD and both the (Hindu) BJP and the (Marxist) CPM seemed unthinkable at first, but pressure from below to form a government increased, and frantic negotiations under the threat of defections gradually established the fact that JD would receive 'critical support' from the right and 'uncritical support' from the left. There was a further prerequisite: a single leader. That, too, was contentious. Rival factions led by Haryana's chief minister, Devi Lal, and Chandra Shekhar from UP staked out their claims. The wrangle continued for three days under the taunts of Congress MPs until a noisy meeting of opposition members gave unanimous support to V. P. Singh. On 2 November he was sworn in as India's seventh prime minister.

Quo vadis?

Many wondered whether the electorate had done the right thing by ousting Congress without giving a full mandate to the opposition. The country had voted for a hung parliament but, as a noted jurist observed, 'that was no reason to hang the country'. What would happen if, over the next five years, the JD lost the support either of BJP or the communists? The simple fact was that it would not be able to survive. V. P. Singh's claim to be able to evolve a national consensus covering the two extremes was bold, illogical, almost inconceivable, not least because there were warring factions within the JD itself, including muscle-men with strong local clusters of militant/criminal support.

And even if V. P. Singh's consensus was actually to hold, the effect might well be to cripple the working of his government. The danger would be that of deadlock at the centre and of economic paralysis. If the electorate then turned once again to Rajiv Gandhi and to Congress, one would have had to conclude that India had in fact not learnt to run its democracy other than by leaning on the crutches of a single dynasty. (These words were written over a year before Rajiv's assassination.)

Such depressing thoughts could, however, be offset by more cheerful indicators in the immediate aftermath of India's ninth general election. We list three of them:

- Nothwithstanding ballot-rigging and violence, India's illiterate millions again showed that they were actively engaged in democratic practice; so too at the very highest level. Although there might have been massive unrest across the Hindi-speaking belt and Rajiv Gandhi did try to remain in office, the fact remains that he resigned gracefully and made possible a smooth passage for the formation of a minority government. V. P. Singh's assumption of office should also strengthen those who believe that the Indian psyche does not follow the dry logic of numbers, there is always room for manoeuvre. The process might have been politically unedifying but it also reflected a high state of the art of the possible.

- The high turnout of over 65 per cent in Punjab saw the election of all the militant Akali Dal candidates, including that of their imprisoned leader, S. S. Mann. There were obvious dangers in that, but it also raised the hope of some form of dialogue. A great deal, then, depended not only on the Akali Dal but on V. P. Singh's attitude, and his early visit to the Golden Temple in Amritsar was at least a large gesture of understanding.[3]
- The emergence of the Bahujan Samaj Party (BSP) as a separate association of the lower castes and *harijans* was one more knot in India's contorted caste-based politics. Its modest electoral success confirmed a trend among the scheduled castes to break from the paternalism of Congress and other national parties, a revolt of caste and class against Brahmins, Jats and Rajputs. The BSP may be a further example, therefore, of the integration of minorities into main line politics.

The belief behind such optimism is that elections in India can integrate secessionists, protect minorities and democratize the terrorist. If the ballot box evokes a measure of violence at the polling booth, it is also, so the argument runs, a form of inoculation against the dangers of a greater violence in society at large, and the failure of the Communist Party of the former Soviet Union to allow such safety valves of dissent is a yardstick of the success of a much greater *glasnost* within India's own form of democratic control.

To sustain success at that level, V. P. Singh's government was required to be active along a broad front. It needed to consolidate its political base and build a new relationship between the centre and the states in place of the dynastic autocracy of Congress rule. It had to diminish the violence which threatened Jammu and Kashmir, Punjab, Assam, Andhra Pradesh and, especially, Bihar where mafia-based campaigns of murder had become commonplace. Abroad, it had somehow to ease relationships with Pakistan and Nepal, and continue the phased withdrawal of troops from Sri Lanka. Domestically, the need was to move the economy forward in order to improve the slum *jhuggis* without losing support from the new Maruti class of the urban élite,[4] and to meet its electoral pledge on rural debt without alarming India's international creditors.

A formidable set of problems. And yet elections had been held, a new government was in place, fresh policies were in train and there was a renewed freedom of national debate. Continuity and change in the world's largest democracy? Long may it be so!

The 1991 election

Within two years of the 1989 election a further contest took place. The ninth *Lok Sabha* had the shortest of tenures and witnessed the most tumultuous events in the parliamentary history of India. Constituted in December 1989, it lasted for just 15 months, 14 months shorter than the sixth *Lok Sabha* which saw the installation of the first non-Congress (I) government under Morarji Desai and later under Charan Singh. As in the sixth *Lok Sabha*, the dissolved house saw two prime ministers take office, V. P. Singh and Chandra Shekhar. (The third *Lok Sabha* of 1962–7 had seen three prime ministers: Jawaharlal Nehru, Lal Bahadur Shastri and Indira Gandhi). The ninth parliament was the scene of bitter controversies, and the government, first of V. P. Singh (for just 11 months) and then of Chandra Shekhar (for only 4 months), lurched from crisis to crisis.

The chronology of events was full of drama: a clash of personalities over the office of Chief Minister in Haryana between Devi Lal, his son Om Prakash Chautala, and V. P. Singh; new evidence in the long-running Bofors gun scandal; the report of the Mandal Commission with its recommendations of a 27 per cent quota for backward classes in government jobs, and the consequent violence across northern India including the suicide, by burning, of young boys and girls; the Rath Yatra protest by L. K. Advani, president of the BJP, against the Mandal Commission and on behalf of the Ram Temple of Ayodhya; the resignation on 7 November 1990 of V. P. Singh after the BJP had withdrawn its support and his replacement three days later by Chandra Shekhar with Congress support; the dismissal of the Dravida Munnetra Kazhagam (DMK) government of Tamil Nadu on 30 January 1991; and the growing rift between the government and its Congress backers first over the refuelling of American aircraft in India, then over the alleged police surveillance of Rajiv Gandhi. On 5 March, Congress announced a boycott of parliament; Chandra Shekhar resigned the following day, but continued on a caretaker basis until fresh elections could be held.

The 1991 election was certainly no less violent than that of 1989 and it brought the terrible death of Rajiv Gandhi on 21 May in a bomb explosion during a party rally at Sriperumbudur near Madras.

Table 12.2: *Lok Sabha* Elections 1989–91

		Cong I	BJP	JD
	1989	510	225	244
Seats contested	1990	493	479	317
Seats won	1989	197	85	143
	1990	225	119	55
Percentage of votes	1989	39.5	11.4	17.8
	1990	37.3	19.9	10.8
Swing %	1989	−8.6	+4.0	–
	1990	−2.2	+8.5	−7

Source: *India Today*, 15 July 1991

Voting was interrupted but not cancelled; it ended with Congress once more in office, though without a majority of seats in the tenth *Lok Sabha* (223 out of 506 seats). There were two unusual features: the new prime minister P. V. Narasimha Rao, a Congress stalwart, was not a member of the Nehru-Gandhi family; he was also from the southern state of Andhra Pradesh. A summary of the results is in Table 12.2.

There is no space here to comment in detail on the results. The BJP now has a strong northern base. It gives voice and a political presence to Hindu sentiments and has struck a chord which will not easily be muffled. On 12 June the Calcutta *Statesman* commented that 'the two major obstacles which have kept the Congress (I) distinct from other parties – its pre-eminence and its dynastic preferences – have disappeared. It is now a "normal party" which may be better incorporated into a democratic framework of politics'. Well, perhaps; one can certainly hope that that will be so. At a time when the economy is in poor shape, when violence disfigures party politics and when the international scene is clouded with danger, India needs as much domestic tranquillity as its half-century of democratic politics can supply.

A note on violence

Violence runs like a dark thread of anguish through Indian politics, violence at different levels of society, violence between different segments of society. It corrupts elections. In the worst cases, in 1989 and 1991, 'politicians and criminals were two sides of the same coin.

During elections, the criminals got money from the politician, and in return they bring him power by capturing polling booths'. A full account was given in a local journal:

> The district administration and the police vied with anti-social elements and criminals recruited by the Congress unit in the region in driving innocent voters out of booths and stuffing already marked ballot papers into the boxes. Sanjay Singh, the Janata Dal candidate . . . and nephew of V. P. Singh . . . was shot at and seriously injured when he tried to chase a gang of hired hoodlums decamping with a set of ballot boxes. He is still fighting for his life in hospital in Lucknow.[5]

In the town of Bhagalpur, Hindu mobs, urged on by local politicians, attacked the Muslim community:

> We were attacked at about 4 in the afternoon . . . the mob went on the rampage and we were attacked with swords, spears, axes. The victims were chased, rounded up and hacked to death. They tried to cut my leg off but the weapon was too blunt. Later, they brought a sharp sword and severed my foot from the ankle. All the bodies and limbs were thrown into the pond. In all some 100 were killed. I do not think more than two or three of the victims survived.[6]

Similarly in New Delhi in October 1984, after the attack on the Sikh Golden Temple in Amritsar and following the assassination of Indira Gandhi, Sikhs were killed and their houses looted in the centre of the capital:

> We were told by residents in the riot-torn area – by Hindus and Sikhs – that certain Congress leaders played a decisive role in organizing the riots . . . and local agents were actively partici-pating in the violence.
> The killings were brutal. One Sikh was pushed into a car which was then set ablaze. Others were hit, thrown on the ground, doused with kerosene and set on fire. Few males survived. Those who lost husbands and sons gave vent to their grief: *ab to sabse accha yeh hoga ki aap ham sab ko jahar dila dain;*

ab ham ji nahin sakte: kaise jiyenge, kis liye jiyenge (it would be best to give us poison, for how will we live and for whom?).[7]

What causes such horrible acts to be committed? There is no single explanation; there is no simple definition of what is meant by violence and terror. Communal killing has to be set alongside the murder of officials by terrorist groups and the shooting of demonstrators by the army and police in Punjab and Kashmir. There are widening circles of complicity: the person who fires the gun, those who supply the money, those who are drawn into the looting of houses and stores, those who, from good or bad motives, protect the perpetrators, and those who profit politically. One must add, too, acts of private revenge and the murder of brides for their dowry and of widows under the guise of *sati*,[8] the killing of *harijans* and scheduled castes by rapacious landlords in the villages and by slum landlords in the towns,[9] and the counter-terror by victims against their oppressors. Since 1947 organized crime and organized politics have joined forces from time to time under an intellectual leadership, notably in the Naxalite movement in West Bengal and Andhra Pradesh, feeding on the disquiet among unemployed young men over the failure of social reform. In this respect, violence in India, as in Sri Lanka and other parts of the world, has been 'a battle of ideas and interpretations as well as deeds'.[10] The deeds, however, have been dreadful almost beyond description.

It seems certain that if remedies are found, they too will be plural. One hope is not of solutions but of amelioration, a falling away of violence through weariness and division among the terrorists themselves, a fragmentation into gratuitous violence for criminal or pathological motives which alienates public support. Another is the ability of the state to remedy the worst forms of economic and social deprivation. A third must be the resolute abstention from illegal acts and repressive violence by the state and its agents. A fourth, liberal in its hopes and prescription, is the patient use of dialogue and negotiation by which a large element of those involved in violence are reabsorbed into political life through parties, elections and parliament. The last is not fantasy. Secessionist threats and violence in Tamil Nadu, Andhra Pradesh and the north-eastern states of India have been diminished by a slow process of absorption into main-line politics.

Even the worst violence at the highest level, for example the murder of Mahatma Gandhi, Indira Gandhi and Rajiv Gandhi, does not herald collapse. Society and state can encompass the violence they engender. And the majority of India's many millions have become not indifferent but inured to the daily reports of violent acts in newspapers or on television. The reader or viewer pauses a little, but then moves on to a different event and another day.

Yet such occasions ought never to be reduced to statistics. There is always suffering, the suffering of those for whom the tragedy is 'permanent and infinite':

Action is transitory – a step, a blow.
The motion of a muscle, this way or that –
'Tis done, and in the after vacancy
We wonder at ourselves like men betrayed:
Suffering is permanent, obscure and dark
And shares the nature of infinity.

The violence recorded does not 'foretell the collapse of Indian society or its politics'. No. But, beyond argument, it disfigures, it tragically mars, the democratic face of Indian politics.

Notes

1. The contract worth Rs14,437 billion (£513 million) was awarded to Bofors when Rajiv Gandhi was prime minister and minister of defence in March 1986 for the supply of 410 155mm-howitzers. The allegations were that commissions worth Rs640 million were paid to Congress members via Swiss banks. V.P. Singh became minister of defence in 1987 (formerly ministry of finance) but resigned in July 1987 and was expelled from Congress.
2. The evidence is overwhelming. See *Who are the Guilty: Report of a Joint Inquiry into the Causes and Impact of the Riots in Delhi from 31 October to 10 November 1984* (New Delhi: PUDR and PUCL, 1984); and *The Truth About Bhagalpur* (Surya, December 1989).
3. The *Statesman* (4 December 1989) saw the election as 'a reassertion of the Sikh's faith in the constitution and the integrity of the country', but that is very optimistic, not least because the Sikh community is itself divided between the Akali Dal, the All-India Sikh Student Federation and numerous local groups. See, too, W. H. McLeod, *Who is a Sikh? The Problem of Sikh Identity* (Oxford: Clarendon Press, 1989).
4. Maruti class = those who own the smart Maruti cars produced under licence from Japan, replacing the sturdy but clumsy Ambassador. The

young upwardly mobile members of the Punjabi *nouveaux riches* are now commonly known as 'puppies'.

5. *Who are the Guilty?* Joint Inquiry into the Riots in Delhi 31 October to 10 November 1984, p. 18. Estimates of the number killed during these days run into several thousand; see, too, *Surya*, December 1989.

6. Ibid.

7. Ibid.

8. See D. Austin, 'Revisiting Delhi', *The Round Table* (1988), p. 376, for an account of the death of Roop Kanwar on the funeral pyre of her husband.

9. A harrowing, detailed account of caste-political violence in Amravati (Maharashtra) is given in Ashgar Ali Engineer, *Ethnic Conflict in South Asia* (Delhi 1987).

10. See David Moss, *The Politics of Left-wing Violence in Italy 1969–1985* (Macmillan 1989). The estimate of terrorist victims during these 16 years was 1,119 killed and wounded, the worst record in western Europe. The most savage incident was the bombing of Bologna railway station in August 1980 when 85 died. Such figures, alas, are small in relation to atrocities in Delhi, Ahmadebad, Bhagalpur, Punjab, Kashmir, Bihar, Hyderabad, Jaffna, etc.

13

THE STRUCTURE OF REGIONAL CONFLICT IN NORTHERN ETHIOPIA[1]

Christopher Clapham

Over the last three decades, no part of independent Africa has been so violently ravaged by conflict as the Horn. Three major conflicts have split the region: the Ethio-Somali dispute, which led in 1977–8 to by far the largest conventional war between independent African states; the Sudanese civil wars; and the war between the central Ethiopian government and movements seeking separate independence for Eritrea. In their wake, and often fomented by the massive build-up of armaments in the region that the major conflicts have brought with them, a mass of lesser, but still devastating, conflicts have proliferated: the civil war in northern Somalia, the Afar and Oromo movements in eastern and southern Ethiopia, the Tigrayan resistance in northern Ethiopia, all the way down to the casual extermination of smaller communities in local conflicts fuelled by the supply of automatic weapons. During the first half of 1991, these conflicts overwhelmed the governments both of Siyad Barre in Somalia and of Mengistu Haile Mariam in Ethiopia, raising immediate possibilities of secession by Eritrea from Ethiopia and by the Northern Region from the Somali Republic.

Such tragedies demand explanation; and at least for the large proportion of conflicts in the region which in one way or another affect its most populous and centrally located state, that is, Ethiopia, such explanations are not far to seek. Very broadly, there is a conventional explanation of regional conflict in Ethiopia, to which I have myself in some measure contributed, which accounts for these conflicts in terms of the political hegemony and economic exploitation imposed by the central Ethiopian state, and by the social groupings from which this is chiefly drawn. The Ethiopian state is, in this view, essentially the creation of the Orthodox Christian peoples of the northern highlands – Amhara and Tigrayan, though with a substantial element of Christian and Amharised Oromo – who are often referred to as Abyssinian. With the powerful political and military organization built on the economic base provided by highland ox-plough agriculture, this state has been able to dominate the surrounding peoples, its hegemony over whom has been justified by a sense of manifest destiny reinforced by religious superiority. With the vast accretion of strength provided in the second half of the nineteenth century by effective indigenous leadership and access to external armaments, the Ethiopian state both extended its territory and imposed on the conquered peoples a highly exploitative economic structure, which turned formerly independent peasants in the south and west into the vassals of central Abyssinian settlers and landowners.

The wars of the late-twentieth century are, in this view, the almost automatic consequence of the conquests of a hundred years earlier, easily summarized in the two words, exclusion and exploitation. Politically, the central Ethiopian government has been dominated by the Christian peoples of the northern highlands who formed the core of the old Ethiopian empire. The incorporated peoples have therefore (save for a small and unrepresentative minority who have been assimilated into the ruling core) been effectively excluded from the state. Not only have the leading positions in the state been overwhelmingly monopolized by Christian highlanders, but the whole structure of the state itself has been set up in such a way as to exclude, or, at least, severely disadvantage, the peripheral peoples. Visibly descended, despite the 1974 revolution, from its imperial predecessor, the state is headquartered in the centrally located highland capital, Addis Ababa, from which roads radiate out to control the periphery. Its language, Amharic, is the dominant language of the highland core, fluency in which has been essential to anyone who aspires to a post in government. Its army, still more obviously than before the revolution, has existed to enforce the diktat of the central power over dissident peoples. And though some of the formal trappings of religious and cultural superiority were discarded after the revolution, these were replaced by the still more stridently centralist rhetoric of Marxism-

Leninism. The economic surplus required to maintain this apparatus of control in turn derived from the exploitation of the very peoples whom it was used to suppress, at first through land alienation and subsequently through the imposition of a centralized state-extractive apparatus. The regions and peoples conquered in the late-nineteenth century produce almost all of Ethiopia's export crops, with coffee normally accounting for over 60 per cent of published export earnings, and also much of its marketable grain. Small wonder, then, that such a state has excited violent opposition, or that such opposition has been directed, unusually in Africa, not simply towards the goal of controlling the state, but to a much more thorough-going rejection of the whole basis of statehood itself.

It should be emphasized that this picture of the Ethiopian state, though inevitably rather crudely drawn, is not basically a false one. The conquest and exploitation of much of southern and western Ethiopia are demonstrable historical facts.[2] The problem is not that it is untrue, nor that it would not amply explain regional resistance, but rather that much if not most of the regional resistance to the central Ethiopian government will not fit into the pattern which this explanation provides. This resistance has come essentially from two sources. The first is the pastoralist peoples of southern and eastern Ethiopia, especially the Somali but also some Afar and pastoral Oromo. These are indeed excluded peoples, lacking any affinity with a central government from which they are separated by language, religion, means of production and social organization. The Ethiopian government has maintained some control over them, not only by force, but also by taking advantage of internal divisions of clan, faction and family. Opposition, especially for the Somali, is also fomented by their nearness to and affinity with the Somali Republic. But even these peoples do not fit into the classic pattern of central economic exploitation. With the exception of the Afar-inhabited areas of the Awash valley which have been taken over for commercial agriculture, and much smaller, and largely unsuccessful, attempts at commercial agriculture in the Webe Shebelle valley, the Somali have been not so much exploited as ignored by the modern cash economy. Their resistance to central government derives from cultural and political alienation, rather than from economic incorporation.

By far the most important military threat to the central government has come, however, not from the pastoralists, still less from the conquered sedentary peoples of southern Ethiopia, but from the northern highlands: from highland Eritrea, from Tigray, and increasingly from Gonder and northern Wollo.[3] In Eritrea, the Eritrean Liberation Front (ELF), which initiated the secessionist conflict against central Ethiopian rule, was indeed drawn largely from the Muslim peoples of the western Eritrean lowlands; but this has now been almost entirely displaced by the Eritrean People's Liberation Front (EPLF) which, under the banner of an Eritrea united across ethnic lines within a Marxist-Leninist framework, draws its leadership and much of its support from the Christian Eritrean highlands.[4] Immediately to the south is Tigray, which after the defeat of the Ethiopian army at Enda-Selassie early in 1989, came almost totally under the control of the Tigray People's Liberation Front (TPLF); this is an overwhelmingly Christian region, which has formed part of the Ethiopian state since the very earliest times, and includes its ancient capital of Axum. But still more strikingly, though the Amhara are universally recognized as *the* core Abyssinian people, whose language, history and culture are essentially those of the central Ethiopian state, even Amhara areas were progressively lost to central-government control. The movement which eventually overthrew the Mengistu regime, the Ethiopian People's Revolutionary Democratic Front (EPDRF), was a coalition of the TPLF and its Amhara offshoot, the Ethiopian People's Democratic Movement (EPDM), which drew its strength almost entirely from the orthodox highland areas of 'traditional' Ethiopia.[5]

In contrast to the collapse of the Mengistu government's authority in much of the four northernmost highland regions, it is important to emphasize the astonishing quiescence of the southern highland areas which were fully incorporated into Ethiopia only in the later nineteenth century. There was certainly an organization, the Oromo Liberation Front (OLF), which sought to challenge the Ethiopian government over the huge area from Welega in the west to Hararge in the east, with the formal goal of establishing an independent Oromia; but in contrast to the EPLF and TPLF, which were able to control large areas of territory in the face of massive and well-armed Ethiopian military, its efforts amounted to little more than hit-and-run operations in western Welega and the more isolated parts of the Hararge highlands. Throughout by far the greater part of southern Ethiopia, including the Hararge and Bale highlands, the whole of Arsi and Shoa, and the highland areas of Sidamo, Kaffa, Gamu Gofa, Illubabor and Welega, there was no sign of any serious resistance to central government. Yet these are precisely the areas which the exclusion and exploitation model of Ethiopian centre–periphery relations would suggest were most at risk. These are the areas where an alien structure of central domination has been imposed, and where landlords and settlers exploited the local peasantry in order to produce the cash crops required by the national market and by Ethiopia's incorporation into the global economy.

In short, the exclusion and exploitation model, regardless of its inherent plausibility, scarcely begins to explain the actual structure of regional conflict in Ethiopia. So far from being a revolt of the politically excluded, regional opposition has been overwhelmingly derived from peoples who have been associated with the Ethiopian state over many centuries. Due to their relatively high level of education, Eritreans have until recently been overrepresented in central government positions. Their progressive exclusion has been due to the war, bringing with it their voluntary or enforced withdrawal, as a result of their own developing Eritrean national consciousness and of central government distrust of their loyalty; the war was not the result of their exclusion. Though Tigray has had a strong sense of its distinctive regional identity, it has also had highly placed connections with central government, under the imperial regime through intermarriage between Haile-Selassie's family and the regional Tigrayan dynasty, and under the revolutionary regime through Mengistu Haile-Maryam's deputy and the then vice-president, Fisseha Desta. The northern Amhara regions have, paradoxically for the stereotype which sees Ethiopian politics in terms of Amhara domination, been rather less well-represented in central government than either Eritrea or Tigray, and much of their resentment of the regime in Addis Ababa was expressed in the view that it was not authentically Amhara at all, but Shoan Oromo. So far from being a revolt of the economically exploited, moreover, the separatist movements have drawn their support from a peasantry which has historically controlled its own means of production, and has not been forced into anything remotely resembling the levels of land alienation and incorporation into a global exchange economy characteristic of the south.

But a war there was, and hundreds of thousands of people died.[6] And an explanation there must likewise be. What follows is necessarily tentative, but does at least try to sketch out an alternative which is broadly compatible with the actual structure of conflict. This explanation needs to approach both the high level of political alienation from the central regime, and also the economic structure and modes of production, which underlie regional separatism. Though obviously linked, these are most conveniently discussed separately.

Eritrea provides the obvious starting point, as the region where the political failures of the Ethiopian state, both imperial and revolutionary, have been most dramatically evident. The distinctiveness of Eritrea lies, of course, in the fact that, although much if not most of it had been associated with Ethiopia from very early times, it was separated from Ethiopia, between 1890 and 1952, by 51 years of Italian colonialism and 11 of British wartime and post-war administration.[7] Its 'reunification' with Ethiopia, under a federal arrangement approved by the United Nations (UN), followed a period of political mobilization which indicated the broad lines of cleavage within the territory. The most obvious of these cleavages separated the Muslims of the lowlands, largely in the western area bordering the Sudan, but also including the Saho and Afar peoples of the Red Sea Plain, from the Tigrinya-speaking Christian highlanders. The Muslims, though with some important exceptions, broadly supported a separate independence for Eritrea, while the Christians, again with exceptions, supported union with Ethiopia. This Muslim opposition carried through into the ELF, after a hiatus while the local population absorbed the effects of federation; armed conflict in the eastern lowlands broke out shortly after the abrogation of the federal arrangement by the Ethiopian government, with the formal though forced approval of the Eritrean Assembly in 1962.

More important, however, in terms of what we now need to explain, was the political evolution of the highlands. Thomas Killion has shown that the commitment to union among Christian Eritreans was always considerably more ambivalent than the broad support of the highlands for the Unionist Party might suggest.[8] The rural population, for whom union represented association with their co-religionists south of the Mareb, and protection against an ever-present Muslim threat, did indeed support unification with Ethiopia; they were understandably urged to do so by the Orthodox Church, which, financed by the Ethiopian government, furnished the basic grassroots organization of unionism, and by elements of the local aristocracy who could see advantages for themselves in an imperial Ethiopia. Some of the intelligentsia could likewise see a role for themselves, either in running the Eritrean government established under the federation, or in the central government in Addis Ababa. Urban highlanders were however, for the most part, considerably more sceptical, a scepticism which was amply vindicated by the experience of federation. Though highly adept at manipulating the politics of faction and family among the northern Ethiopian aristocracy, Haile-Selassie's regime appears to have had no idea of how to come to grips with organized urban groups or the political parties which represented them, groups which in any event went unrepresented in the no-party state south of the Mareb. It viewed the autonomous government in Eritrea as a threat to its own authority (differing little in this respect from newly independent governments which were obliged to inherit federal arrangements as part of the decolonization settlement throughout the continent), and sought from the start to absorb Eritrea as an administrative region within the ordinary centralized structure of Ethiopian local govern-ment – while dissolving the Unionist Party which had previously served as its instrument for achieving unification. Job opportunities for educated Eritreans within the regional administration were thus reduced, and the sense of regional identity which had emerged over the colonial period was affronted.

The outbreak of the Ethiopian Revolution in 1974 appeared at first to offer opportunities for reconciliation. It had long been an article of faith among radicals in Addis Ababa that the conflict in Eritrea echoed their own differences with the imperial regime: that it was essentially a clash between feudal and progressive forces, which could be resolved by the accession of fellow progressives to power at the centre. The first chairman of the Provisional Military Administrative Council (PMAC), General Aman Andom, was moreover an Eritrean who, though associated with the central government since the liberation campaign in 1941, made it his first priority to secure a settlement in Eritrea. It is by no means certain that he could have succeeded; he sought to win over the local population by direct appeals, rather than negotiating with the separatist movements, and the level of actual autonomy which he would have been prepared to concede remained unclear. At all events, he never got the chance. His search for reconciliation aroused the hostility of the jacobins within the PMAC, led by Mengistu Haile-Maryam, who made Eritrea the pretext for ousting, and killing, Aman in November 1974.

The support, or at least adherence, which the central Ethiopian government was able to command in Eritrea was not as negligible as the separatist movements claim. By far the greater number of admin-istrative positions in Eritrea after 1974 were held by native Eritreans.

These were, however, drawn heavily from sections of the population, and often individuals, associated with the Unionist Party, many of them from the old Unionist stronghold of Seray; elsewhere, for example among the Kunama people around Barentu in western Eritrea, the central government was able to call on the artificial unionism derived from local ethnic rivalries. Never after 1974, however, was the post of chief administrator in Eritrea, or after 1980 that of party first secretary, entrusted to an Eritrean.

The other disaffected regions of northern Ethiopia, Tigray, Gonder and northern Wollo, had neither Eritrea's experience of separate colonial rule nor its special constitutional status. Though continuously part of Ethiopia, they nonetheless had longstanding internecine grievances against the Shoan-dominated government in Addis Ababa. Tigray, additionally distinguished by its different language, was the homeland of the Emperor Yohannes IV, whose death in 1889 opened the way for the Shoan hegemony. His descendants continued to exercise great authority within the region, and at times to harbour unrealizable hopes of the imperial crown. Wollo had provided the core of opposition to the *coup d'etat* which brought Haile-Selassie to power as regent in 1916. Ras Gugsa Wolle of Gonder had rebelled in 1930. But although the common view of the Christian highlands as a homogeneous political unit is thus far from accurate, these historical rivalries appeared to have been brought well under control by 1974. The regional governor in Tigray was a great-grandson of the Emperor Yohannes, married to the granddaughter of Haile-Selassie; another granddaughter was married to the governor of Gonder. Haile-Selassie's eldest son was titular governor of Wollo.

It was partly the very success with which these regions had been associated with the central government under Haile-Selassie that led to their alienation under his successors. The overthrow of the monarchy aroused the opposition of regional aristocrats who saw the new regime (quite rightly) as a threat to their own position, and who also retained the loyalty of their local peasantries. And while the aristocracy had much to lose from the new dispensation, the peasantry did not have much to gain. Unlike the peasantries of southern Ethiopia, they largely controlled their own means of production, and the new government's land-reform proclamation, which nationalized all rural land, could be seen more as a threat than as the deliverance from landlord exploitation which is how it appeared in the south. The two governors, Ras Mengesha Seyoum of Tigray and Nega Haile-

Selassie of Gonder, launched a 'white' opposition, the Ethiopian Democratic Union (EDU), which, though it failed within a few years, helped to set a pattern of political mobilization against the central regime.

This pattern of alienation was then reinforced by a further set of circumstances. The first was the counterproductive brutality of many of the regional rulers appointed by the central government; particularly notorious in this respect was Melaku Teferra in Gonder. Imbued with the centralizing jacobinism of the regime which they represented, viewing the territory which they ruled as implicitly hostile, they interpreted any expression of regional identity or dissent as counter-revolutionary activity, and alienated not only the rural population, but also many of the regional intelligentsia who should have been their natural allies. This process was reinforced by events in Addis Ababa, where the Ethiopian People's Revolutionary Party (EPRP), much of whose leadership was of northern origin, was defeated in the terror of 1976–7 by an alliance between the military regime and the rival party of the Marxist intelligentsia, Meison. Fragments of the EPRP retreated to their northern homelands in pursuit of a Maoist strategy of rural liberation, eventually being incorporated into the TPLF and its sister organizations.[9] Finally, despite considerable differences between EPLF and other northern opposition movements, the EPLF had an obvious interest in fostering resistance to the central government in the regions immediately to the south of Eritrea.

While the revolution thus greatly intensified the political basis for northern separatism, this in turn may be seen as the reflection, or superstructural manifestation, of its economic foundations. These in turn derive, not from the exploitation of regions which were being incorporated, by way of a repressive and extractive state apparatus, into the global economy; but, quite the contrary, from the marginalization of regions which were progressively excluded from the market at both national and international levels.

The economics of alienation, like the politics, were at their sharpest in Eritrea, where the Italian colonial rulers had built up an urban infrastructure which went into profound recession on their departure. The artificial war economy of the 1930s would in any event have been difficult to sustain; but the British military administration had little interest in the economic development of the territory, in contrast to the measures which it took to encourage political awareness, and compounded its problems by removing industrial equipment inherited from the Italians. Federation in 1952 with one of the least developed states in the world was little help, still less so since the axis of development in Ethiopia was centred on Addis Ababa, with its links to the coffee-growing regions in the south and west, and via new roads and the line of rail to the Awash valley, and the coast at Djibouti and Assab. Economically as well as politically, federation had little to offer to the urban classes of the Eritrean highlands.

Eritrea was, however, no more than a special case of the general economic predicament of the northern highlands. Over many centuries, the centres of economic and political power in Ethiopia have tended to move southwards, from the original capital at Axum near the Tigray/Eritrean border, to Lalibela and Gonder in the central highlands, and eventually to the late nineteenth-century capital of Addis Ababa. While the old centres were conveniently placed for trade with the Red Sea basin and the Nile valley, they were correspondingly vulnerable to Muslim, and eventually colonial, attack, and Ethiopia's rulers retreated to the safety of the mountains. When commercial links with the external world regained their central importance to the Ethiopian state in the later nineteenth century, these turned on the export of cash crops, notably coffee, which were grown not in the highlands but at lower altitudes to the south and west. This was a process from which the southernmost old Ethiopian province of Shoa was the natural beneficiary. The very fact that peasants in the northern highlands controlled their own means of production may have inhibited their incorporation into the world market, since it was not possible for an indigenous Ethiopian state to impose on them the exploitative mechanisms of land alienation and surplus expropriation through which the newly conquered areas of the south and west were harnessed to the needs both of the state and of the international economy. With the exception of the grain-producing region of Gojjam, the peasant farmers of the northern Amhara and Tigrayan highlands produce very little marketed surplus for either export or domestic consumption.

Finally, and perhaps most important of all, the northern highlands have been a zone of progressive agricultural degradation, from which people as well as power have seeped steadily southwards to avoid the dangers of drought and famine. The catastrophic famines which hit the region in 1973–4 and 1984–5 demonstrated the effects of drought on areas already badly hit by overpopulation, uncertain rainfall, increased pressure on land and the resulting erosion and deforestation.

Although the revolutionary land reform of 1975 had been intended to promote the productive forces of the countryside, paradoxically it accelerated this process of agrarian decay. Land reform guaranteed to peasant families a roughly equal share of the land within their own peasants' association area and, as an automatic corollary, denied them access to land outside that area. The overall result, in regions such as Tigray and northern Wollo where the pressure of people on land was already high, was to lock peasants into a local community in which increasing population led only to declining plot sizes and further degradation, a process which Dessalegn Rahmato has aptly defined as agrarian involution.[10]

Opportunities for peasants to compensate for the inadequacy of their family farms by seeking additional income from the monetary sectors of the economy were systematically, though for the most part inadvertently, removed by the economic policies of the revolutionary government. First, since peasants who left their home areas could lose their rights to land there (unlike under the pre-revolutionary system, in which land rights derived from inheritance, and were inalienable), the flow of migrants to the towns was sharply reduced, and in the first years of the revolution possibly even reversed; food, job and housing shortages in the towns in any event made them an unattractive proposition, and a high proportion of urban immigrants are women who, lacking land rights in the countryside and forced from their homes by marital breakdown, often support themselves by prostitution.[11] Second, opportunities for peasants to supplement their income by seasonal labour in the cash-crop sector of the economy were removed by the nationalization of privately managed plantations and estates, and the prohibition of the private hire of agricultural labour. These opportunities had been critically important, especially in Tigray. Huge numbers of temporary workers from Gonder and Tigray – estimates vary between 100,000 and 300,000 each year – converged for the sesame harvest on the Humera lowlands bordering the Sudan, where the urgent need for labour and the peculiar characteristics of the crop enabled them to gain, by peasant standards, high rates of pay. For peasants in Wollo and south-eastern Tigray, similar opportunities were offered by cotton-picking and other seasonal labour in the Awash valley. Peasants from all over the northern highlands went at picking time to the coffee-growing areas of the south and west. With the revolution, all of these opportunities were drastically reduced, if not totally halted. Sesame production in the Humera area was badly affected by the fighting between the government and the EDU, and although attempts at rehabilitation were made after the EDU's defeat the area was subsequently abandoned. At Humera and in the Awash valley, the new state farms recruited casual labour at punitively low rates of pay, and could only get the necessary workforce by levies on peasants' associations, dubiously voluntary campaigns among urban workers, and in extreme cases by methods which fell little short of slavery. Coffee-picking was also badly affected. Excluded from the world economy even in the marginal role which they had previously taken as seasonal labour for export crops, the peasants of the northern highlands have re-entered it as the recipients of famine relief.

The political and economic bases of revolt in northern Ethiopia are tragically clear. Politically, the people of the region were alienated from a national government of which they had historically been not only part, but an often dominant part. Their previous incorporation into a national political structure was indeed reflected in a leadership, whether drawn from an old aristocracy or from a new radical intelligentsia, which resorted to local resistance following defeat at the centre. The political marginalization, indeed often destitution, of the local population, provided a setting in which dissident élites, aided by the brutality and ineptitude of the central government and many of its local representatives, could readily find support.

The situation in southern Ethiopia was different. Precisely because of the level of exploitation under the imperial regime in the newly conquered southern regions, these areas gained immediate and important benefits from the revolution which were not available in the north. Land reform removed the settler and landlord class, enabling peasants to gain at least usufructory rights in the land which they farmed, and relieving them of their previous obligation to deliver a high proportion of their crop to the landlord. They were incorporated into a cash economy which strengthened their links with central government, at the same time that the northern peasants were being progressively marginalized. The apparatus of revolutionary government, that is, peasants' associations, marketing organizations, villagization, the party, was installed in most areas without evident difficulty.

It should not be assumed that this quiescence is permanent. The old exploitative apparatus of landlordism was replaced by the new more centralized and perhaps more systematically exploitative apparatus of a revolutionary socialist state. The villagization programme through which the Mengistu government sought to extend its control over peasant agriculture throughout the country, but especially in the south where it was easiest to implement, was disastrously counterproductive. Old resentments remain to be exploited, and organizations such as the OLF have sought to foment them, with results that may yet bring to much of southern Ethiopia the levels of bloodshed and devastation already experienced in the north. Although the new EPRDF regime that took over provisionally in May 1991 was more committed than its predecessor to regional autonomy, it had very few links with the economically vital southern regions, where it might indeed be as readily associated with the domination of central government by the northern highlanders, as with the overthrow of the Mengistu regime. But it is at least clear that the stereotype of the Abyssinian state is in urgent need of revision.

Notes

1. This chapter is based on a paper presented originally at the symposium on 'Contemporary warfare in Africa: the local experience', held at the African Studies Centre, University of Cambridge, by the UK African Studies Association in May 1989. It also draws on material published in Clapham, *Transformation and Continuity in Revolutionary Ethiopia* (Cambridge University Press 1988).
2. See, for example, an excellent recent study: Charles W. McClellan, *State Transformation and National Integration: Gedeo and the Ethiopian Empire, 1895–1935* (East Lansing: Michigan State University, 1988).
3. This chapter refers to the regional boundaries of Ethiopia as these existed up to 1987, and refers to the Gonder region even for the period before 1975 when it was called Begemder and Semien.
4. The most detailed and objective account of the origins of the resistance movements in Eritrea and Tigray is by John Markakis, *National and Class Conflict in the Horn of Africa* (Cambridge University Press 1987).
5. Virtually nothing, to my knowledge, has been published on the EPDM, which is not even referred to in Markakis, op. cit. There is a brief report, 'Ethiopia's forgotten liberation movement', *New African* (July 1985); a congress was held in May 1989, reports from which appear in *Summary of World Broadcasts*.
6. Dawit Wolde Giorgis, as first secretary for Eritrea of the Commission to Organise the Party of the Working People of Ethiopia, estimated that 379,000 people had died in the Eritrean conflict alone up to 1983, 280,000 of these being civilians, 90,000 Ethiopian soldiers and 9,000 soldiers of the resistance movements; see Dawit Wolde Giorgis, *Red Tears: War, Famine and Revolution in Ethiopia*, (Trenton NJ; Red Sea Press, 1989), p. 113.

7. Eritrea was also formally united with Ethiopia within the Italian colonial empire from 1936 to 1941.
8. Thomas Killion, 'The development of nationalist political consciousness in the Eritrean Christian community, 1952–1978', conference on Prospects for Peace and Stability in the Horn of Africa, Michigan State University, April 1989.
9. See Markakis, op. cit., pp. 248–58; one section of the EPRP continued to operate in opposition to TPLF/EPRDF in Gojjam.
10. Dessalegn Rahmato, *Agrarian Reform in Ethiopia* (Uppsala 1984).
11. See Christopher Clapham, *Transformation and Continuity in Revolutionary Ethiopia*, op. cit., p. 130.

14

THE ENDING OF BRITISH RULE IN HONG KONG

Norman J. Miners

The transfer of sovereignty over Hong Kong from Britain to China on 1 July 1997 will be without a parallel in the post-war decolonization of the British Empire. In every other colony Britain has followed the principle of self-determination, that the indigenous inhabitants should be allowed to decide their own future political status. This was true even in the case of Palestine, where the Arabs and Jews living in the trust territory were left free to settle their fate through a bloody civil war. But in the case of Hong Kong, the Sino-British Joint Declaration which transferred the whole of the colony to China in 1997 was negotiated between the representatives of Britain and China without the participation of any representatives of the local population. The nearest parallel is the transfer of the German colonies and the provinces of the Ottoman Empire to the victorious allied powers in 1919, or the return of Taiwan to the Republic of China in 1945 after 50 years of Japanese colonial rule without any consultation with the local inhabitants. There are a few cases where a British colony has attained independence by merger with another state: in 1960 the Somaliland Protectorate chose to unite with the Republic of Somalia immediately after attaining independence; in 1961 the Southern Cameroons chose to split away from Nigeria and join the United Republic of Cameroon; and in 1963 Singapore joined the Federation of Malaysia. But in all these cases the choice to join another state was made by an elected legislature, or as the result of a referendum of the entire population.

Hong Kong is also exceptional in that in every other colony except Palestine Britain had set up the institutions of parliamentary democracy, that is, a legislature elected by universal suffrage with a ministerial executive responsible to it, before relinquishing imperial control.[1] However, until 1985 all the members of the Hong Kong Legislative Council were appointed by the governor. The reason for this anomaly was China's objections to any form of constitutional development. This has never been publicly stated by any secretary of state while in office, to avoid diplomatic embarrassment, but the point has been freely admitted by ministers and officials when speaking off the record or in retirement.[2]

Only a small part of the crown colony of Hong Kong is ceded territory. The island of Hong Kong was annexed to the Crown by the Treaty of Nanking in 1842, and the peninsula of Kowloon opposite the island was ceded by the Convention of Peking in 1860. But nine-tenths of the land area of the colony is held on a 99-year lease negotiated in 1898. Such leasehold tenure was very rare in the colonial empire and was practically confined to China where the territory of Weihaiwei, relinquished in 1930, and various concessions in the treaty ports were all held on leases with no fixed terminal date. Outside China the only leased colony was the island of Cyprus, which was administered by Britain from 1878 under a Convention of Defensive Alliance made with the Sultan of Turkey. When Turkey entered the war on the side of the Central Powers in 1914, Cyprus was annexed to the Crown by order in council. This annexation was subsequently recognized in 1923 by the Treaty of Lausanne.[3] One governor of Hong Kong, Sir Cecil Clementi (1925–30) suggested that the Cyprus precedent should be followed and the New Territories should be annexed at a time when relations between Hong Kong and Canton were very strained, but the Foreign Office rejected the proposal, since China would never recognize such a violation of the 1898 treaty.[4] The Chinese government had acquiesced when the British seized possession of the Walled City of Kowloon within the New Territories in 1899, contrary to the 1898 treaty, but had subsequently laid claim to continued jurisdiction over this area in 1934, 1948 and 1962.

The nationalist (Guomindang) government of Chiang Kai-shek recognized the validity of the three treaties which constitute the colony, but sought to secure the premature rendition of the New Territories by agreement with Britain. His government particularly pressed for this in 1943 when negotiations were in progress for the ending of the privilege of extra-territoriality and the restoration of the foreign concessions in the treaty ports. Britain rebuffed the Chinese demand for the return of the New Territories, but promised that the lease should be discussed after the war was over.[5] In the expectation that Chiang Kai-shek might renew this demand at any time the China department of the Foreign Office drew up a position paper on the future of Hong Kong in July 1946.[6] This recorded the opinion of the Chiefs of Staff that Hong Kong could not, under modern conditions, be defended against a major power in occupation of the Chinese mainland, and pointed out that China could paralyse the colony's trade and administration for the purpose of enforcing any political demand, as had been done during the general strike and boycott of 1925–6. Accordingly the Foreign Office recommended that Britain should anticipate any Chinese demand by offering to terminate the lease of the New Territories and restore Chinese sovereignty over the whole of the colony, provided arrangements could be made for continued British administration of Hong Kong and Kowloon for 30 years. This recommendation was never acted upon by the foreign secretary, Ernest Bevin, but he also refused to allow any affirmation of Britain's determination to remain in Hong Kong to be issued, for fear of provoking China.[7] However, moves were initiated in Hong Kong, as in other colonies, at this time to institute elections as a first step towards the establishment of a democratic form of government.[8]

Fortunately for Britain and Hong Kong the nationalist government of Chiang Kai-shek was too preoccupied with the war against the Communists to raise the question of Hong Kong before Chiang's defeat and flight to Taiwan in 1949. The imminent prospect of a Communist victory led to the abandonment of all plans for constitutional reform. At first this was intended to be only a temporary postponement, and new proposals were elaborated up to 1952. But in that year the secretary of state for the colonies announced in the House of Commons that the time was inopportune for constitutional changes of a major character, and this remained the position of the British government for the next 32 years until 1984. The prospect of a communist government in China caused the British government to revise its view as to the feasibility of holding on to Hong Kong. In December 1948 a Foreign Office minister informed the House of Commons that the government intended to maintain its position in Hong Kong, and in 1949 the garrison was massively reinforced.[9] The chiefs of staff had revised their previous views, and now believed that

Hong Kong could be held even against an open attack, since the Chinese Communists, even if they controlled the whole of China, could not be classed as a major power. The governor was also confident the colony could hold out indefinitely against other methods of coercion such as blockade, boycott and the instigation of internal unrest, though this might involve feeding the population by seaborne supplies.

Accordingly the Cabinet decided in August 1949: 'We should not be prepared to discuss the future of Hong Kong with the new government unless it were friendly, democratic, stable and in control of a united China . . . These conditions do not exist at present and are unlikely to exist in the foreseeable future. Until conditions change, we intend to remain in Hong Kong'.[10]

Communist troops reached the northern border of the colony in October 1949, but made no attempt to penetrate further. There was a number of minor frontier incidents, but reasonably amicable relationships were soon established with the new Communist regime. The official position of the Chinese government was that all three treaties on which Hong Kong's separate existence was based were unequal and therefore invalid, but no attempt was made to seek the retrocession of the colony. The topic was never once raised in the negotiations between China and Britain from 1950 to 1954 over the question of British recognition of the People's Government of China. In 1972 China informed the United Nations (UN) that Hong Kong and Macau should not be included in the list of colonial territories covered by the declaration on the granting of independence to colonial countries and people: 'The Chinese government has consistently held that the questions of Hong Kong and Macau should be settled in an appropriate way when conditions are ripe'. Britain was happy to acquiesce. So long as China obtained up to 40 per cent of its foreign exchange earnings from exports to Hong Kong and other economic transactions conducted through the colony there seemed to be no reason why this convenient arrangement should not continue indefinitely.

In 1952 the newly elected Conservative government in Britain decided that Hong Kong was no longer defensible and that the task of the military should be to insure internal security and, if attacked, to cover an orderly evacuation.[11] The garrison was gradually run down during the 1950s. In effect this meant that the colony was now at the mercy of China. It was commonly said that Mao Zedong could take over Hong Kong at any time by lifting the telephone and putting a call through to London. But nothing ever happened. Various understandings and agreements were concluded with the Communist authorities covering such matters as the supply of water to the colony and the return of illegal immigrants to China. But the colonial government was careful to maintain its freedom of action. Sir David Trench, governor from 1964 to 1971, defined the position as follows: 'Hong Kong does not do anything silly and against China's legitimate interests, but at the same time does not allow herself to be pushed around unreasonably'.[12] His successor, Sir Murray MacLehose (1971 to 1982) told a House of Commons committee:

> Apart from intervention during the Cultural Revolution, which was major and then disowned by the Chinese government, direct intervention in Hong Kong's affairs has been really very small, relating to quite small things, border incidents, complaints about the treatment of compatriots in Hong Kong, but not really very much in the way of direct pressure ... When I was there I had this constantly in mind: was there encroachment about this or that, because if there was one had to stop it at once, otherwise you would fear a flood of intervention would follow.[13]

This happy state of co-existence might have continued indefinitely but for the expiry of the lease of the New Territories on 30 June 1997. This terminal date was referred to in the order in council of 20 October 1898, which is the basic British legal document incorporating the New Territories into the existing colony. Unless this was amended, or a new lease negotiated, British rule must come to an end in 1997. All land leases in the New Territories expire on 27 June 1997, and by the end of the 1970s landowners and business firms were becoming increasingly concerned about the security of their future property rights.

In March 1979 Sir Murray MacLehose paid an official visit to Beijing, and raised the issue of the land leases. It is probable that he was then told that China intended to resume sovereignty over Hong Kong in 1997, but no mention of this was made in the official account of the meeting.[14] Sir Murray brought back the message from Deng Xiaoping that investors in Hong Kong should 'put their hearts at ease'. However, 15 months later, in June 1989, the Hong Kong government unexpectedly issued a Green Paper proposing a new pattern of local administration under which 18 newly created district boards would have one-third of their membership elected by universal suffrage. This first tentative move towards Western-style democracy was seen by some as connected with the approach to 1997, since the new district boards, when further developed, might be a legitimate organ to give expression to public opinion on the colony's future. Representatives of the Chinese government expressed their disapproval of this constitutional innovation.

In 1982 Britain took the initiative in asking that negotiations on the future of Hong Kong should begin. Humphrey Atkins, lord privy seal, visited Beijing in January, and Mrs Thatcher had further discussions with the Chinese leaders during her visit in September. Talks were held soon afterwards and substantive negotiations began in July 1983. The British team comprised staff from the British embassy in Beijing, the Foreign Office, and Sir Edward Youde, the governor of Hong Kong. When Sir Edward stated that he was representing the Hong Kong people, the Chinese side promptly denounced this, claiming that China alone could represent the interests of the Chinese population of Hong Kong.[15] The colony's Executive Council was informed of the course of the negotiations on a confidential basis but had no influence on the outcome. At first Britain hoped to convince China of the need for continued British administration of Hong Kong in order to retain the confidence of the business community, in the belief that China could not afford to do anything that would jeopardize the stability and prosperity of the colony which made such an enormous contribution to the Chinese economy.[16] China was not persuaded by these arguments and insisted on China's sovereignty over the whole of the colony together with full rights of administration. Once this was conceded China was prepared to allow that the Hong Kong Special Administrative Region should possess a high degree of autonomy, that the government should be in the hands of the local inhabitants, and that the existing social and economic systems of the territory should be preserved for 50 years after 1997. The Chinese position had been communicated to the British government in April 1982 before the talks started, and no significant modification of its stand was achieved in the course of the negotiations.[17] The British negotiating team, working to a deadline of September 1984 imposed by the Chinese government, eventually conceded all China's demands. In exchange China agreed that its future plans for Hong Kong should be spelled out in detail in a binding international treaty. This was the Sino-

British Joint Declaration on the Question of Hong Kong which was initialled in September 1984, signed in December and formally ratified in May 1985.

Once China had made clear its determination to repossess the colony Britain had no alternative but to acquiesce. Britain could only appeal to China's self-interest by arguing the need for a continued British presence in the administration to safeguard business confidence, and could point to the unwillingness of the mass of the population, as shown by numerous surveys and opinion polls, to become part of China.[18] The Chinese rejected both these arguments as irrelevant. The one bargaining counter which might have been effective in persuading China to modify its demands would have been a willingness on Britain's part to offer full British passports to all Hong Kong's businessmen, enabling them to quit the colony and leave its economy in ruins. But the British government was as anxious as China to prevent an exodus of Hong Kong Chinese to Britain, and had altered the laws defining British nationality in 1962, 1971 and 1981 in order to prevent such a mass migration occurring.[19]

The foreign secretary, Sir Geoffrey Howe, claimed that the final document was a triumph for British diplomacy. Hong Kong had no elected legislature to express its views on the final settlement. The appointed Legislative Council gave its reluctant approval to the Joint Declaration; only two members voted against and one other member resigned his seat. There was no referendum to test the views of the population. Instead an Assessment Office was set up and members of the public were invited to submit their opinions. Few did so, since it was made clear that the declaration was not subject to amendment and that the alternative to acceptance of the agreement was a takeover by China in 1997 with no agreement at all. All 18 district boards discussed and endorsed the agreement, but this was not a valid expression of popular opinion since one-third of their members were government officials and one-third government appointees. Nevertheless the Assessment Office Report claimed: 'All the principal, representative bodies have unequivocally placed on record their views that the draft agreement is acceptable'.[20]

Although the British government was unable to allow the Hong Kong people to exercise any right to self-determination it still made a belated effort to install a democratic constitution before quitting the colony. When Sir Geoffrey Howe visited Hong Kong in April 1984 to announce that the British administration would not continue after

1997 he immediately went on to promise: 'During the years ahead the government of Hong Kong will be developed on increasingly representative lines'.[21] In July 1984, before negotiations on the Joint Declaration had been completed, the Hong Kong government issued a Green Paper entitled 'The Future Development of Representative Government in Hong Kong' containing detailed proposals for reform, the aim of which was 'to develop progressively a system of government the authority for which is firmly rooted in Hong Kong, which is able to represent authoritatively the views of the people of Hong Kong and which is more directly accountable to the people of Hong Kong'. It sketched out a scheme under which, by the 1990s, a majority of the members of the Legislative Council would be elected, a majority of the Executive Council would be chosen by the Legislative Council, and the governor would be selected by a joint meeting of all the unofficial members of the legislative and executive councils. In essence this proposal was that the government of Hong Kong before 1997 should become a modified form of parliamentary democracy with the executive chosen by and responsible to the legislature.

This went somewhat further than the vague outline of the future government of the Special Administrative Region (SAR) set out in the Joint Declaration. This stated merely that the future chief executive should be selected by election or through consultations held locally; that the legislature should be constituted by elections; and that the executive authorities should be accountable to the legislature. At the time the Green Paper was issued the Chinese government had not yet even agreed that the SAR legislature should be constituted by elections. This point was only conceded at the end of the negotiations.[22]

The Chinese authorities made clear their disapproval of the Green Paper in private briefings, but made no overt protest, presumably waiting until after the Joint Declaration had been signed and ratified. In November 1984 the Hong Kong government published a White Paper setting out in detail the constitutional reforms which it proposed to implement as a first stage in the progress towards representative government. Elections were to be held in 1985 to fill 24 out of the 56 seats in the Legislative Council, with 12 members elected indirectly by members of district boards and the urban and regional councils and 12 members elected by 'functional constituencies', that is, by business group and professional organizations. The White Paper promised that a further review of constitutional arrangements would take place in 1987 at which it would be decided whether to introduce some members chosen by direct elections into the Legislative Council in 1988. It was noted the bulk of public response was in favour of this as the next step.[23]

This vision of steady progress towards the institution of a functioning democracy before the handover to China in 1997 was rudely shattered in October 1985. The director of the New China News Agency, who is effectively the senior representative of the Chinese government in Hong Kong, called a news conference at which he denounced the Hong Kong government's plans and accused Britain of breaking the Joint Declaration. China made plain its view that any constitutional changes in the transitional period up to 1997 must conform to the pattern laid down in the Basic Law, a mini-constitution for the future of the Hong Kong SAR which was then being drafted by a committee appointed by Beijing. At first Britain attempted to claim that constitutional development in the interim remained its responsibility, while admitting that the constitutional structure in place by 1997 must converge with China's blueprint for the future government of the SAR. This did not satisfy the Chinese government, which insisted that the work of the Basic Law Drafting Committee should not be predetermined by decisions made by the colonial government.[24]

The 1987 constitutional review was held as promised, but every effort was made to ensure that the result would satisfy China's wishes. A Green Paper was published setting out 36 options for constitutional change in 1988 in which the institution of direct elections to the Legislative Council was buried among a mass of minor and inconsequential proposals for change. The Green Paper was so confusing that practically half the respondents questioned in a public opinion survey sponsored by the government were unable to answer the question. A Survey Office was set up to receive comments and suggestions from the public. A total of 368,431 people wrote individually to the office or signed petitions and group letters. Out of these 361,398 individuals gave their views on the question whether there should be direct elections to the Legislative Council in 1988. Among these 265,078 were in favour and 94,565 against; 1,755 gave no clear views. A similar result was obtained in opinion polls conducted by newspapers which asked specifically whether there should be direct elections in 1988. At least 68 per cent of those with a definite opinion said Yes. But in spite of this the government White Paper of February 1988 claimed that 'Among submissions to the Survey Office from individuals, groups and associations more were against than in favour of the introduction of direct elections in 1988.[25] This extraordinary conclusion was reached by ignoring the 223,886 signatures collected by signature campaigns and counting only the views of those who had sent in signed letters to the Survey Office. Most of these were in fact identical copies of letters distributed by Communist-owned businesses in Hong Kong to their employees, who were required to sign them and send them to the office.

In December 1987 the governor paid a visit to Beijing to consult with officials of the Hong Kong and Macau Affairs Office of the Chinese government. The White Paper published in February 1988 announced that ten seats in the Legislative Council would be filled by direct elections, but that this development would not take place until 1991, and the new directly elected members would replace the ten members indirectly elected by the district boards. The paper made clear that any further progress must await the final version of the Basic Law. The publication of the White Paper marked the complete capitulation of the British and Hong Kong governments to China's demands.

The final version of the Basic Law was ratified by the National People's Congress of China in April 1990. Only 20 out of the 60 members of the 1997 Legislative Council will be directly elected. Ten will be chosen by an election committee, and 30 by functional constituencies. The chief executive of the special administrative region, who will be responsible to Beijing, will be chosen by a selection committee of 400 members themselves nominated by a committee appointed by the National People's Congress of China. He will enjoy greater powers over the legislature than a British colonial governor. The executive authorities of the SAR will be accountable to the legislature only in the sense that they must present reports before it, answer questions and obtain its approval for taxation and public expenditure. It cannot dismiss the executive. This structure of government was arguably in accordance with the words of the Joint Declaration, but was far from the interpretation put on it by Sir Geoffrey Howe and other ministers when commending the agreement to the House of Commons.

Since the signing of the Joint Declaration the colonial government in Hong Kong has effectively been operating under the supervision of China. The Sino-British Joint Liaison Group, consisting of 5 representatives each from the British and Chinese governments, meets every few months to discuss matters relating to the smooth transfer of government in 1997. All changes in Hong Kong law which are expected to continue beyond 1997 and all important administrative decisions come within its purview. Since 1985 it has discussed a new pension scheme for civil servants, terms of service for judges and magistrates, the expansion of the Police Force, the timetable for the withdrawal of the British garrison, the wording and validity of new identity cards, the establishment of a Hong Kong Register of Shipping and the relocation of the British naval base. According to the Joint Declaration all matters on which there is disagreement within the Joint Liaison Group shall be referred to the two governments for solution through consultations. This means that consultation must continue until both China and Britain are satisfied. In effect this gives China a veto power over any changes in the government of Hong Kong which may be proposed between now and 1997.

Even on matters not raised at the Liaison Group the Hong Kong government is now anxious to anticipate China's wishes in every respect.[26] Since the Tiananmen massacre of June 1989, the Chinese population of Hong Kong has lost all confidence that the Chinese government will adhere to the promises of autonomy and non-interference made in the Joint Declaration. All those who have the necessary capital or professional qualifications are seeking to obtain foreign passports and emigrate elsewhere. It is doubtful whether it will be possible to maintain the stability and prosperity of Hong Kong in the remaining years until the formal transfer of sovereignty to China on 1 July 1997.

Notes

1. This was not true of protected states: the Sultanate of Brunei was an absolute monarchy when it became a sovereign independent state in 1984.
2. See for example the remarks by Mr Peter Blaker, a former minister of state at the Foreign Office in *House of Commons Debates*, 16 May 1984, p. 455: 'There are very good reasons why we have not developed representative institutions in Hong Kong: Peking would have viewed such a development with alarm.' See also the remarks of Lord Goronwy-Roberts in *House of Lords Debates*, 21 July 1976, p. 844 and 22 November 1978, p. 975.
3. Sir Kenneth Roberts-Wray, *Commonwealth and Colonial Law* (London 1966) p. 678.
4. Clementi's despatch is missing from the CO 129 records. It is referred to

in a minute from Grindle to Wellesley, 9 January 1931, FO 371/15484, p. 493.

5. There is a detailed account of these negotiations in Chan Lau Kit Ching, 'The Hong Kong Question during the Pacific War', *Journal of Imperial and Commonwealth History*, Vol. 2 (1973–4) pp. 46–77.

6. FO 371/5365 (FIO572).

7. In June 1948 the colonial secretary A. Creech Jones was pressed by his officials to raise the question of the future of Hong Kong in Cabinet. He minuted, 'I have urged the Foreign Office and Bevin for a statement often. Bevin has taken a strong line. If we go to Cabinet we shall get a decision we do not want. Bevin fears that the effect on China of any statement may lead to new difficulties on Hong Kong. We must act on the assumption that the situation remains unchanged' (Minute dated 22 June 1948 in CO 537/3702).

8. An account of these plans and their abandonment is given in N. J. Miners, 'Plans for constitutional reform in Hong Kong, 1946–1952', *China Quarterly* 107 (September 1986), pp. 463–82 see also S. Y. S. Tsang, *Democracy Shelved* (Hong Kong 1988).

9. *House of Commons Debates*, 10 December 1948.

10. Cabinet Memorandum CP(49)177, 19 August 1949. This document is closed for 50 years at the Public Record Office, but a copy is available in Creech Jones' papers at Rhodes House, Oxford.

11. This decision is still closed in the Cabinet papers, but it is referred to in CAB 131/12 Memo D(52)5 para. 9: 'We do not consider that our strategy in Hong Kong should be changed by a French withdrawal from Indo-China, although it may be necessary to maintain a larger garrison to insure internal security and, if attacked, to cover an orderly evacuation'.

12. Sir D. Trench, *Hong Kong and its Position in the Southeast Asian Region* (Honolulu, Hawaii 1971), p. 6.

13. *House of Commons Session 1988–89 Foreign Affairs Committee, Second Report, Hong Kong Volume II, Minutes of Evidence*, p. 254.

14. Sir S. Y. Chung stated that he had been told by high officials in China that MacLehose was told in 1979 that China would regain sovereignty in 1997. See the interview with Sir S. Y. Chung in *Asiaweek*, 1 June 1984.

15. *South China Morning Post*, 8, 9 and 10 July 1983.

16. The talks in Beijing were confidential, but Chinese officials released a steady flow of information on their progress to visiting delegations and to pro-communist newspapers in Hong Kong. A reconstruction of the course of the negotiations can be found in I. Scott, *Political Change and the Crisis of Legitimacy in Hong Kong* (Hong Kong 1989), pp. 171–219.

17. In April 1982 Mr Edward Heath visited Beijing and had a long audience with Deng Xiaoping at which he was given a comprehensive outline of China's plans for communication to the British government, *House of Commons Debates*, 16 May 1984, p. 427.

18. Numerous surveys and opinion polls were conducted in Hong Kong while the negotiations were in progress. Their findings are summarized in J. Y. S. Cheng, *Hong Kong in Search of a Future* (Hong Kong 1984).

19. See the letter from R. M. Purcell, a former civil servant in the Foreign and Commonwealth Office in *The Times*, 19 June 1989.

20. *Arrangements for testing the acceptability in Hong Kong of the Draft Agreement on the Future of the Territory Report of the Assessment Office* (Hong Kong 1984) p. 16.

21. *South China Morning Post*, 21 April 1984. A more detailed account of these events can be found in N. Miners, 'Moves towards representative government 1984–1988' in K. Cheek-Milby and M. Mushkat, *The Challenge of Transformation* (Hong Kong 1989).

22. This fact was revealed by Sir Geoffrey Howe in his evidence before the Foreign Affairs Committee, *Volume II, Minutes of Evidence*, p. 24.

23. *White Paper: The Further Development of Representative Government in Hong Kong* (Hong Kong, November 1984), p. 8.

24. *South China Morning Post*, 22 November 1985. In September 1988 Mr Szeto Wah, a member of the Legislative Council and of the Basic Law Drafting Committee visited Beijing and met Zhao Ziyang, the general secretary of the Communist Party. He told the delegation that China had objected to direct elections in 1988 since the Basic Law to be promulgated in 1990 might then need a proportion bigger than 25 per cent by direct election, and then they would be led by the nose.

25. *White Paper: The Development of Representative Government: The Way Forward* (Hong Kong, February 1988). p. 8

26. In October 1989 the Hong Kong government allowed a Chinese student Yang Yang who had asked for political asylum in the territory to depart for the USA instead of deporting him back to China. In retaliation China refused to accept back other illegal immigrants detained by the Hong Kong authorities for two weeks until the colonial government apologized to China. The letter from the political adviser to the governor to the New China News Agency (NCNA) was subsequently leaked to the press by China, and was published in the *South China Morning Post*, 26 October 1989. It runs as follows:

> Subsequent to our meeting on 17 October, you asked whether the Hong Kong government could provide further explanation relating to our discussion on the statement made by Ambassador Ke at the thirteenth meeting of the Joint Liaison Group. I am happy to do so.
>
> The Hong Kong government has no intention of allowing Hong Kong to be used as a base for subversive activities against the People's Republic of China. NCNA will have noticed the arrest of members of the April 5th Action Group outside their National Day reception. They will also have noted that the 10 October celebrations passed off in a low-key way, and that the Hong Kong government has recently rejected a proposal for a permanent site for a replica statue of democracy. No group in Hong Kong has any more tolerance than the law allows. The Hong Kong government will continue to have a prudent regard for the special circumstances of Hong Kong and the interests and concerns of the Chinese government.

CONTRIBUTORS

Dennis Austin was formerly Professor of Government at Manchester University

Holger Bernt Hansen is Research Professor of Political and Religious Studies at Copenhagen University

T. H. R. Cashmore was formerly Head of Research at the Foreign and Commonwealth Office

Christopher Clapham is Professor of Politics at Lancaster University

David Fieldhouse is Vere Harmsworth Professor of Imperial and Naval History at Cambridge University

Anirudha Gupta is Professor of Politics at Jawaharlal Nehru University, New Delhi

John D. Hargreaves was formerly Professor of History at Aberdeen University

John Kent teaches International History at the London School of Economics

Maryinez Lyons is currently researching into the social history of medicine in Uganda and Zaïre at the Institute of Commonwealth Studies

Shula Marks is Director of the Institute of Commonwealth Studies and Professor of Commonwealth History

Norman J. Miners is Head of the Political Science Department at Hong Kong University

W. H. Morris-Jones was previously Professor of Commonwealth Studies and Director of the Institute of Commonwealth Studies at London University

Colin Newbury is Fellow of Linacre College, Oxford

Stanley Trapido lectures on the politics of new states at Oxford University

Michael Twaddle teaches politics and history at the Institute of Commonwealth Studies

Donald Wood was formerly Dean of the School of African and Asian Studies at Sussex University

ACKOWLEDGEMENTS

Grateful thanks to staff at the Institute of Commonwealth Studies for preparing drafts of contributors' papers on disk; to Lester Crook, Emma Sinclair-Webb and colleagues at I.B. Tauris for expert assistance; to the Thornley Bequest of London University for financial help; and to the Royal African Society and the University of Copenhagen for ensuring that copies of this volume are available for consultation in university libraries within the Third World itself.

INDEX